THE BAREFOOT REVOLUTION

BERTRAND SCHNEIDER

The Barefoot Revolution
A Report to the Club of Rome

English Version by A. F. VILLON

IT PUBLICATIONS

Intermediate Technology Publications
9 King Street, London WC2E 8HW, UK

© IT Publications, 1988

ISBN 0 946688 19 2

Printed in Great Britain by
Short Run Press Ltd, Exeter

Project Team

TECHNICAL COORDINATION
Bertrand Schneider
Nicole Rosensohn

FIELD SURVEY
Carried out in
Bolivia, Brazil, Colombia
Ecuador, Mexico, Peru
Burkina Faso, Cameroun, Egypt
Kenya, Mali, Nigeria
Togo, Zaire
Bangladesh, India, Indonesia
Philippines, Thailand
By
Wally Clinckemaillie
Louis Coignard
Guy Delbrel
Daniel Durand
Pierre Espagne
Didier François
Marie-Christine Guéneau
Catherine Guernier
Mark Mosio
Nicole Rosensohn
Bertrand Schneider
André-François Villon

DOCUMENTARY SURVEY
Centro Febbraïo 74
Rome

IN MEMORIAM
Maurice Guernier
who inspired this work
and
Aurelio Peccei
who made it possible

CONCLUDING SEMINAR
April 10–12, 1985
Bogotá, Colombia

Honorary Chairman
H. E. Belisario Betancur
President of Colombia

Mario Calderon
Jaime Carvajal
Ricardo Diez-Hochleitner
Pedro Gomes
Alexander King
Giancarlo Quaranta
Gabriele Quinti
Nicole Rosensohn
Bertrand Schneider
Alfredo Solarte
Dao Spencer

FUNDING
Caisse des Dépots et Consignations (France)
Fondation de France
Ministry of Foreign Affairs (Spain)
Ministry of Foreign Affairs (Italy)
U.T.A.

PROJECT SECRETARIAT
Denise Vergniol

Contents

Introduction

Never since navigators first charted and divided the globe have the latitudes marked greater disparities. While the post-industrial societies of the northern hemisphere shoot their technology into the skies, below the equator, the 'developing' world battles hunger, drought, indebtedness, and underdevelopment — the *mal de siècle*.

All the statements, strategies, and well-intentioned policies of international co-operation and solidarity have as yet been incapable of altering the implacable fact — half of humanity still lives in want, misery, and malnutrition. Although rescue operations are mounted from time to time by the 'North' to stem the terrible toll of human lives, these do not adequately address the root causes of underdevelopment, one of which is the apparent inability of the rural populations of the Third World to produce enough food. The symptoms are temporarily alleviated, but the problem remains unsolved.

Since the oil crisis of 1974, the terms of the North–South dialogue, or what might be more appropriately termed the North–South confrontation, have been profoundly altered. While an increasingly complex web of economic and strategic relationships renders the rich and poor nations inescapably interdependent, the industrialized nations have retreated to their traditional spheres of influence and have revised the more generous concepts of the sixties in favour of 'market' approaches in their dealings with poor countries.

Yet the conflicts, economic crises, and social upheavals that convulse the southern hemisphere inevitably wash over the breakwaters of the North. The plight of the underdeveloped half of the planet is a political priority which cannot be ignored, even if a coherent response has yet to be offered. This predicament is at the very heart of what the Club of Rome has termed the world 'problématique'.

The emergence of a new phenomenon may revolutionize this problématique. Although it has yet to be clearly perceived and accurately measured, a new pattern of development is taking shape at community and village level in rural areas of the Third World. In a spirit of self-reliance, numerous 'grassroots' groups have decided to take charge of their own development in rural villages throughout Latin America, Africa, and Asia. As yet this trend has not demonstrably altered the challenge facing the world's rural population of roughly two billion people, but it can no longer be considered marginal for it extends even to the furthest reaches of a vast and neglected rural hinterland which progress and the modern world have left behind. These non-governmental, spontaneous development initiatives are the subject of this book. How they organize and devise small-scale programmes to tackle the problems of agricultural production, health care, and education in rural areas can perhaps indicate a positive trend for the future of poor nations. And though results are often modest and failure at times unavoidable, the movement continues to spread through the supposedly backward and cautious rural Third World. Apparently irresistible, this 'barefoot revolution' is essentially a peaceful one, but if too many obstacles or barriers are placed in its path, it is difficult to predict what course it might take. Despite their impoverishment and isolation, the rural communities of the Third World are beginning to realize that they are capable of assuming responsibility for their economic development. Thanks to a new awareness of their economic and demographic strength, they see the possibility of emerging from their vulnerability.

This new trend is radically changing the tenets of development that have prevailed until now, for it entails a complete overhaul of twenty years of economic strategy that has not fulfilled its promises. The respective roles of the various partners in the development process will have to be redefined in order to open the way for a reorientation of efforts and resources based on a clearer analysis of a complex and rapidly changing reality. The importance and urgency of the barefoot revolution require from governments, international institutions, and non-governmental organizations new thinking and novel approaches, closer co-operation and greater responsiveness to the growing expectations of rural communities. Failing such a response, the quiet revolution might very well grow more radical and fall prey to the temptations of violence.

Rural development in the Third World is not only a life and death matter for two billion peasants, but also a problem affecting the peace and security of every nation. In 1983 the Club of Rome commissioned a study to determine why this crucial issue had not so far been given proper consideration. In the course of the subsequent study, the role of non-governmental organizations in both rich and poor countries became apparent through their support of rural development projects in villages throughout the developing world.

The study brought to light hundreds of similar efforts aimed at providing immediate responses to familiar imbalances, even though the contexts varied from region to region. These projects are financed and supported by non-profit, non-governmental organizations (NGOs), volunteer and charitable agencies or institutions which channel aid and assistance, provide training through personnel in the field, and encourage innovation and the use of simple local technologies wherever possible.

These organizations, which exist by the thousands in both hemispheres, are the moving force behind what are often termed 'microprojects', small-scale, community- or village-based development projects under way in a hundred different countries. These projects address vital concerns such as food production, health services, and education. The NGO network is extended and backed up by scores of informal groups without precise legal attributes — co-operatives, churches, and religious communities — but also by governments and international institutions.

The activities of NGOs remain unknown to a large segment of the public. While the media have begun to give NGOs and their activities broad exposure, in some quarters they are still regarded as well-meaning amateurs engaged in charitable activity. However, a growing number of observers is beginning to take them seriously, recognizing their enormous economic and human potential as a very positive development for the future. NGOs are beginning to emerge as a significant force for development. Despite the normally cautious attitude of governmental agencies and international institutions towards groups outside their purview, they have not only granted most NGOs official recognition, but have also established formal ties with them. Daily co-operation occurs within the numerous NGO liaison offices set up within the United Nations system and its regional bodies. This is ample evidence of the high regard in which the non-governmental sector is now held. It is therefore surprising that no overall study of NGOs has as yet been undertaken.

This book is based on the results of surveys of 93 small-scale development projects carried out by six teams of researchers in nineteen countries of Latin America, Africa, and Asia from September 1983 to January 1985. Each team was made up of two professionals, one from the social sciences — sociologist, anthropologist, historian — the other an economist, agronomist, or experienced development field-worker. Each team spent an average of a week to ten days at the project site, interviewing its participants, beneficiaries, NGO workers, villagers, officials, religious leaders, local organizations. The teams also sought out people in neighbouring villages and areas to determine the local impact of the project and how it was perceived by outsiders. Were they eager to emulate the project, or did they have reservations about joining in the experiment? Why were they reluctant? For cultural, ethnic, or socio-political reasons? The teams were also free to select any other projects for study which they felt would be of significance to the overall report. Thus, in the course of the field visits the 60 projects initially earmarked for study soon expanded to 93. This expansion broadened the research base, resulting in more varied and representative material.

The field surveys were followed up by a documentary study of a further 227 small-scale projects primarily supported by organizations in the developed world. This phase of the project was conducted by a prestigious Italian research team at the Centro Febbraio 74 in Rome. Appendix I outlines the methodology of the entire project.

Our purpose, then, is to identify and measure the impact of small-scale operations on the severe problems affecting rural areas in the Third World. The type of project selected for the study corresponds to what we termed 'endogenous' criteria, in other words, each project was entirely aimed at supporting and reinforcing a given group within its natural organic unity, respecting its cultural integrity, traditional structures, and values. We felt that in order to ensure lasting social and economic progress, the communities had to achieve a certain degree of self-reliance and regain the initiative, choice, and responsibility for their own development. The ultimate aim of the study was to determine whether small rural development projects really offer a valid development alternative for the Third World. Could this type of operation begin to provide some answers to the urgent needs of the world's two billion rural dwellers, and even be extended throughout the developing world?

The results of the study and the overall findings more than justified our initial hypotheses. As we shall see, a very encouraging grassroots movement is bringing hope to thousands in rural areas. In view of the failure of twenty years of development efforts patterned on Western industrial society's models, it is clearly time to try less ambitious and more pragmatic approaches.

Acknowledgments

Without the trust and co-operation of hundreds of villagers and development workers throughout rural Latin America, Africa, and Asia, this book could not have been written. These men and women were willing to share with us the story of their 'barefoot revolution', their struggle for self-reliance and dignity. They opened their villages, schools, farms, and homes to us so that we could listen and learn.

I am equally grateful to the talented individuals who carried out this study in the field, often in difficult and dangerous circumstances. Their observations and insights form the raw material and core of this work.

My thanks also go to all the non-governmental organizations, both in 'developing' and 'developed' countries, that have advised and assisted us in this enormous undertaking.

I should also mention the dozens of people to whom I am indebted for their ideas, suggestions and encouragement: the list would require a volume to itself. In particular, my deep gratitude goes to Giulio Fossi, José Luis Pardos, Gianpaolo Calchi Novati, and Maria Isabel Vega for their help and support through every phase of this project.

Lastly I should like to thank the Société Sycor in Paris for its kind assistance and for making its offices and dedicated staff available to me for this study.

B.S.

PART ONE

CHAPTER 1
Twenty Years of Misguided Development

Development experts and economists the world over are quick to denounce as misguided and ineffectual the development policies applied in Third World countries over the past twenty years. They criticize the near-systematic reliance of developing nations on large industrial projects based on Western models that are totally alien to local needs and requirements. In most cases, the huge amounts of capital invested in these schemes benefit only a minority of a country's population, while in rural areas, such policies often come into conflict with local cultures, upset traditions, and are ultimately rejected by the very people they are supposed to benefit.

Another consequence of the fundamental misunderstanding of the real needs of the developing world is the widening disparity between rich and poor nations and its attendant inequities. Among the many adverse consequences of misguided or inappropriate economic policies is environmental damage, such as depletion of natural resources, desertification, deforestation, and drought. The countryside is drained of its vitality through the migration of large numbers of peasants to the already overcrowded cities in most Third World countries, a direct consequence of poor development planning and the incapacity to promote economic activity in rural areas.

Regional conflicts which strain national resources and paralyse local economies can often be traced back to economic rivalries and an unwillingness to acknowledge mutual interdependence. Ultimately, the failure of development in the Third World renders these economies perennially dependent on the industrialized North.

THE DEVASTATING EFFECTS OF LARGE-SCALE
DEVELOPMENT SCHEMES
To quote a villager from Cameroun, one of many local development workers who was interviewed in the course of the field

survey, 'We've seen quite a few economists come through to set up
big projects, and their development schemes invariably bring ruin
and devastation in their wake. The problem is that they don't take
human beings into account.'

In most cases, the internationally funded projects on the draw-
ing boards of western engineers absorb vast amounts of capital and
require sophisticated technology. The intended beneficiaries of
these projects, on the other hand, are generally incapable of
adapting them to the local needs and environment and are consequently not in a position to profit by them.

The Namarigunu irrigation project on the River Niger provides
water for 1,500 hectares of arable land. The cost per hectare of the
irrigation infrastructure amounts to a monstrous $17,000 ($25.5
million for the entire project). About a mile away, cropland lies
fallow where an earlier irrigation scheme had been set up and then
abandoned through lack of money, eventually becoming totally
inoperative. It stands as a haunting reminder of the fate of
grandiose and hastily executed development schemes.

At Mopti in Mali, since a similarly costly irrigation system was
inaugurated nine years ago, rice production has fallen from 50 to
15 bags per hectare owing to the spread of wild rice and weeds in
the fields and the inability of the more vulnerable imported
varieties to survive unseasonal rains and flooding.

On the other side of the continent, near Arusha in Tanzania, an
experimental wheat farming project was set up in 1970 with the
help of Canada which contributed $44 million in funding in the
hope that the Tanzanian government would be able eventually to
take over management of the project. Fifteen years later, this had
still to be achieved, even though Tanzania matched Canada's initial
investment. The land for farming the wheat was taken from the
Barbaig, a pastoral tribe that for centuries had grazed its cattle on
the land, and who are now obliged to use nearby natural pastures
for grazing, contributing to soil erosion and desertification. The
agricultural technologies applied in the project are far too intensive
for the delicate tropical ecology and, as noted in a recent report on
farming and grazing in the Arusha valley, these practices, modelled
on the wheat farms of Canada's western prairies, resemble the
farming methods which provoked the catastrophic dust bowls of
the thirties. The Tanzanian experimental farms are totally unsuited
to an environment subject to periodic tropical floods: the land is
already seriously eroded and infertile rifts cover extensive areas. As

a result, the entire project is being reconceived and traditional Tanzanian wheat farming techniques such as strip-cropping on contoured terraces are being introduced to replace the Canadian technologies.

In Africa, as in Latin America, the goal of food self-sufficiency is often undermined by the channelling of scarce financial resources into large agro-industrial schemes aimed at increasing production of exportable tropical cash crops such as sugar cane and coffee.

In Sudan, this type of project has always been given high priority. The Kenana sugar cane production project is probably the largest of its kind in the world. When it was set up in 1974, sugar prices were at their highest level in years — £665 sterling a tonne. Five years later, when the project finally became operational, the price per tonne had fallen to £63, and it was to be another two years before any sugar was actually refined. While the project was no doubt profitable for the foreign investors and managers involved, the advantages for the Sudan have yet to be demonstrated. Frequent power failures render the irrigation system periodically inoperative, the high cost of oil products slows down the highly mechanized agricultural production, the road system is costly to maintain, and the extension of irrigation has spread debilitating water-borne diseases such as bilharzia — a deadly sickness carried by river snails — throughout rural villages.

Since exportable cash crops bring the highest immediate financial return, the necessary investment is generally made and the best land found for raising them. These lucrative crops apparently justify the construction of roads and storage facilities and make investments in transportation and research worth while for governments. However, in terms of satisfying domestic food needs, the results have been devastating, particularly in Africa. Food production per capita has dropped 1.4% annually since the sixties. According to the 1983 World Bank Development Report, average food production per capita increased in only eight African countries — Burundi, Cameroun, Central African Republic, Ivory Coast, Ruanda, South Africa, Sudan, and Tunisia. The food self-sufficiency ratio for Africa was 98% in the sixties; today it has dropped to 86% and it is diminishing rapidly. Between 1970 and 1980, food imports increased by 8.4% yearly and the cost of grain imports for human consumption alone represented $5 billion each year and continues to grow. The priority given by the majority of African governments to cash crops for export at the expense of

domestic food production has made the continent more dependent
and deprived subsistence agriculture of sorely needed resources.

THE BIG DAMS — AN ENVIRONMENTAL AND HUMAN
TRAGEDY

Officials at the Inter-American Development Bank do not hide
their misgivings regarding the forty giant projects that have been
carried out in recent years on the world's major water systems. In
their view, 39 of these large dams and hydroelectric energy projects
are patent failures. The only one that even partly met its much-
vaunted objectives was the Koussou Dam in the Ivory Coast. A
relative success at that, since the Ivorian engineers estimate that the
system will never be able to function at more than 30% of capacity.
The original technical estimates turned out to be inaccurate and the
predicted export of electrical power to neighbouring countries —
calculated to permit reimbursement of the loans — never material-
ized. The construction of the dam initially caused the forced and
hasty displacement of 100,000 people in particularly inhuman
circumstances.

In Egypt, the Aswan High Dam, inaugurated in 1970, was
originally viewed as a daring step into the future which would
permit the spectacular modernization of a poor country. Today,
Aswan has become a symbol of the absurdity of technology when
it is not mastered and is not conceived to meet real human needs.

The High Dam was designed to generate half of Egypt's electric
power, control the annual flooding of the River Nile, and extend
arable land through irrigation, making year-round farming possible. Detrimental side-effects soon appeared. The fertility of the
arable land steadily declined, while ill-conceived and inadequate
drainage resulted in soil waterlogging and salinization. Egypt's
sardine industry was destroyed as a result of the loss of the rich silt
deposits, which were an essential element of the aquatic food chain
in the Nile Delta. The fish simply stopped coming into the delta
and the country lost an annual catch of 18,000 tonnes.

The introduction of year-round irrigation and cash-cropping
entailed the use of chemical fertilizers and insecticides, resulting in
an alarming accumulation of toxic substances in the soil and
groundwater of rural areas, particularly as the groundwater table
had been raised by the dam. These substances also filter into the
Nile, which is a major source of drinking water for the country's

inhabitants. Besides the rise in chemical pollutants, a serious increase in water-borne diseases has been observed since the completion of the High Dam and the new irrigation canals. The infection rate of bilharzia has increased from zero to 80% in areas with new canals.

Because of the almost totally negative effects of the construction of the High Dam, the Egyptian authorities have been understandably reluctant to provide detailed information on the consequences of the project, an unfortunate attitude which has deprived other nations of the valuable experience Egypt has gained regarding the dangers of such large-scale water development projects.

According to most engineers and water experts, the great majority of the giant water projects underwritten in Third World countries since the sixties by the World Bank and the Inter-American, African, and Asian Development Banks have had devastating ecological and human effects. The first, and no doubt the most brutal, consequence has been the threat of physical and cultural extermination of isolated indigenous peoples, often accompanied by the destruction of potentially valuable unexplored tropical ecosystems, including the virtual extinction of hundreds of species of flora and fauna. Among other detrimental effects cited are the production of noxious gases from biomass decomposition and water-weed infestation of newly formed reservoirs as well as the rapid spread of diseases in which water is implicated, such as parasitosis, malaria, and bilharzia.

The example of the world's largest power dam, Itaïpu, on the Parana river, located between Brazil and Paraguay, is more recent than Aswan, yet it has not been as widely publicized. Although construction began twenty years (1975) after the Aswan project was launched, it proves that the lessons of the past have been either misunderstood or disregarded.

A total of 50,000 people were relocated out of the area to be inundated by the reservoir. The problem of compensation of former residents of the area was only partially solved: for example, 27 Ava-Guarani Indian families received only 20 hectares in exchange for the 1,500 hectares they originally occupied. Some of Brazil's and Paraguay's best farmland, already at a premium, was flooded by the dam's catchment lake. Guaïra Falls, the world's largest natural falls, seven times larger than Niagara in terms of volume of water, has been submerged by the dam reservoir.

In Togo, the damage wrought by the Akossombo Dam,

constructed in neighbouring Ghana between 1962 and 1973, became apparent only twenty years after work on the project began. A 200-metre strip of Togo's coastline was swallowed up by the sea, fishing villages were destroyed, and others are condemned to disappear in the future. The advance of the ocean threatens lakes, particularly Lake Togo which abounds in fish and wild life, not to speak of the fresh-water systems vital to the residents of these areas. A veritable disaster threatens the industrial sea wharf where Togo processes the phosphates on which its economy largely depends — exports of phosphates represent a third of the country's gross national product.

A report recently issued by the University of Lomé in Togo warned, 'The immediate cause of the loss of coastal land is the construction of the Akossombo Dam which retains almost all the sediment carried down-stream by the River Volta. The coast along the Gulf of Guinea, from the mouth of the Volta all the way to Benin, has undergone massive erosion since the opening of the dam began to prevent sediment from flowing down-stream and reinforcing the coastline. The construction of the Port of Lomé had already caused a loss of coastal land, but it was a much slower and less brutal process than the erosion caused by Akossombo. Something must be done before it is too late.'

The engineers who designed Akossombo did not foresee that a quarter of a century later they would provoke an ecological disaster which will no doubt cost as much or more to repair than the dam initially cost to build.

Yet other serious environmental consequences, including a growing threat to agriculture, continue to appear which call into question the very usefulness and economic value of these large water development projects. The example of India, which for the past 50 years has pursued a vigorous policy of developing hydro-electric power in order to sustain its industrial growth, is also very enlightening. On the subcontinent, the large water projects and irrigation schemes have produced only mediocre financial and agricultural results. For example, instead of the predicted yields of 4–5 tonnes of grain per hectare, harvests rarely exceed 1.7 tonnes per hectare.

In the India of the sixties, most of these programmes never paid off financially or socially. The irrigation systems were so designed that they only benefited wealthy landowners and farmers who were in a position to take advantage of the new agricultural opportunities spawned by the Green Revolution. The fragmented holdings of the poor farming class were too widely dispersed to make efficient use of centralized irrigation facilities. The power output of large dams, conceived and built by industry, ultimately did not truly serve the surrounding rural areas where the use of firewood continued, further aggravating the problems of erosion and siltation.

Ironically, while most dams were built to control seasonal flooding resulting from the torrential monsoon, the ribbons had hardly been cut on most of the new installations before engineers realized that they were incapable of preventing or stopping flooding. In fact the dams contributed to it. First, uncontrolled tree-cutting and farming at the dam sites around the catchment reservoirs resulted in greater flooding as the land became less able to absorb rainwater. Then, following the rapid deforestation and erosion of areas surrounding the dams, sedimentation due to upstream erosion further reduced the retaining capacity of the dams, eventually completely destroying their ability to control floods. The conflicting goals — the need for flood control versus the need for water to generate power and for irrigation — have resulted in reservoirs being kept full even during the rainy season. Emergency discharges, to prevent structural breaches, have caused man-made flash floods that have killed thousands in India.

Severe criticism of large-scale water development schemes is hardly ill-founded. The promises of their advocates rarely coincide with the real impact of the construction and operation of these projects. The enormous waste of resources they entail has prompted many observers to ask whether investing the same amounts of money in more modest projects which would benefit larger segments of the population might not be a wiser course for ensuring lasting development. The answer to this question is not as obvious as it might seem, as we shall soon see, for the major obstacles to development are often not financial. It is not a matter of simply condemning large-scale development projects for the sake of it, but of examining the actual impact they have on the overall development process and the standard of living of the entire population of a country. The challenge facing the economies of Third World countries today is to combine large and small projects so that they reinforce one another to ensure more equitable and sustainable forms of development.

The villager from Cameroun drew, in his own manner, the

conclusion that many people in the Third World seem to have come to with regard to large projects.

> Most often, as peasants we are not in a position to oppose the international experts who are not really familiar with our problems. I mean the difficulties I have to face every day. So we thought that it was up to us to set up our own development projects, to make them succeed, to help one another rather than wait for help to come from a large development scheme.

While there appears to be something of a consensus regarding the failure of recent development policy, no one school of economic thought has prevailed. As economists and development experts debate alternatives, the rural populations of many developing countries are busy setting up their own innovative approaches to development.

CHAPTER 2

Microprojects — A New World-wide Phenomenon

Various terms have been used to designate the thousands of grassroots initiatives that are springing up in the rural villages of Third World countries throughout Latin America, Africa, and Asia — microprojects, small-scale development projects, small farmer development programmes, community development, village-level development. Rural groups are engaged in a wide range of activities: well-digging, irrigation, seed selection, reforestation, fish-farming, road-building, managing rural clinics, training rural health workers, developing and testing local technologies, mastering accounting procedures, learning credit management, marketing agricultural products, creating small cottage industries, organizing co-operatives, and so on.

Three short histories collected by our teams in the course of their field visits in Ruanda, India, and Bolivia told with all the passion of the people involved, make this multi-faceted reality more easy to grasp.

'Listen to me, listen to what I have to say, and go and tell others!'

THE PRIDE AND PROGRESS OF A FLEDGLING RUANDAN CO-OPERATIVE

Simon Musengimana, project co-ordinator and son of a rural schoolteacher and a peasant woman, graduated from a Belgian university and then returned to his native Ruanda in 1974 to join the Ministry of Agriculture. He told us how he decided to start an agricultural co-operative on his own.

I decided to leave my post at the Ministry to go back to the Giclye Hills to help the villagers organize so that they could tackle their problems. But the people at the office said I only wanted to show the Government that I could do without it, that I could go it alone.

During the first eight months, I had to stretch the little money I had managed to save when I was studying and working in Belgium. But I finally obtained financial support from some Belgian organizations which I located thanks to contacts I had maintained from my days in Brussels.

At our founding assembly on 11 February 1979, 43 charter members — unheard of in Ruanda — decided officially to set up the 'Twese Hamwe Co-operative'. The cost of a founding share in the co-operative was set at 1,000 Ruandan francs, about $11. The by-laws also required each member to contribute a day's work a week to the co-operative. A month later we were already operating. First, we began organizing the farms, then we built offices for the co-operative, making the adobe bricks ourselves, set up a grain mill at Ntosho and a shop for marketing basic foodstuffs. Now we even have a savings plan for the workers and members of the co-operative. From time to time new projects are launched which we generally manage to finance by ourselves. And, despite a few cases of 'sabotage', the co-operative has managed to survive and is highly regarded in the area.

The Twese Hamwe Co-operative is part of a much broader programme called Action for Integrated Rural Development (AIRD). This non-governmental association plans and co-ordinates community projects such as setting up a village drinking-water system, or building a road to open up an isolated area. In each instance, AIRD carries out preliminary research and feasibility studies and secures funding, generally in Western Europe.

Quite a few development initiatives have been attempted by people from the capital, but these 'well-meaning' people are generally not willing to go all the way because of the risks involved. They want to continue living in the city while they attempt to do something for the rural poor.

Gradually they are overwhelmed by the difficulties and privations they encounter in rural areas and then decide to designate others to manage the projects, people who are often less experienced and less open-minded than the original promoters. The projects ultimately fail because it is impossible to control operations from afar and the promoters soon lose touch with the daily lives of the rural communities they are supposed to be helping.

Greed is another downfall of my countrymen. Most people think twice before sacrificing material security to work in a rural area where the pay is very meagre.

Simon concluded his testimonial by adding:

Many people blame villagers for their plight, considering them backward and closed-minded. But, in fact, the city dwellers are the ones who are afraid of change and innovation. It's truly ironic that they are the ones that claim they are struggling to develop the country. The truth is that they are scared to death of change.

BRINGING WATER AND HOPE TO 100,000 BENGALI PEASANTS

'My Bengal, golden, beloved land', Bengali fishermen chant in chorus as they cast their colourful nets from their dug-outs on the shallow reservoirs surrounded by coconut palms and banana trees. Then, as they return home at dusk, they blow their conch shells to salute the arrival of the goddess of the night. Mritunjoy Mukherjee, a Brahmin priest, told us of the poverty of this land of rice paddies and reservoirs. He described the perennial floods that sweep away houses, roads, and cattle, bringing in their wake malnutrition and disease.

In the 40 years he has lived in his native village of Jikhira, Mukherjee has set up a small Gandhian ashram to help the poor, but lack of money limits its effectiveness. The peasants who own their own plots generally have only a half or a quarter of an acre of land to farm, not enough to survive without working elsewhere. The others, the vast majority, are landless farm workers, and they rely solely on the beans they grow on their rooftops in order to feed their families. Their daily wage averages eight rupees, about $0.40, but they work only five to six months of the year, at planting and harvest time.

According to Mukherjee, when things get rough or disaster strikes the only alternative left for the local farmer is to move to the slums in Calcutta. The small farmer who has lost his home and crops owing to drought or flooding has nowhere else to go. The priest described the inexorable process.

> The first year after calamity strikes a farmer mortgages his land, then the year after he is forced to borrow from the local moneylender at exorbitant rates, for he has to feed his children. The third year his wife sells the jewellery from her dowry. Then the cow and oxen are sold. That's the end of it for him! He's ready for the slum and the life of a coolie. His son will end up pulling a cart like a donkey, and he will probably die of tuberculosis at the age of 30 or 35.
>
> His children will suddenly be uprooted from their peaceful village life to be cast into the havoc and destitution of Calcutta with its gangs and city vices. The only way out of this infernal cycle is irrigation. If the small farmer could have irrigated his plot, he could have harvested three crops a year and his life would have been transformed.
>
> Take the small farmer, for instance, who works a quarter of an acre.

He harvests 450 pounds of rice each year. He needs two pounds of rice a day to feed his family of six. That is the bare minimum to ensure survival. And on top of that he has to pay back the cost of the seed, set aside enough for next year's planting, pay his debts, perhaps even provide for his daughter's dowry, a funeral, or sickness. This man lives in doubt and fear, always with the threat of ending up in Calcutta hanging over his head. Yet, with water flowing from the pumps through canals and irrigation ditches, he could harvest 450 pounds of rice three times a year or even alternate his crops and find a degree of peace of mind.

Following the catastrophic floods of 1978, a team of Indian volunteers which since 1966 had been working under a local physician, Dr Sen, with the inhabitants of Pilkana, one of Calcutta's largest slums, arrived to help the villagers. Mukherjee's encounter with the field workers of this volunteer, non-governmental organization, Seva Sangh Samiti, was to be momentous for the peasants of Jikhira.

The Seva Sangh Samiti team first set up quarters in Mukherjee's ashram while a professor of literature in a Paris lycée collected funds among students and colleagues to set up a 'Help Seva Sangh Samiti Committee'. The funds collected enabled Mukherjee and the team to set up the vast irrigation and drainage scheme which the Brahmin had been dreaming of for years. It was the beginning of a full-scale development effort to irrigate hundreds of acres of farmland, build twelve schools, set up health care facilities for 400 patients a day, organize cottage industries, and sink 50 wells at a depth of 60 feet to supply clean drinking water to the villagers who up until then had been plagued by amoebas, acute gastro-enteritis, and typhoid. Now thousands of farmers are harvesting three crops a year instead of one. As Mukherjee and Seva Sangh Samiti continue their work, 100,000 Bengali peasants have found new hope for the future.

BOLIVIAN VILLAGERS OPEN THEIR ROAD TO DEVELOPMENT

Bundled in their woollen scarves, caps, and earth-coloured ponchos for protection against the icy wind, members of the Aymara Indian community of the village of San Francisco enthusiastically recount the epic of their road. A circle of children listens nearby as the elders begin by intoning the litany of their miseries. Don Paco, the community leader trained by the first team of foreign development workers from the French non-governmental organization CICD (International Centre for Co-operation for Development), waits his turn to tell his version of the story.

San Francisco, perched at 3700 metres in the Bolivian Andes, is a tiny cluster of adobe houses recently roofed with bright orange Spanish tiles that finally arrived by truck from the other side of the world — La Paz, the capital.

Here the land is fertile, thanks to a temperate micro-climate protected by the surrounding chain of mountains crowned by the legendary twin peaks of Illampu rising to 6500 metres. But these plots of 'warm' land, which provide more than enough food to feed the community, belong to the *patrones*, or landowners, of Ambasia, a small rural town in the valley eight miles below.

Don Luis, community leader and member of San Francisco's village council, tries to get our attention.

> Listen to me, listen to what I have to say, and go and tell others! We still have to break our backs for the *patrones*. And when they think we are not producing enough on 'their' land, they slug us with their bare fists, kick us, or club us with shovels. We set up our community council to fight the *patrones* of Ambasia with the help of the Pastoral Committee for the Land of the Diocese and Paulino, an Aymara like us. He was born here and now works as an agronomist.
>
> Thanks to Jean-Marc from CICD, who came all the way from Europe to help us, and our hard work, we have brought life back to our community. We built our community centre by ourselves. Our children attend school here and the adults learn how to read and write. We are planning to build a grain mill to make our lives easier.

Paulino, our guide in this forgotten corner of the planet, translates Don Luis's Aymara into Spanish. Earlier, our jeep had climbed the track hewn out of the granite mountainside at 4500 metres altitude. It wound along eight miles before it came to a dead end in San Francisco's Plaza de Armas. Don Paco, picking up from Don Luis, begins to tell how the people of San Francisco conquered the mountain with their 'hand made' road.

> Here in San Francisco, we can grow anything, more than we actually need for our own consumption. Corn, fruit, vegetables, beans. But it used to take hours on foot to take our produce to the market in Ambasia once a week. And in Ambasia the *patrones* run the market and make the rules. We couldn't go any further on foot or reach other markets. The road ended at Ambasia. All we had was a small footpath

wide enough for a single person with a load on his shoulders. First, we went all the way to La Paz to beg the government to build us a road so trucks could come up here from Ambasia. They replied, 'We can't afford it. There's no credit.' For us that meant, 'There's nothing for the Aymaras way up there.' What could we do? Resign ourselves to submitting to the *patrones* in Ambasia, to their insults and blows, and the injustice of the local judges. We decided to ask the Pastoral Committee and Jean-Marc to help us buy shovels, pickaxes, and dynamite. There are not many of us up here, not more than 1,000 to 1,200 Aymaras in the entire valley. But together we decided in our assembly to build the road ourselves. It took four years to carve the road out of the mountain, with the entire community working with picks and shovels and their bare hands, until we had opened eight miles of road for the trucks to come through. While the men and women split through the rock, the children pushed the debris down the mountain into ravines below. Four years of hard work and at last the first truck could come through to load our corn, beans, fruit, and vegetables. Now it comes every week. Its capacity is eighteen tons and our road is strong enough for it. We also travel on it to La Paz to sell our produce and buy what we need to fix up our houses, build the community centre, the mill, and soon maybe even a silo.

In the middle of the Plaza waits a large, brightly coloured truck, loaded with 4,000 kilos of corn for La Paz. On the way back it will bring another load of tiles for the roof of the mill.

The rapid spread of microprojects and the growth of non-governmental organizations working in rural villages has been observed on the five continents. However, two notable exceptions to this trend should be mentioned.

In the socialist countries of Europe and Asia non-governmental organizations are rare and relations with developing nations are normally restricted to purely governmental channels.

Non-governmental organizations are also almost non-existent in the Arab world, with the exception of Egypt where most of the local NGOs have been set up by the Coptic community. This situation is all the more surprising since a number of Arab nations are affected by the problems of underdevelopment and, in particular, are plagued by shortfalls in domestic food production. The reasons for this situation, unique among developing nations, are hard to understand. Perhaps the explanation offered by an Arab sociologist may cast some light on this matter.

The religious origin — Christian in particular — of many of the pioneer European NGOs caused many Arab Muslims to regard them with a certain amount of suspicion, fearing that they might in fact be more concerned with proselytizing than with humanitarian goals. It should also be noted that the Koranic tradition places greater emphasis on individual charity than on organized efforts other than those carried out within the *uma*, or community of the faithful, the symbolic centre of which is the mosque. It should also be pointed out that the rise in Arab societies of an affluent class which, like those in the West, is more concerned with maintaining its standard of living and enjoying the benefits of the consumer society, has resulted in a general lack of interest in the social and economic problems facing these nations.

There are no doubt other explanations for the absence of private volunteer movements working to address development problems in the Arab world. It would be enlightening if authoritative voices in Arab countries spoke out to explain or justify this apparent lack of concern or, better yet, to suggest development alternatives like those in progress in other areas of the world.

The case of China deserves special attention. In fact, one of the major targets of the economic reordering under way in China since 1979 is agriculture, a sector of great economic potential. The earlier collectivist approach is being gradually replaced by a more flexible agricultural system. In the words of Wan Li, a member of the Chinese leadership, in a speech made in 1984, 'Affluent farmers are the avant-garde of productive forces in rural areas.' This certainly represents a radical change of policy.

This shift was also underscored by a surprising request made by the Chinese government to the regional office of the United Nations Development Programme in Beijing, in December 1983. The Chinese authorities apparently suggested that UNDP initiate exploratory contacts with European NGOs, private groups, and foundations, to determine to what extent they would be interested in participating in a co-operation programme with China. The Chinese government showed an interest both in promoting NGO financing of projects in China and in their participation in technical assistance in the field. The programme would involve setting up scholarships for trainees from developing countries, inviting volunteer technical assistance (Transfer of Know-How through Expatriate Nationals, or TOKTEN), and training of rural co-operative personnel, as well as rural development projects for minority population groups numbering over 60 million who live in outlying and often inaccessible areas of the Republic.

The success of China's 'barefoot doctors' has already shown that a rudimentary assistance programme geared to meeting the needs of large segments of the population can have a significant impact on health problems. The request for assistance from European NGOs shows an openness on the part of the Chinese to innovative approaches which will be interesting to observe in the future.

CHAPTER 3

Development of the Third World — a Continual Concern of the Club of Rome

When it was founded in 1968, then again in 1972, in its comments on the Meadows Report, *Limits to Growth*, the Club of Rome solemnly emphasized the importance of the difficulties confronting the Third World within the global 'problématique'.

> A substantial improvement of the situation of the so-called developing nations is a *sine qua non* of world equilibrium, an improvement necessary in absolute terms as well as in relation to the developed nations.[1]

New expressions were coined: 'new world order', 'planetary strategy'. It was in the hope of inspiring more concrete recommendations that, following a meeting held in Salzburg in February 1974 which was attended by heads of state or government from Mexico, Senegal, Canada, Sweden, the Netherlands, and Austria, the Club of Rome asked Nobel laureate Jan Tinbergen, professor of economics, to prepare a report on the 'new international order' which came to be known as the 'RIO' (reshaping the international order) Report. This study, which was extensively discussed and debated at a meeting in Algiers in October 1976, did not have the hoped-for impact on public opinion and world leaders, perhaps owing to its rather academic presentation and generalized proposals.

Yet the problem is one of the issues most often discussed at the Club of Rome as well as in the major international forums. In 1977, an official report of the Canton of Geneva estimated that over 52,000 experts had debated the problems of the Third World that year in some 1,020 meetings representing a total of about 14,000 working sessions. These *ad hoc* meetings do not include the daily work of 20,000 international civil servants throughout the

[1] Maurice Guernier, *Tiers-Monde: Trois Quarts du Monde. Rapport au Club de Rome*, Dunod, Paris, 1980.

110 world organizations which have headquarters in Geneva. To this inventory should also be added the scores of meetings held at UN headquarters in New York, at the World Bank in Washington, DC, at the European Economic Community in Brussels, at the Organization for Economic Co-operation and Development (OECD) and UNESCO in Paris, the UN Food and Agriculture Organization (FAO) in Rome, the Organization of African Unity (OAU) in Addis Ababa, the UN Environment Programme (UNEP) in Nairobi, and so on. The succession of meetings continues to increase exponentially with each passing year, contributing no doubt to one of the greatest bureaucratic wastes of all time.

Recognizing the inefficiency of many of these endeavours, Maurice Guernier presented a new report to the Club of Rome in 1980, *Third World, Three-Quarters of the World*, which set the stage for immediate and concrete action. His most innovative recommendation concerned the creation of large development communities within the Third World.

Facing the five major communities of the northern hemisphere — North America, Europe, the USSR, Japan, and China — Guernier recommended setting up five or six communities in the southern half of the globe:

in Latin America (already called for by such distinguished Latin Americans as Paul Prebish and Felipe Herrera)
in Africa
in the Middle East — from Morocco to Iran
on the Indian sub-continent
in Southern Asia.

Maurice Guernier's ideas were warmly received and became the subject of a special meeting of the Club of Rome held in 1980 at the United Nations in New York, which was attended by a host of high-level officials, including the Secretary-General himself as well as the Chairman of the Security Council and the President of ECOSOC.

As a result of this meeting, the UN and the Club of Rome decided jointly to consider Guernier's new approach. However, after four years of efforts, the final recommendations never moved beyond vague generalities, without any mention being made of realistic goals for regional co-operation or any attempt to define strategies to attain well-meaning objectives. This failure showed how difficult it is to persuade people to accept a practical approach to problem-solving.

In 1984 another Club member, René Lenoir, presented and published yet another report, *The Third World Can Feed Itself*, in which two 'scenarios' are put forward concerning food supply and the dependence of Third World countries on food imports into the next century. The first scenario, more or less corresponding to the status quo, predicts a dramatic deterioration of economic and social conditions in Third World countries if top priority is not given to domestic food production. Lenoir suggests an alternative course, recommending the mobilization of rural populations which would assume full responsibility for their own development at village or community level, while governments would commit themselves to a pricing structure in line with the real costs of agricultural production and provide the necessary infrastructure (roads, transportation, and communication networks) to ensure ready access of products to markets and consumers. The latter hypothesis, of course, would imply that governments should radically reassess the policies they have been committed to in the past. Shifting the emphasis from the individual farmer to the village or community, this approach would reinstate the group as the most effective agent for economic development and social change.

The Club of Rome has devoted a succession of reports and studies to the problems of the Third World because it feels that this is the major challenge of our time, while its members also recognize the complexities and difficulties of the issues involved. For the present study the Club has decided to change its customary approach and work, as it were, from the ground up, in the hope that the report will have a greater audience.

The Barefoot Revolution, then, is the result of keen observation in the field and analysis of work in progress at village and community level in dozens of areas of the Third World. These small-scale projects undergo a continual process of trial and error — thousands are launched, progress, succeed, or get stuck and fail, while others are constantly springing up. The wonder is that up until now no one has attempted an overview of this phenomenon, despite the plethora of books and studies that have appeared on its theoretical aspects and case studies in selected areas. Perhaps the vast number and human dimension of these operations, as well as their extraordinary diversity, have discouraged many from attempting a global approach, combined with the fact that most of these undertakings still remain isolated and their achievements are difficult to evaluate with the stock tools of the economist and sociologist.

In the final analysis, however, this neglect is probably due to the fact that development efforts are normally not considered exciting fare. There is really nothing very spectacular about a field of wheat, a well, or a rural clinic if the real story of the battle waged and won is not told. What is spectacular is underdevelopment, with its trail of powerful and obsessive images — starving children in Biafra, Bangladesh, and Ethiopia, food riots in Brazil, and so on. This is probably the reason why the media prefer to cover underdevelopment, rather than attempting to show the slow and painstaking efforts of those who are building their future with their own hands.

The goal of the present study, then, is not only to attempt an overview of a major development trend, through the detailed analysis of a series of grassroots rural initiatives in nineteen Third World countries, but to provide the forgotten men and women encountered in the course of the survey with the opportunity of speaking for themselves.

Their words have been carefully set down following interviews conducted during field visits by several teams. The stories, admonitions, recommendations, complaints, illustrate the reality of the rural Third World and are intended to ensure that the voices of the rural poor be heard expressing their hopes, expectations, or disappointments, sometimes even their revolt, but almost never their resignation.

PART TWO

CHAPTER 4
First Aid, then Development

'When many Third World countries won independence and nationhood in the sixties, the former charitable activities of humanitarian groups suddenly turned into fully fledged development projects,' Akpalo Kouassivi, Executive Secretary of the Council of Non-governmental Organizations in Togo, pointed out recently in interviews with our field survey team in West Africa. He went on to underscore what he regards as the crucial situation facing African rural societies today: 'It is not so much a matter of promoting development as arresting underdevelopment. This means first and foremost slowing migration to the cities by reinforcing the cultural identity of the rural poor while at the same time offering them a way of staying on the land and farming.'

In rural villages throughout the Third World, in Brazil and Kenya, Zaire and the Philippines, Indonesia and Egypt, two contradictory forces are at work — the entropy of poverty and the dynamic push to provide genuine development alternatives. On the one hand, development projects seem to be spreading to even the most remote rural areas, giving the impression that a vast movement is in progress. Yet in the immediate vicinity of a project, in the next village or even in the next field, the familiar symptoms of poverty and underdevelopment can still be seen. In many cases the latter end up by cancelling the positive effects of the former.

The statements of the dozens of villagers interviewed in the course of this study confirm the sombre assessment that the overwhelming majority of the Third World rural population is caught up in the spiral of poverty and hunger. In the words of one African villager, 'Rather than talk of development, what we urgently need is rescue, in other words first aid.'

The situation becomes more complex as one attempts to account for the persistence of poverty and its causes. To understand the impact of small-scale village-level development initiatives, we must first examine the factors contributing to rural impoverishment in the light of observations and information gathered during our field surveys. The data collected in the course of these visits has enabled us to complement the extremely fragmentary information culled from numerous theoretical works and publications.

Some of these factors are structural, others are related to the economic situation; some economic parameters have existed for so long that they have become structural. Some characteristics are common to most poor countries, others are specific to individual areas, and, before analysing these factors, it must be emphasized that their effects vary considerably from one country to another. Far from constituting a homogenous group, the Third World is a collection of contradictions and paradoxes. There is not one Third World, but many.

Over the last twenty years the overall standard of living has improved in some countries, such as Brazil, Cameroun, the Ivory Coast, Malaysia, South Korea, Taiwan, Hong Kong, and Singapore. Other nations, such as India and China, by a variety of means have managed to attain food self-sufficiency and to continue their economic progress. To underrate the development efforts of these nations would be a grave injustice. None the less, few of the 125 countries officially regarded as 'developing nations' could claim that this euphemism reflects their actual economic situation: 'underdeveloping' would be a more appropriate term. Consider such populous countries as Bangladesh, Egypt, Kenya, Indonesia, Burundi, Ruanda, or Malawi, where land and resources are scarce. Despite increased food production, the growth rate of these nations has not kept pace with that of the population. According to the latest World Bank estimates, in Bangladesh, Nepal, and 27 of the sub-Saharan African countries, the birth-rate has completely overtaken and mortgaged future economic growth. The world-wide shortage of arable land further reduces many nations' chances of ever becoming self-sufficient. Yet possibilities remain for feeding a growing population — it is not so much a problem of availability of food as one of distribution.

Economists have even introduced a further category among the poor nations, that of the 'Least Developed Countries', the LDCs — the majority of this group of 36 countries are African — in which per capita income is at the bottom of the international scale. Given that per capita income appears to be a fairly inaccurate indicator in the case of the poorest nations, even that income continues to slide and is in the process of disappearing altogether.

Lastly, socio-cultural characteristics, political regimes, underlying ideologies, and administrative systems contribute no less to defining the complexity of each situation. Even within these so-called developing countries, disparities between different geographic areas or social and professional groups are increasing rather than diminishing. Brazil and Kenya represent two good examples of social and economic contradictions within their very borders.

In Brazil there is the enormous imbalance between the heavily industrialized states in the south and the depressed north-eastern region, the 'nordeste' where alongside pockets of industrial development, government-supported agro-industry has developed anarchically over the past fifteen to twenty years at the expense of small farmers and landless peasants. In the State of São Paulo, 50 children out of every 1,000 live births die before reaching the age of five. In the nordeste, only 500 of each 1,000 children born will survive beyond their first year in school. These figures were quoted to the press in October 1984 by the Brazilian Federal Minister of Health himself.

In Kenya, the desert is rapidly overtaking the impoverished and overpopulated areas. If a line is drawn from the island of Lamu, at Kenya's northern coastal border with Somalia, all the way across the country to Mount Kenya, the population living on the 180,000 square miles north of this line would not be more than half a million people, while in the 130,000 square miles of territory south of the line over eighteen million people live. In fact, in the north-east, the population density in particularly arid zones falls to one inhabitant for each two square miles, while in the populous south it rises to 500 in the Nyeri and Fort Hall districts and even 700 around Kiambu.

Compounding the extraordinary disparity of population in Kenya are the extremely diverse levels of development. Primitive bushmen are still to be found alongside a modern managerial class including sophisticated trade union and political leaders. The disparities between areas within Third World countries, as well as other no less flagrant contradictions, often divide poor nations against themselves, while the destinies and interests of the industrialized North and impoverished South continue to drift further and further apart.

To begin to understand these complex differences, the very classification of these areas needs to be revised. The eminent French economist Jacques Lesourne, founder of OECD's forecasting

'Interfutures' group, proposed five categories, more or less corresponding to the widely diverging levels of economic and social development prevailing in these areas.

At the top of the list are the nations of East and South-East Asia which have already experienced two generations of industrialization. A first sub-group includes the 'gang of four' — Hong Kong, Singapore, Korea, and Taiwan, with Malaysia coming immediately behind. These countries have all experienced fairly advanced industrialization and some have even managed to attain a more or less equitable distribution of income. In most of them education and training have helped ensure development and acquisition of skills, in both industry and agriculture. This group also benefits from the proximity of Japan, and it is gradually emerging as a coherent economic zone in the western Pacific.

The second group covers the whole of Latin America. Here the situation is entirely different, first of all because investments have been channelled into more capital intensive industries. Income, although very unevenly distributed, has tended to increase during periods of growth, including the seventies when the population as a whole benefited from the economic boom, particularly in countries such as Mexico and Brazil. However, this growth was achieved at a tremendous cost, an almost intolerably high level of indebtedness.

The third group consists of 'continent' countries such as India and China. In recent years these countries have made strides justifying a certain amount of optimism. The shift of policy in China has led to a considerable increase in agricultural production, vital to the country's development, and prospects for improving industrial production, in view of the measures which have been taken, are far from negligible. Annual GNP growth rates of five and six per cent in China no longer appear impossible between now and the end of the century. India, the other major 'continent' country, has a very low per capita income. Although a vast agricultural country, India possesses a strong industrial base, particularly in heavy industry. Like China, India maintains a very independent political stance, and accordingly it does not suffer from debt problems. The World Bank estimates that India could easily attain annual GNP growth rates of 4.5 per cent.

A fourth group is made up of several intermediate countries where the process of industrialization is still recent or fragile. In these countries, the major development problems confront the agricultural sector. North Africa and the Middle Eastern nations make up the greater part of this category.

The fifth and final group includes the poorest regions — Africa south of the Sahara in particular — for which the World Bank has sounded the alarm in view of the extremely pessimistic outlook for agriculture in these countries. Here, per capita agricultural production has fallen considerably in recent years. Prospects for industrialization are limited, government administrations are weak and policies uncertain. Many observers consider the future of these countries to be threatened, all the more so since demographic pressures continue to squeeze already scarce resources.

Referring euphemistically to the countries which make up these diverse Third Worlds as 'developing countries' seems almost irresponsible. A good many of them are 'underdeveloping countries'. It might be more accurate to refer to them simply as poor or Third World nations, keeping in mind the extreme diversity of the regions under consideration.

In the course of our study, we soon realized that the term 'underdevelopment' designated more than insufficient economic development. It generally described an inexorable process of impoverishment afflicting vast areas in the southern hemisphere. We began to look closely at the causes, or 'factors of impoverishment'. In the interviews with villagers, development workers, local officials, village chiefs, political leaders, and others, the factors of impoverishment which were invariably cited as being direct causes of underdevelopment were: political instability, indebtedness, misuse and misappropriation of land, uncontrolled migration and population growth, the loss or rejection of cultural identity, and finally corruption. Again and again dozens of examples of their devastating effects were given. Before we attempt to define a set of 'factors of development', we shall review, using some of these examples, the regressive factors.

CHAPTER 5

Factors of Impoverishment

POLITICAL INSTABILITY

In a rapidly evolving and violent world, where ideological and economic conflicts threaten rich and poor societies alike, Third World nations tend to be more dependent than interdependent or aware of the basic ties of mutual interest and solidarity which should unite them. They feel their voice is seldom heard, and when it is, it is even less understood. History has bequeathed to them fragile, often artificial boundaries. From former colonial powers they have also inherited notions of national sovereignty which in some cases run counter to local secular tradition and custom. While civil strife threatens areas of Latin America and Africa, wars and constant violence have become a daily feature of life in the Middle East and South-East Asia. Caught between the super powers, many of these countries struggle to resist coups, minority revolts, and rebellion among the poorer sectors of the population.

There can be no better way of illustrating this instability than by chronicling some of the events of the past two decades. The example of Africa is particularly eloquent in this respect: in the past 25 years over 70 heads of government in 29 African countries have been overthrown by assassination, purges, coups. Of the 41 states south of the Sahara, only six permit opposition parties, seventeen are one-party regimes, and a further eighteen are governed by the military. Taking a quick glance over the events of 1984, for example, we observe:

8 coups
Burkina Faso: 1 successful, 1 attempted.
Mauritania: the Prime Minister deposed the President.
Nigeria: coup by General Buhari.
Cameroun: attempted coup followed violent fighting which re-
    sulted in many deaths.
Guinea: a military committee for national recovery took power
    one week after the death of Sekou Touré.

Niger: attempted coup.
Grenada: successful coup.

14 riots or demonstrations
Chile: successive demonstrations and protest days, in each case resulting in dozens of people killed and hundreds injured.
India: fighting between the Indian army and militant Sikhs resulted in at least 2,000 dead and thousands of arrests.
South Africa: (official figures) 31 dead.
Sri Lanka: fighting on several occasions between security forces and Tamil separatists led to the deaths of several hundred people.
Nigeria: several hundred dead in fighting between police and the Muslim Brotherhood.
Dominican Republic: rioting against the austerity policy resulted in 45 dead.
Plus riots in Pakistan, Philippines, and Senegal.

21 executions or political assassinations
Benigno Aquino in the Philippines, Indira Gandhi in India, Malcolm Kerr, President of the American University in Beirut, are among those which have most influenced public opinion; but various political opponents in Jamaica, Turkey, Iran, South Africa, Sudan, Peru, and Lebanon were also killed.

30 bomb attacks
Explosions in airports, trains, shops caused the deaths of approximately 500 people in Afghanistan, Chad, Israel, Kuwait, Burma, Angola, as well as in the United Kingdom, Northern Ireland, Italy and France.

Wars and guerilla attacks
Conflicts, more or less bloody, breaking out, dying down, or flaring up again after semblances of cease-fires and negotiations. In all cases, the victims are without number.

A summary of violence in 1984 would be incomplete if it did not include mention of the various natural catastrophes — cyclones in the Philippines, over 1,000 dead; earthquake in Turkey, more than 2,000 victims; famine in Ethiopia, 6 million endangered — or accidents caused by industrial civilization — as in Mexico where the explosion of tanks containing liquid gas caused almost 500 dead

and 4,000 injured, or in India where a leak of poisonous gas at
Bhopal caused the deaths of 2,500 people and will have dramatic
consequences for another 100,000.

The world has also seen a terrifying increase in violent crime. In
Lagos several murders are committed every day on the public
highway. A thief who wishes to steal a car does not think twice
about murdering its occupants, a burglar kills all the inhabitants of
a house or apartment in the course of a robbery. Because the death
penalty is applied to all armed robbers, even if they have not used
their weapons, witnesses must not be allowed to survive. Taxi and
bus passengers are held to ransom by armed individuals. After
eight o'clock in the evening it is practically impossible to find a taxi
driver prepared to take passengers to the airport from Lagos,
because the ten-mile highway to the airport is occasionally overrun
by gangs of armed youths who stop cars to steal money, identity
papers, and luggage. The army and police have increased road
blocks and controls in vain: crime increases daily.

This type of violence takes place most frequently in large urban
areas such as São Paulo, Bogotà, and Mexico City, Manila and
Bangkok, where the cumulative effects of urban sprawl and
poverty make it almost impossible to enforce the law. The inability
of public authorities to assure security in the major political or
economical capitals could well endanger the power of the State and
the effective exercise of its authority over the country as a whole.
This is one of the factors of political instability which is becoming
increasingly important, and its results can be felt even in rural
communities. More seriously, the weakness of the State, sometimes its absence, in these rural areas can create a temptation to
establish 'peasant power', which could only increase the existing
gap between urban and rural areas.

INDEBTEDNESS

In considering factors of impoverishment, it is well to recall, albeit
briefly, that the current strength of the dollar, by increasing the
indebtedness of countries, constitutes a burden which weighs on
their financial equilibrium. According to the OECD, loans granted
in 1982 to poor countries amounted to no more than 7% of the
overall amount of domestic and international credits of Western
banks and made up 30% of all international credits. Three countries,

Brazil, Mexico, and Argentina, alone account for 40% of this total, the remainder being shared between the 50 other countries concerned.

For example: Brazil's debt, now more than $110 billion, has been caused for the major part by the following projects:

the Itaïpu Dam which cost $25 billion and produces electricity 30% more expensive than that previously supplied.

a nuclear project which has already cost $35 billion.

the planned railway line to link the state of Minas Gerais with the states of São Paulo and of Rio to transport iron ore; not one single mile of track has been laid, the various elements of civil engineering — bridges, tunnels, etc. — are rusted and overgrown, and $100 billion has been swallowed up by this project.

a considerable amount of irrigation work currently under way; these irrigation and hydroelectric projects will benefit only a small number of people, major agro-industry plants, agrofood units working for export, high technology industry, all to the detriment of small farmers.

The increase of $480 billion in the debt of non-oil-producing countries between 1973 and 1982 can be broken down as follows:[1]

oil price increases in excess of inflation in the United States, cumulative total between 1974 and 1982: $260 billion.

above average interest rates between 1961 and 1980 and effects in 1981 and 1982: $40 billion.

deterioration in the terms of trade and export losses in real terms as a result of the world-wide recession: $100 billion.

Of this $480 billion debt in 1982, $80 billion alone represented indebtedness resulting from the policies of non-oil-producing countries themselves. The slowing down in world growth and the increase in interest rates resulted in projects, profitable at the outset, running into losses.

Thus, on the strength of phosphates which were bringing in substantial resources, Togo set up a prestige and industrialization investment policy in the seventies. Industry received 72 billion francs CFA for major projects. However, the price of phosphates has fallen drastically since 1975 and Togo is now saddled with a large number of unprofitable industrial complexes which have had

[1] Study by the Institute for International Economics, Washington.

to close down (for example oil refineries). Today Togo has a per capita debt almost equal to its per capita GDP. Nevertheless, like many other countries, even among the poorest, Togo devotes almost one-third of its investments to purchases of military equipment and to expenditure on prestige items.

The poor countries are strangled by debt, the weight of which mainly results from measures imposed from the outside, but also because policy options do not take account of the basic needs of the population. It is not clear how these countries could in the near future find the means of acquiring capital goods, since the OPEC countries are no longer in a position to extend credit or grant loans; furthermore, the United States, the richest country in the world, instead of lending to others, continues to exploit the world's available resources, paying for these resources at rates which make the rich even richer and the poor poorer. Lastly, within the frame of the vast change which the world is undergoing today, industrialized countries, paralysed by their own economic and social difficulties, have increasingly tended to limit public aid to poor countries.

If the poor countries are beginning to feel that they must rely on themselves rather than on others, it is because they see their development efforts being abruptly brought to a standstill through lack of resources and aid, at least official, from governments in the countries of the North.

LAND MISUSE

Whether by the violence of nature or by the hand of man, land is continually being misused.

Violence of climate

In the village of Gaban in Cameroun, a couple of volunteer workers from Volontaires du Progrès and some villagers described the situation to us. Gaban is situated in arid savannah in the north of the country, that is to say at the southern edge of the vast Sahel region. This is an alluvial plain covered with a sedimentary layer between six and twenty metres thick, under which is a layer of marl enabling the formation of fresh ground-water reserves. Village wells are on average twelve metres deep. A considerable number of 'mayos', wadi-type rivers, cross the plain from east to west, rising in the marshy region which is the southern prolongation of Lake Chad and winding their way through the sandy bed: these are tributaries of the Mayo Kibi, which itself is a tributary of the Bénoué. Each village is built on the banks of a mayo which fills up during the rainy season and overflows, depositing a thin layer of fertile alluvium on the surrounding fields. Gaban is built at the confluence of two mayos.

'For more than ten years now,' the villagers say, 'the mayos of Gaban haven't been filled with water for more than eight days a year, right at the time when the rainy season starts. This year, although large tropical rain clouds burst over the hills and the marshlands of the Logone and on the plain a few kilometres from Gaban, there wasn't enough rainfall to fill up the mayos again. The water ran over the parched earth without penetrating it and the seeds which were sown according to tradition just before the first rains came were roasted before they had time to germinate.'

The average depth of the fertile layer in the fields around Gaban is approximately 5–6 cm. It is a mixture of sand and decomposed vegetation, either the meagre bush vegetation (in the case of a field which has been cleared for the first time), or of millet or cotton stems or groundnut twigs (in the case of fields which have been farmed over a long period). Despite this annual deposit of organic material, and despite manuring from cow or horse dung, this layer very rapidly becomes infertile.

There would have to be a considerable urea input to enrich the earth. Sodecoton (national company for the development of cotton growing), responsible for piloting the food crops project in the north, is holding in its warehouses there sufficiently large stocks of urea or plant protection products (fungicides and insecticides), but it does not distribute these to the farmers. The selling price is too high for the farmer who is constantly in debt because of insufficient yields in food crops, which also leads to speculation on millet.

Water hand pumped from wells is insufficient to ensure irrigation of the crops. Neither tradition nor imported technology has resulted in the construction of mini-dams on the mayos to create a large number of small reservoirs during the rainy season which would enable watering and irrigation of food crops over a longer period.

On the other hand, according to all water engineers, the construction of a gigantic dam at Maga-Kéléo to the north-east of the plain where Gaban is situated, has modified the already sensitive regime of the mayos, and may also have disturbed the ecosystem of a vast area, by the same token endangering the traditional food crop (millet). Camriz (Cameroun Rice Company) uses the water from the dam to produce rice in the north of Cameroun where rice is not eaten (eating habits are based on millet and difficult to change). Rice is exported to the south over 1,800 kilometres of track, although the south, thanks to its own rice fields, is self-sufficient in rice. In attempting to counteract the vagaries of the weather, decisions counter to common sense, or no decisions at all, end up aggravating an already difficult situation.

Real desertification and false drought
In certain regions of India if the monsoon is late, no harvest is possible. When drought lasts for ten consecutive years in the Sahel, all the Sahel economies, already fragile at the outset, are scorched by the sun. Rapid desertification is destroying the fertile earth. The poor are becoming still poorer, and people talk of the 'curse of drought'. It is true that for over five years the rainfall deficit in the nordeste of Brazil has been considerable. However, lack of rain has not affected the vast reserves of ground-water, nor has it had any appreciable effect in reducing the regime of the rios. Those in charge of what has been called the 'Radan Project' have carried out a detailed study on the problem of water in the nordeste. The current reserves in the area examined, which covers 67% of what has been called the 'drought polygon', stand at 70 billion cubic metres of surface water and 240 billion cubic metres of ground-water. As far as the largest rios running through the nordeste are concerned, Jaquaribe, São Francisco, and Parnaiba, 3% of their waters are used for irrigation purposes, 97% flows into the sea.

The same goes for the wastage of rain water. In the present period of drought, in the state of Céara alone, there is an average overall annual rainfall of 720 mm, or 110 billion cubic metres of water. Since there are no reservoirs, because reforestation plans have not been implemented, most of this water trickles over the eroded earth into the rios and is lost in the sea. With this rainfall alone, and allowing for evaporation and water losses on steep eroded hillsides, it would be possible to constitute water reserves of 30–40 billion cubic metres; the state of Céara would thus be able to increase the total area of irrigated land to 6,000,000 hectares, compared to the present figure of barely 60,000 hectares.

In 1983, Professor Iprides Macado, Vice-President of the

Brazilian Association for Water Resources, talking of the state of Céara, said: 'With the construction of 6 large and 24 medium-sized water reservoirs, and a network of aqueducts, it would be possible to provide all the water necessary for all agricultural activities. These reservoirs and the distribution network could be built for a cost of 220 billion cruzeiros (US$80 million), i.e. 120 billion cruzeiros less than the government supplied in "charity" to the state of Céara under the heading of drought grants.'

The money for these drought grants, apart from a few crumbs which trickle down to the small farmers, has disappeared no one knows where, the greater part probably going to the large landowners (the *fazenderos*) and to the 'clients' of politicians.

Land misappropriation

'Land without farmers — Farmers without land.' It is not just that millions of peasants are stripped of any means of earning a living; the land itself is misappropriated, by landowners eager to increase their properties, diverted from its primary use in providing food, degraded and impoverished by the misuse to which it is subjected.

In India, it is easier than you think to lose your piece of land. Lose it, you say? In the shade of a banyan tree, Palani, now landless, tells how his grandfather lost his five acres all because of some dried fish:

> Sahul Rawther, a trader in the village, was a friend of my grandfather. Each time he went into town for his own business, he never forgot to bring back some dried fish for the old man, who was very fond of it and bought this fish on credit. One day the shopkeeper demanded immediate payment from my grandfather, or his land in exchange. My grandfather could not pay back the money he owed and had to hand over his land, literally swallowed up by the dried fish.

Munuswami is a Harijan farmer who lost his piece of land, as many lost or are still losing theirs. He used to farm a three-acre field which yielded enough for himself and his family for the major part of the year. The remaining three or four months, when he did not have enough, he worked for wages on the farm of a landowner. Everything was more or less satisfactory until the region was struck by drought and famine at the end of the fifties. Nine out of ten people in the region were without food, sometimes for several days. One of the children was dying of hunger and Munuswami went to the landowners, begging for a little food for his children. One of them offered him 10 kgs of sorghum. Munu's daughter was saved, but it cost him dearly: he had to hand over his land in exchange.

Illiteracy also costs dearly, if we are to believe the tale told by a Brazilian peasant from Carquija:

> Before I knew how to read, I used to get papers which I was to sign. I didn't know how to write so the person who had brought me the papers signed for me. And then I had to leave the land which I was working because the paper said that I agreed to go away in return for money. I don't know how much. I think it was 300,000 cruzeiros. I don't know where the money is, probably in the Banco Agraria or somewhere else, because I couldn't fill in the papers to get the money. That was ten years ago. Now I know how to read, and nobody can cheat me any more, because written words are written and no one can say anything other than what is written. That's what is good for my family and myself, because I can read now.

Failure of land reform

In Brazil, development is first and foremost a problem of land. In this country, fifteen times the size of France, there are more than 5 million landless farmers, another 500,000 who farm less than 5 hectares that they do not own, and 750,000 small owners with less than 5 hectares. Osmundo Rabouça, Secretary for Economic Planning in the government of the state of Céara:

> A close examination of the land structure of Céara shows that a handful of people own most of the land, but this land is not farmed, that a few small landowners do not have the means to farm their land, and that a vast number of landless farmers have absolutely no possibility of working the land. This combination of 'land without farmers and farmers without land' is a factor of extreme social tension.

The dimension of the land factor can be found particularly in all the countries of Latin America. Until 1968, more than 60% of farm land in Peru belonged to less than 2.5% of the population. We asked one of the country's political leaders to explain the aims of the agrarian reform of 1969.

> The basic idea of our land reform was to set up in areas of agricultural production co-operative structures for production and distribution, around which village communities would spring up. In this way farming communities would be brought on to the economic scene, so that they could produce beyond self-sufficiency and control the marketing of their products. The profits of the co-operatives were to be reinvested in rural areas. However, at the same time, a balance had

to be established between the food crops necessary to satisfy the food requirements of the country and the cash crops for export which create foreign currency and which would have enabled the development of a modern agro-industry, without destroying small farmers ...

The land structure was that inherited from the aftermath of the Conquest when the large estates were set up on the fertile land by the Spanish settlers, to the detriment of the Indians who were banished to the mainly arid sierras and to the *puña* (the bleak Andean plateaux). Although the Indians' right of ownership to the lands in the sierra was recognized, it did not remain so for long, because once stock-raising (*ganadería*) proved profitable, the Indians were dispossessed.

After independence the descendants of the Spanish settlers started to multiply, and a half-breed farming class emerged, which gradually divided up the estates in the western valleys and on the coastal plains into *minifundia* by the interplay of inheritances.

The breaking up into *minifundia* resulted in the landowners being unable to produced in sufficient quantities to modernize their farms. The large estates (*latifundia*) were thus reconstituted, the small landowners selling their *minifundia* (sometimes at a loss because of their debts) to the large landowners. These small farmers became tenant farmers and even share-croppers on their former land, or left to go and live in the city.

The aim of the agrarian reform was to encourage a return to the *minifundia*, these being linked to a co-operative structure, in this case the SAIS (Social Interest Agricultural Companies). 'The problem we were unable to control is that most of the SAIS started to operate like the *latifundia*, which we had dismantled. That is to say that the management structures of the SAIS were extremely bureaucratic, and simply replaced the *latifundia* owners.'

Regrettably, he said, only one SAIS was still operating in the way he had intended and actually set up. The others had been restored to their original owners, in the case of land, or had allowed foreign agrofood or agro-industry companies to come and establish themselves, companies which reinvest their profits not in Peru but in other countries.

What were the consequences of this failure?

'However much the agrarian reform is criticized, it was Peru's only chance to survive the crisis and many farmers in the valleys and coastal plains managed to pull through. However, for the Indian peasants in the sierra and the Altiplano, poverty took on frightening proportions, and in the southern provinces of the country these Indian peasants account for almost half of the country's population.'

Is this the beginning of a revolutionary process?

'Despite our efforts, the Indian peasants have been neglected by the agrarian reform. Distrusted both by the white and the mestizo populations, banished from the economic scene, they no longer have the feeling that they belong to the national community. The fact that Sendero Luminoso, the Shining Path revolutionary guerilla movement born fifteen years ago, has managed to take root in the Ayacucho region without encountering any obstacles in the last four years, is because it has found an attentive audience for its extremist speeches among some of the neglected indigenous peasants. In order to gain access to these close-knit Indian communities, Sendero has managed to bring into conflict groups with divergent interests, semi-nomadic shepherds against the settled population of the high valleys, for example, even inciting them to internecine war in order to bring its influence to bear on one or other of the parties, or to appear as the sole arbitrator of these various interests.'

The failure of agrarian reform in Brazil, together with government land policy, favoured the large landowners and allowed them to dispossess thousands of families of the lands which they had worked for several generations. However the *camponeses*, the small farmers of the Sertao, could not and are still unable except in a few instances to prove their right to the land. They are thus obliged to give up their farms and come, as in Salvador, the capital of the state of Bahia, to fill up the shanty towns where they already constitute one-sixth of the population.

The violence of the *fazenderos*, the large landowners, towards these small farmers results from the fact that Brazilian society, at least in the countryside, still functions according to a feudal system.

To this day more or less everywhere the hard and fast rule of what is called 'cambao' still exists; this rule dictates all relations between the *fazendero* and the small tenant farmer. If he is a hired labourer of the *fazendero*, the farmer must work the landowner's property for a given number of days every year before working the plot of land that he rents from his employer — one acre (in Brazil one tarefa), that is to say, some 4,000 square metres for the head of a family, half an acre for his wife and each of his children. In exchange for this concession, the farmer must in addition hand over half of his crop to the *fazendero*. The 'cambao' is nothing more nor less than hard unpaid labour; but if the farmer has lost his land as a result of illegal extension of the *fazendas*, he cannot find work as a day labourer unless he accepts it.

Nor does the small farmer suffer any less from the violence of the *fazenderos* if he is not a farm worker subject to the 'cambao'. There is a land rule in Brazil known as 'usucapia', which gives the right to 'own one piece of land per head'. If a small farmer can prove that for five consecutive years he and his family have had as sole source of income the produce of the land which he has farmed, then the ownership of the land is theoretically granted to him by a federal service (Instituto Nacional Cadastral e de la Reforma Agraria). Once he has this first document, the farmer then has to obtain from a state body a provisional five-year title deed. If the title is granted to him, and at the end of the five years no one has come forward to contest his claim, then the provisional title deed becomes definitive.

However, three practices come to light which question the meaning of this pseudo agrarian reform:

in a vast number of cases, the state body has issued simultaneously a title deed for a given piece of land to a small farmer and to a *fazendero*. The case goes to litigation and the judges practically always declare in favour of the *fazendero* against the small farmer, who is dispossessed.

although the small farmer has received the documents which enable him to exercise his right to the land, a *fazendero* supplies the proof, even if he himself has never exploited the land, that it belongs to him; the emperor Dom Pedro granted his family ownership in the 19th century, in return for which the *fazendero* had a duty to protect the people who lived on that land. (In fact, the *fazenderos* who obtained this exorbitant right from Dom Pedro, at the time they received the right of ownership either banished or massacred the indigenous population.) In such cases the judges declare in favour of the *fazendero* and order the expulsion of the small farmers.

through successive expulsions of *camponeses* the *fazendero* increases his lands, gradually surrounding the smallest holdings. This is what the farmers call the 'grilhagem technique', after the mole cricket which devours the roots of plants thus killing off the crops. Once the smallholding is completely surrounded by the *fazendero*'s lands, he can refuse the farmer right of way. The *campones* can no longer go to work his fields and eventually, at the end of his tether, flees to the city. He may try to fight it out through the legal system, but the *fazenderos* employ *pistoleros* to resolve in their own way the open conflict with the farmer. In 1983, in the State of Bahia alone, 21 small farmers were murdered by *pistoleros* in the pay of *fazenderos*. Between January and October 1984, six were murdered. A young lawyer who undertook the defence of small farmers whose right to the land was being contested by law, was gunned down by a *pistolero*. By way of reprisal, the *camponeses* managed to kill two *pistoleros* in the pay of the *fazenderos*.

The banking system, willingly or no, is becoming the accomplice of the *fazenderos* against small farmers: no capital credits are granted to *camponeses*, because they cannot present sufficient guarantee and the mortgage value of their land is insufficient, even in cases where they can in fact prove that they own the land.

A vicious circle of violence has been set up; everything works towards concentrating all the lands in the hands of a few land-owners, to enable export-intensive agriculture, while subsistence agriculture is in the process of dying out. All that is left for the small farmer to do is to rent out his labour to the *fazendero*, but he then falls again into the 'cambao' system which does not permit him to survive and to provide for his family.

This problem of land wrested from small farmers to increase the large estates, of land diverted from food production to favour export agriculture, is one of the most striking features of the situation in Latin American countries. It also exists to a lesser degree in Asia. In Africa, at least so far, it is still the exception.

The price of all-out industrialization
The states in the nordeste of Brazil have an enormous agricultural potential. This region alone could produce enough to meet half the food requirements of the population of Brazil. However, forced to earn foreign exchange, the state governments give priority to setting up vast estates — the *fazendas* — to produce rice, sugar cane, corn, soya, cashew, and citrus fruits in order to promote the development of agrofood industries. In particular, the desire to industrialize the country has led the Brazilian government to promote the development of immense sugar cane plantations to produce alcohol, the 'miracle fuel'. The Proalcool plan, launched in

1979 in an attempt to reduce oil imports since domestic production of crude oil could meet only 32% of requirements, has favoured the growth of even larger units at the expense of small farmers.

These extensive farming practices reduce soil fertility and do not take into account the priority food requirements of the inhabitants. Progressive mechanization of the large estates has resulted in many farm workers becoming redundant.

In the province of Cavité (Philippines), our team unearthed a typical case of land acquisition by foreign companies. The village of Barangay in 1975 had 678 inhabitants in 122 households, of which 82 were farmers. Of the total land of the village, 114 hectares were used for agriculture. The main crops were rice and maize, and 70% of the harvest went to the share-croppers, 30% to the mayor.

In the sixties the mayor decided to convert all the land to sugar cane plantations and to build a refinery. The share-croppers, who were opposed to this change, met and set up an Organization of Farmers of A——; this later became affiliated to the Federation of Free Farmers. Thanks to help from the FFF, the case was brought before the court for agrarian affairs, which declared in favour of the mayor. The share-croppers appealed to the Supreme Court. Four years of negotiations followed, resulting in a memorandum of agreement in 1972 according to which each share-cropper would keep 2 hectares on lease. Meanwhile the Minister of Agrarian Reform had decided that the farmers were entitled to own their land and certificates for the transfer of land titles were prepared, but were not distributed to the farmers since the case was still under jurisdiction.

Several years later, the mayor declared he would like to buy out all the leases of the share-croppers, who would each be given a plot of land along the road on which to build new houses. Many share-croppers consented to this agreement only after they had been subjected to considerable pressure. Subsequently the mayor sold the land to a company which in its turn sold it to a real estate agent. Most of the land was lying fallow.

About 80 families in this village and something like 40 households in a neighbouring village were involved in these transactions. In addition to losing their right to lease land, most of them had to sell their animals in order to pay the cost of removal and of building new houses on the plots of land for which they to this day have no title deeds or ownership agreement. And they are now without work.

Similar land speculation operations are under way in neighbouring villages, but most farmers now seem determined to resist. Moving tenants off the land in order to convert the agricultural land to industrial zones has become commonplace in the province of Cavité.

This is also one of the serious problems affecting farmers in Nigeria. Impoverished by the water shortage which is the direct consequence of large water catchment schemes, they see their water being diverted for the industrial farming of cereals such as sorghum. The grain produced is not destined to be consumed locally, but is sent to large breweries owned by Belgian and German companies and partly financed with Nigerian capital. As local chief Alhaji Adewumi pointed out: 'Once the irrigation projects from the Bénoué River are completed, the industrial production of sorghum will enable us to reduce imports of European malt for beer production.'

What is surprising is that those in charge of the agricultural economy do not seem to be fully aware of the problem. It would appear that their main aim is to make maximum use of the foreign currency earnings from oil exports to undertake still greater projects for the benefit of agro-industry and the agrofood business. Dr Vincent Egbema considers that famine will increase considerably in the years to come:

> It is impossible to say how many people are in a chronic state of starvation. There are certainly thousands in the north. But today most of the population, both rural and urban, is definitely at the lowest acceptable limit for calories and proteins. This has not yet reached extreme dimensions, but the Nigerian economy is so vulnerable that it could become extremely serious within a few years' time.

And another of those we interviewed confirms this:

> In Nigeria, particularly in the last year (i.e. 1984), the fact is that nothing works any more in agriculture. With the exception of a few private initiatives, which started out with financing from outside Nigeria, and the development programmes largely financed by the oil companies, it could be said that Nigerian agriculture is self-sufficient for barely half the rural population. The other half is on the threshold of malnutrition. And the urban population, for its part, is entirely dependent on imports.

Similar conditions can be found in Colombia and in South-East Asia. Bolivia, too, is a country where the majority of the population live in rural areas, but the constant drama of the country is undernutrition. Elisabeth de Frias of the National Nutrition Division in the Ministry of Health:

> 43% of children under the age of five are currently in a serious state of malnutrition, that is to say suffering from protein and calorie deficiency. This means approximately 480,000 children. Also 31% of children between 5 and 14 years of age are suffering from nutritional deficiency and this means 350,000 children. There is another serious deficiency, iodine deficiency, which is causing irreversible damage for 60% of children between 6 and 19 years of age. This affects 1,124,000 people. The whole infant and adolescent population is concerned, but in rural and urban areas we are as yet still able to measure the consequences which such deficiency will cause in the longer term.

Many Bolivians accuse the State itself. Of course since the arrival of civilian government and the democratization of the regime, a series of measures have been taken to try to turn the tide, but the amount of work still to be achieved is staggering.

Michel Urioste, the Government Minister, states:

> In the sixties the State devoted 10% of its budget to the rural sector (agriculture and livestock). In 1975 the share of the State budget devoted to the rural sector was 14%, but in 1982 this share fell to 2%. And this money is appropriated by large agricultural projects or livestock projects run by large companies. The small farmers on the other hand, who are the main agents in agricultural production, get practically nothing. But what is also serious is that of this infinitesimal part of the budget, 2% of the State budget, one half is taken up by the bureaucracy.

Also in Bolivia, cocaine growing has become an activity of prime importance, and everyone is convinced that the government is impotent to put a stop to the activities of the financial forces involved in the network and of the peasants who live from this. Jaime Zallez, head of the integrated development project of the SEAS described the situation as it is now:

> Why would a peasant from the temperate zones, even with North American subsidies, change back to maize growing, tomato growing, or whatever else? He would need to start working for several hours a day again in order to make a profit of several thousand pesos. However, with a few coca trees hidden in the forest, harvesting the leaves three or four times a year, which isn't a very tiring job, in one year he will make what he would have earned in 200 years of maize

growing. All the small coca planters know how to make the pasta, the basic product. All they need is còca leaves and kerosene. They can sell the pasta in the cities and towns directly to the large dealers, who then transform it into pure cocaine. However, now almost all are able to produce pure cocaine from their pasta. It takes a little time, a few old basins, and some sulphuric acid. It's really child's play. With one harvest and few hours' work, the peasants make enough money to be able to laugh at all the arguments put forward by the government or the gringos to persuade him to become an 'honest peasant'.

Economic consequences of land misappropriation

DROP IN FOOD PRODUCTION

Diverting farmland from agriculture for other purposes, such as we have seen in the case of Cavité in the Philippines, leads to losses in food production which can ultimately have a severe impact nation-wide and aggravate a country's food deficit. At the local level, the effect is often even more serious, with the local community suffering from a drop in available foodstuffs. The families which were producing their own food and selling some of it on local markets — thus increasing locally available sources of food at reasonable prices — now have to find other ways of earning money and must buy a greater proportion of their food, or all of it. The landless peasants who were working the land of tenant farmers have also lost a source of food, since part of their income was in the form of produce. Furthermore, many landless peasants were allowed to farm small plots during the dry season in exchange for their work, so they could feed their families. These various means of obtaining food directly disappear when land is diverted from agricultural uses. Two extremely vulnerable rural groups suffer most from this upheaval — landless peasants and tenant farmers. They are also the classes that are most vulnerable to changes in the prices or availability of basic foodstuffs. When there is a lapse of time between the moment when the farmers leave their land and the land is put to other uses (which is frequently the case), these two groups are often tempted to return to the fields to grow crops they need for family consumption.

JOB LOSS OR JOB CREATION?

Agriculture provides jobs both for the farmer and his family, as well as for other farm workers whom he hires for ploughing, planting, and harvesting. When the farmland of a community is converted to other uses, all these employment opportunities dissappear. Do new opportunities for employment emerge?

Many people believe that industrial development in rural areas creates sufficient jobs to offset losses in agricultural activities. However, this point can only be clarified by a careful case-by-case study. In Cavité, one of hundreds of examples, we saw a directly opposite trend: the conversion from agricultural to industrial uses of the land turned out to be a disaster, in fact it was years before the land was actually put to a productive use. There can be many reasons for this — lack of necessary investment for financing industrial activity, speculation, etc. — but the result is that the land lies dormant and unproductive for long periods.

In many cases, the failure to make use of converted land is due to speculation. Land is bought and held in the hope that its value will increase. During this time, the farmers are evicted in order to avoid problems such as complaints to the authorities responsible for implementing land reform or other legislation protecting farmers' rights to the land. In some cases, land is diverted from farming to be subdivided into plots for housing construction. In the majority of these situations, no new employement is created for the local population and the new housing generally does not go to the people who have been displaced or the former residents.

As we saw in the Philippines, most of the jobs created in industry benefit the new 'colonies', for example in Dasmarinas, a suburb of Manila. According to the information our team gathered, around two-thirds of the new jobs were held by the inhabitants of this new colony who came there from the urban areas, rather than by the original population of the area. Of the other one-third, only a few people came from the surrounding villages, the majority from Manila. The reason frequently given is that the local population, in particular those who were formerly employed on the farms, have neither the skills nor the training necessary to hold the interesting jobs. The few people who have managed to obtain employment are restricted to menial jobs at low salaries, such as guards or janitors.

In the case of Cavité, then, the only possibilities available to the local population have appeared in the service sector and in the aid granted to the new populations to move from industrial to residential areas. This includes running jeepneys and tricycles, small food stalls, night clubs, mini-bazaars. Although this does not constitute a substantial source of income for the farmers and their displaced workers, it is nevertheless one of the few possibilities offered to them.

The problem of land appears to be one of the main factors of impoverishment. Too many farmers, particularly in Latin America and to a lesser extent in Asia, find themselves landless or dispossessed of the little land they had. The land is insufficiently protected from the climatic conditions to which it is subjected, nor is it protected from the consequences of major works programmes. The amount of farmland is diminishing, food crops are abandoned in order to grow industrial crops and crops for export. Many attempts at land reform have tried to remedy this situation but in most cases they have either failed or been sabotaged. The difficult but vital task of attacking and solving land problems must devolve upon the governments of the different countries concerned.

UNCONTROLLED MIGRATION

Population migrations, by their dimension, destabilize rural areas and, for a variety of reasons, generate millions of rootless people: people who have been displaced because of major works projects; political refugees escaping from warfare; peasants evicted from their land without receiving any welcome or hospitality in the cities; migrant workers far from home trying to find the means to survive which they cannot find in their own country.

People displaced by major works projects
We were told that they were 13-year-olds; perhaps they were younger, these children who greeted us with smiles and, above all, with the faraway look of those who expect nothing more from life. Or at least nothing more than a greeting. Deported, in the real sense of the word, from the small villages along the banks of the Nile, 300, 500, 600 kilometres downstream, they live, or rather survive, cut off for several months of the year from the rest of the world, alone with the eternal mists of Lake Aswan. Their only refuge is the shelter built by CARE, an American NGO. In this particular one, there are twelve of them, fishermen by necessity. Almost all are children, yet already men. Fishermen by night, under veritable house arrest by day by vipers and scorpions, they listen for the slightest hiccough of their 'leader', who makes all the decisions and is the master after God, sometimes even before, in

the shelter. He alone negotiates with the fishing company in Aswan which organizes the collection of fresh fish, the sale of dried and salted fish. He alone knows how much the men earn, since he depends on the quantity of fish caught every day and the profit he usually takes for himself.

The paradox of these huge works programmes, built by the hand of man and costing millions of dollars, is that each time a dam is built, tens of thousands of families are forcibly displaced without any provision for their accommodation or to enable them to work new land, let alone cope with the psychological shock of being forced to leave the land of their ancestors:

> in the Ivory Coast, 100,000 persons displaced by the Koussou Dam.

> in Brazil, 75,000 for the Itaïpu Dam.

> in the Philippines, 100,000 from the Bantoc and Kalinga tribes for the dam on the Chico River.

> in Sri Lanka, 25,000 for the dams in the Mahaweli Ganga project.

More than a million people have thus been officially displaced in the last fifteen years, forming new pockets of poverty in the areas to which they have been transplanted and abandoned.

— and for aesthetic reasons
The car pulls up by the roadside in the Philippines. The view is magnificent: you can see far out on the China Sea, which at the moment is as smooth as a millpond. The ground falls away steeply to the sea, into the Bay of Subic. To the left you can just make out the buildings of the American naval base whose geometric lines break the gentle curves of the landscape. On the right, nearby, a beautiful estate. 'That belongs to the mayor of the town,' Father Shay tells us, 'and where we are standing now used to be the village.' It is hard to believe that a village was once situated on this little terrace, which has barely room for three or four cars. 'The houses were built here and down the slope to the sea.'

Some 250 people, 65 families, used to live here. Poor fishing families, in poor houses made of whatever material came to hand, a kind of miniature shanty town — an eyesore — hanging on the hillside. Rosalie, who used to live in the village, tells us how she found herself banished along with her three children.

My husband was a fisherman, like the other men in the village. One day the government decided that our village was going to become a private holiday club. We were told that our village was ugly for the American tourists to look at. We were ashamed that our village was so ugly. We wanted to stay there, it was all that we had. Neighbours and students tried to help us. We managed to hold out for several years. The mayor didn't want to know anything about it. He was embarrassed by our village. We wanted at least to be rehoused elsewhere, and we got up a petition to the government asking for this.

One day, the demolishers came, eleven men with hammers and four armed soldiers. What could you do? They demolished our houses and we didn't know where to go. For three days we slept in the open air, and this was during the rainy season. It rained a lot and everyone, the children, pregnant women, the babies caught cold. Some of them had to go to hospital. We didn't have anything to eat for a week.

The fact that they are not all dead is because an Irish priest, who looked after young drug addicts, installed them on the land which belonged to his Foundation. He helped them in those first days and is still helping them to build a new life.

Political refugees
In most African countries tribal rivalries are stronger than nationalist feelings, particularly in rural areas.

Burundi gives us a particularly gory example of ethnic rivalries. The Tutsi ruling minority in this country (15% of the population), under the pretext of an attempted coup, murdered 200,000 Hutu tribesmen in 1972. Ten years earlier in Rwanda, the Hutu (89%) had seized power by eliminating 100,000 of the Tutsi tribe. In 1970, Biafra, the breakaway state, came under Nigerian control again. The number of victims of the secessionist conflict is estimated at more than one million, of which 80% are of Ibo origin. Since independence five years ago, the ruling Shona tribe in Zimbabwe, which also controls the army and police force, has been eliminating the rival Ndebele tribe led by Joshua Nkomo.

These tribal conflicts have been one of the main difficulties in constructing African states following decolonization. In Kenya, President Daniel Arap Moi, member of a minority tribe, the Kalenjin, talks of tribal rivalry as 'a cancer which is eating away at the construction of our nation'.

Political oppression in Africa can assume awesome proportions. In 1983, 2 million Ghanaians were expelled from Nigeria, in an attempt to reduce increasing unemployment among Nigerian nationals. 700,000 Somalis, victims of the war with Ethiopia, are living in refugee camps in Somalia. The Sudan is home to some 650,000 refugees from the rebel state of Eritrea, fleeing from Ethiopia, as well as 200,000 Ugandans escaping the civil war in their country. Zaire has several tens of thousands of them, as well as 335,000 other refugees from Angola, Rwanda, and Burundi. In 1983 hundreds of thousands of foreigners (from Togo, Benin, Cameroun, Niger) were expelled from Nigeria. Only a few stayed behind, those with firm contracts from large international companies, or working at embassies. Although the frontiers are still effectively closed to these populations, clandestine immigration has been organized.

In Mexico, the United Nations High Commission estimates the number of refugees at 350,000 Salvadoran peasants and 200,000 Guatemalans. According to an NGO official who works with these refugees, 'the Mexican Government only concerns itself with these refugees because of the frontier problem with Guatemala — there are large oil fields and oil reserves in that region — and for strategic reasons. This explains the policy of transferring refugees from the frontier regions of Chiapas to the State of Campeche.'

Nor can we omit mention of the refugee camps for Palestinians who are caught up in the violence and misery of the Middle East, or the constantly increasing numbers of Cambodians in Thailand. Entire populations in Asia, Africa, and the Middle East, and major groups in Latin America, are thus condemned to wander aimlessly and are forced to regress to a kind of nomadic lifestyle, following no law, no organization. The sole aim is flight in order to survive.

Economic and cultural pressures
Hundreds of thousands of men and women are forced to pack up and leave their native villages and fields following natural calamities, drought, hunger, in search of a new life or hope in the city. Eugène Severin tells what he overheard in Endoum:[1]

> There's more money in town and it's easier to earn it. There's more freedom. In the village you have to work every day, on land which is sometimes unproductive. The harvest is never sure. Drought, locusts, or other pests frequently threaten to spoil everything. It's difficult to sell. The village is far from the town centre. Roads leave a lot to be desired. Very often the dispensary is far away and you are more prone

[1] Extract from the bulletin of Promotion Collective (Maberon, Cameroun), notes by Eugène Severin MVOE.

to disease. If development doesn't come to the village, you have to go and find it where it is, that is to say in the town. That's why the town is attractive. It attracts young people who have been to school. It also attracts parents; some of them send their children to schools in town, saying, 'That way, my son won't end up like me here in the village.'

One girl who had stayed in the village of Endoum says:

Our sisters from the town came back here with beautiful clothes, necklaces, driving in cars; they go to the cinema and dancing while we just grow old fast. You can't even find a husband here. The workers from the CIFOA take advantage of us and give us diseases instead of money. They make us pregnant and then refuse to pay for the upkeep of their children. The best-looking and strongest men have all gone away to the town. Those who have stayed behind are here because they are incapable of doing anything else. So you can see why the boys who have stayed behind in the village don't manage to find wives.

A young hunter says:

Life in the village is deteriorating. Changes today are dividing the village. We don't enjoy ourselves as much as we used to and people have become less tolerant. The village no longer has any social structure to solve these problems and so anarchy rules.

A priest:

First of all there is the division between young and old people. They accuse one another. Young people no longer respect the customs and the authority of the old people. Family relations are dying out. The old people want young people to work for nothing. They don't want to give them any land.

A young man from Nlong (ZOA settlement) tells us:

I stayed the whole year with my father to clean up his patch of cacao trees. He gave me an old pair of trousers, not even good enough to wear to the market or to visit a girl friend. Young people can't participate in decisions concerning the village, because old people think, 'If I accept this child in the village council, I may lose my authority.' Thus the young people are afraid of the old people's magic.

A group of young people:

In Endoum, everything is depressing. Everything is dead from seven in the evening. Different diversions can help young people forget their boredom. In rural development projects, who thinks about young people's needs? We are laughed at when we ask for a record player and ten records along with the wheelbarrows and watering cans. To my mind, young people need the record player just as much as the watering can.

Nothing is happening in the village, also, because since the time of colonization all decisions concerning the village are taken in town. Before that the village used to manage to get along on its own and to look after its own future. Nowadays other people take the initiatives on their behalf. If there is a conflict between villagers, or someone is not satisfied, he can always go and see the administrative or political authority; so what is the use of trying to solve your problem with the village chief?

An old man, when asked about life in the old days, tells us:

> Then we used to live in our village, we had a say in the life of our village. If we left the village, it was because there was a war somewhere. Now they have opened up the roads and brought cars here. You can travel far away. We old people see that having a say in village life isn't enough for young people; they have to have a say elsewhere. We old folks stay here in the village with our say.

Eugène Severin:

> For me, this old man is speaking the truth. Times have changed and a certain adaptation is necessary, otherwise the village will die. But this new lease of life, does it have to be looked for elsewhere? Surely all the villagers of Endoum, young and old alike, have to look together within the village itself for this new ideal, this new way of life?

It is difficult to chart accurately the drop in Nigerian food crops because this is due principally to three reasons. First, in the northern regions on the border with Niger, the advancing desert and shortage of rainfall have combined to reduce the amount of land under millet, as well as to reduce the overall yield for this crop. According to some people interviewed, in the states of Sokoto, Kano, Kaduna, Bauchi, and Botno millet production has fallen by 30–40% in the last ten years, while the population has increased by 25%.

Secondly, the extension of highly mechanized rice production using dams along the River Niger and the Kaduna and Bénoué rivers has paradoxically had a negative impact on Nigeria's domestic food production. Although large areas have been converted into paddy fields for industrial rice production, down-stream of the dams water has almost disappeared and the parched land has stopped producing in sufficient quantities. This means that even if the harvest is sufficient for ten to twelve months' subsistence, the farmers are not able to build up stocks to insure against problems. Since there is little or no surplus for sale, farmers are unable to save enough money to buy substitute products in times of scarcity. 'Rice production was a double gamble. First of all to make it one of the staple elements in the diet of Nigerians; but the farmers in the bush don't accept it. Secondly to produce it in sufficient quantities to have a surplus for export; in terms of quality it is far surpassed by Asian rice. Moreover, part of it has to be used for animal fodder. Given the investments involved in the major irrigation projects, the production cost per pound is higher than its sale price.'

The third reason is the impoverishment of the countryside. The oil boom led the government to encourage the establishment of large-scale industrial production units (steel works, automobile assembly plants) with an enormous service sector around these structures, typical in developing countries. 'In some sectors of the Nigerian economy, there are more than twenty administrative jobs for one production job.' A large number of young people in the last fifteen years have rushed to the industrial areas, mainly Lagos and Port Harcourt, and in some villages this rural exodus has left behind a population either too young or too old to work the land. Today, despite a tailing off in industrial activity, rural migration, although not as extensive as it was in the seventies, relentlessly continues. In the far north for example, desertification, drought, installation of a few industries, have all combined to increase the population of the town of Kano from 200,000 in 1970 to one million in 1984.

In Brazil, in Feira de Santana (state of Bahia), José tells us:

> Here in the *favela* [shanty town], as in all the surrounding countryside, it's not a question of setting up structures, the means for development as such. The absolute priority is to organize the rescue of the entire population, whose very survival is threatened. In rural areas, survival can be coherently organized only through community action. It is through these cohesive social structures, which are the means for reorganizing the peasant economy, that the peasants will be able to defend themselves against exploitation, expropriation, and violence; this will help them more than any instruments for major reorganization of agricultural production or consumption.

He goes on to describe the process of rural migration which is relentlessly forcing small farmers to give up their land and emigrate to the town.

The families of small farmers, despite the force of Christian tradition in Brazil, which solidly anchors family links, are today threatened with being split up. The family head, wracked by the daily anguish of being unable to satisfy the food requirements of those in his charge, chooses seasonal migration in winter, to go and work as a farm labourer in the large rice fields belonging to the *fazenderos* or agrofood companies. During his absence, the plots of land are badly cared for by the women. After a few years, during which all kinds of pressures are exerted on them by the *fazenderos* — with increasing violence — the family migrates to the city.

If by good fortune, the head of family finds a job, the salary is insufficient (around 150,000 cruzeiros — US$50 a month for a labourer in the building industry). So he has to give up all his spare time to doing a whole range of jobs in the 'informal sector'. The absence of the head of the family from dawn until dark, seven days a week, is a destabilizing factor in family life. The *favelados*, like the peasants who have stayed behind in the countryside, are also subjected to vicious threats.

In the state of Céara there is a major drama of massive rural migration of landless peasants, displaced by the extension of large estates or quite simply fleeing the countryside because of lack of the means of subsistence. Month after month, they come and swell the numbers in the *favelas*.

The population of the municipality of Feira de Santana today is 400,000 inhabitants; 350,000 are concentrated in the town itself and 50,000 in outlying areas. Among the many *favelas*, there is one where 25,000 people live, which has grown over the years on a stretch of unused and undeveloped land, slightly to one side of the town centre. Most of the population of this *favela* are of rural origin. The owner of the land, the widow of a *fazendero*, wanted to effect a property deal and started a lawsuit at the magistrate's court in Feira to have these 25,000 persons, 4,000 families, evicted.

The daily newspaper *Estado* of Fortaleza, the state capital, on 31 October 1984, quotes Osmundo Rebouças, Secretary in charge of the State's Economic Plan, as saying: 'The state of Céara can step up its efforts but the gaps in federal policy, combined with natural catastrophes, make the problem almost insoluble. This is all the more so in that the economic and social structures of our state are additional barriers to the development effort which we consider to be our responsibility.'

The displaced farmers of Bolivia may become miners in order to survive. When Chahuaca is on holiday, the *bandas* or miners' orchestras set the men and women dancing, drunk on *pisco* and beer, kicking up the fine dust blown about by the wind. The women's costumes are brightly coloured, but they wear them as little as possible, only on special occasions one of them told us, because what their husbands and children earn in the mines is so absurdly low. While one of the *bandas* is letting its hair down, an Indian in charge of security down the mine explains to us what 'Matilda' is:

> You sign a contract with the company to become a miner because the land cannot provide a living any more, or because pressure from the *patrones* is so strong that there is nothing for it but to leave. Age is of no importance, but you have to be at least 16. That's how old I was when I first went down the mine seventeen years ago. At that time they were looking for ore at 3,500 metres, now they're down to 5,000 metres. At that depth it's so hot, you just work in underpants.
>
> A young lad of 16 who goes down the mine, knows that he will certainly die before he reaches the age of 38. I have 100% silicosis [*sic*]. But I must go on working because I've signed a contract with the company. What's terrible is that everything here belongs to the Matilda Company: the houses, the roads, the cantinas, the miners. Today, because it's a holiday, we're pretending to be free men, but we are Indians and mestizos, some of us, and we belong to the company. There is no future, there is no way out. We never look at the sky above our heads because in the sky the birds are free and they tell us that we are slaves — five days a week, ten hours a day including the time to get to the workface and back to the surface, as well as the short break in the middle of the day, all for a salary of 5,000 pesos a day.

At the time that this miner spoke, coughing his lungs out between two gulps of beer or *pisco*, the official rate for 5,000 pesos was one dollar. The black market exchange rate for one dollar was 15,000 pesos.

> For five years you have to buy all your food, paraffin for oil lamps, alcohol (because miners drink a lot), in the cantinas that belong to the company. When you ask for your account at the end of the contract, they show you the papers. And you see that in fact you owe money to the company. What else is there left for you to do? You live in a house that belongs to the company, the company built the schools that the children attend. The company directors explain that they are making your children happy and that without the company they woldn't know how to read or write. So you sign a new contract for the joy of working again down the mine, in the heat and dust. A new contract for the pleasure of having alcohol on tick. Until such time as you die,

down the mine or in the sun, it's all the same, and then your children go down the mine, in the 'mierda de la tierra' to provide for their mother and for the pleasure of getting alcohol on credit.

In many areas, children are no better off than adults. According to our team that visited Bolivia, in the silver mines of Potosi, where the ore is mixed with quartz and the seams often less than a foot wide, adults have difficulty working the mines, and cutting machines cannot be used in such narrow seams. The 'perritos', or 'little dogs', twelve- to thirteen-year-old boys, do the work. With a light fixed to their foreheads, they crawl on their knees along the narrow tunnels, breaking through the quartz with pick hammers, while other perritos load and haul the little wagons to the conveyor belt in the main gallery. How many are there? No one knows for certain, since no one in Bolivia is willing to admit that children work the mines. The children themselves lie when they talk to investigators from international organizations or unions who come to investigate: they know that they might lose their jobs and an indispensable source of income for their families. The mining companies lie because they do not want to say how much they earn from the cheap labour of children. The Bolivian authorities lie because it is better to hide the terrible truth. Somewhere behind these mining villages there are small graves of the children crushed to death when a gallery deep in the mine caved in.

When we arrived at the airport in Manila, we saw a whole convoy of West Germans. We saw them again later, these 'tourists', them or others, in the streets, looking for exotic thrills, in the company of local adolescent girls and boys, sometimes even pre-adolescent children. Perhaps when they leave Manila, they will return to their families and their roles as good fathers and husbands.

The next lot of young boys or girls who will bring foreign currency into the country are at this very moment sleeping with their parents on the sidewalks of Manila. There is a young woman arranging a rag under her baby's head, nestled on the ground between herself and her husband. This spectacle can be seen again and again all along the streets of Manila and its suburbs, the only varying element being the number of children. You tell yourself that these children have little chance of ever escaping the streets. (Our team in the Philippines.)

Besides extreme examples of child exploitation such as these, we noted that in many countries child labour is almost always a factor of impoverishment, primarily because the wages of children (other than those who help out on family farms) are in no way competitive with those paid to adults. The profit (or saving) an employer makes on a child's labour stays in the employer's pocket. Children who work cannot attend school, or have to leave their studies at an early age. Consequently, they are unable to break out of the ignorance–poverty spiral in which their own parents are often caught. They will never be in a position to assume responsibility for their own self-reliant development.

Even apart from any economic considerations, the attraction of the city is very strong for young people who demand more out of life than just three meals a day. 'You can't hold back a young person who wants to go away. Here you don't earn enough money from farming to be able to buy yourself a moped. In any event, soon there will be only old people left in the village.'

Dialogue in Cameroun with a young villager:

After school, what are you going to do?

Take the exam for the civil service.

Which exam?

One to get into the army, the police, the customs. I don't know yet.

Why do you want to go into the police, army or the customs?

Because you can tell other people what to do.

What does your father do?

He's a farmer.

Does he have much land? A large herd?

Yes, a lot.

But then why don't you stay with your father on the land?

You don't earn enough to live here and there's nothing to do. There's no cinema, no electricity, nothing.

Do you get well paid in the civil service?

I don't know, but you're in the town and there's everything that you need.

It is the same in Togo, where an enquiry carried out among 104 young school-age people to find out how they see their future, came up with the following results: 53 would like to become civil servants, 20 would like to become tradesmen, 31 would like to become farmers. Almost half of the children would like to stay in the village, but only as civil servants in order to 'be respected', 'own large fields', and 'never have any problems of food shortage'. The others wanted to go to the town to 'have everything', 'be civilized', 'become an important person', 'find a lot of money'.

Civil servants, who seem to enjoy such a reputation among at least the younger members of the rural population, do not reciprocate. 'First of all, without doubt, in most African countries the countryside is of little value in the minds of civil servants. In addition to that, there are mixed feelings with regard to farmers themselves. Not infrequently managers in rural areas mention the backward, primitive attitudes, not to say narrow-mindedness of the farmers. Feelings generally run between contempt and indifference.'[1]

A serious problem for Egypt at the present time is the emigration of *fellahin* (Egyptian peasants) who go to work in the Gulf States. Although this phenomenon has existed for a number of years, it has worsened considerably: in 1984 50% of the Egyptian workforce sought employment abroad, especially in Iraq where salaries average 200 to 300 Egyptian pounds a month.

The number of Egyptian workers is 4 million of which 2.5 million are *fellahin*. It must be remembered that 95% of land owned in Egypt consists of small plots (less than 2 hectares, and 0.21 hectares on average). Income is therefore very low (except if the *fellah* is able to maintain greenhouses to grow fruit or vegetables). Moreover, the type of farming is controlled by the government. The Iraqis use Egyptian manpower mainly for farming activities. It is estimated that £3–4 billion is repatriated into Egypt from the Gulf States annually.

Thus, the economic income of Egypt can be described as follows: oil, income from expatriate workers, the Suez Canal, then tourism, and lastly foreign aid. The consequences of this situation are serious in rural areas. The labour shortage during the rainy season is sorely felt and the farming cycles are no longer completed normally, leading to a loss in yields.

Accordingly, children now work in the fields for two or three pounds a day; adults receive 4–5 pounds for half a day's work. In fact, since everyone sits up very late in the evening watching television, the *fellahin* do not get up as early as they used to and so they work less during the day. They are not interested in working for such small salaries. Thanks to the money sent from the Gulf and distributed within the families, they live well enough. Sometimes family groups of 100 people live off the external manna. As

[1] J. Bugnicourt, Enda.

the standard of living is constantly increasing (television sets, dowries, lands), 90% of *fellahin* could not carry out the customary ceremonies — marriages, religious feasts — without the money from the Gulf. The rural situation in Egypt would be catastrophic, everyone agrees, without this financial contribution.

However, this is an economic factor which can change radically from one day to the next, as has been seen in countries such as Algeria, Morocco, Turkey, the Philippines, India, or Pakistan. Nationals of these countries found themselves sent home each time the country which received them as immigrant workers was confronted by an economic crisis resulting in unemployment.

UNCONTROLLED POPULATION GROWTH

Two new facts have come to light in the long-standing debate which the Club of Rome and Aurelio Peccei, its founder, contributed to launching. First of all, during the conference on population held in Mexico in August 1984, unanimity was expressed for the first time with regard to population policies, whereas in the past there had been a tendency to affirm that 'development was the best contraceptive' (Bucharest Conference, 1974). This shows a certain change in attitudes.

Secondly, for the first time in ten years, the world population growth rate has fallen. In ten years it has declined from 2.03% to 1.67%, which is a considerable decrease and may be the sign of a certain awareness. Nevertheless, the population of all developing countries continus to increase extremely rapidly whereas that of industrialized countries (apart from migratory movements) is increasing very slowly, stagnating, or even in some instances is no longer capable of renewing itself (Western Europe, in particular the Federal Republic of Germany).

Between 1955 and 1981 the share of the countries of the South in world population grew from 68% to 74%. By the year 2025, the span of one generation, the countries of the South will represent 85% of the world's population, which will be more than 7 billion, China and India alone accounting for one-third of the total. Also by that time the total population of Africa will be around 1,110 to 1,850 billion, that is to say in the case of the upper hypothesis, equal to the present population of China and India.

Such are the main trends outlined by population experts. It is true that growth rates are tending to fall in South America and in

Asia, areas where birth control policies are showing a certain degree of success and there is increasing awareness with regard to the problem among both the rural and urban populations. In Mexico and Colombia, for example, where the governments have adopted vigorous population policies, fertility fell by around one-third between 1970 and 1980, whereas within the same period it dropped by less than 20% in Brazil where the government has not taken any stand in favour of a population policy. In Thailand we attended a press conference of the Minister of Health where it was said that the population growth rate over ten years had fallen from 3.3 to 1.6, attributing this result to the powerful Thai NGO, PDA (Population and Development Association) with whom we spoke on several occasions. However, many rural villagers still explain their attachment to large families by pointing out that few of their children actually survive to adulthood, and these will ensure the care of the parents when they grow too old to work or farm.

Population growth rates are being maintained at a high level in Africa, where fertility rates remain very high with a considerable potential for reducing death rates. Whatever the rate of progress — ranging from spectacular to almost non-existent depending on the country concerned — the hard facts are as follows: two billion children have just been born or will be born despite the considerable efforts to control population growth, the effects of which will only be felt some considerable time later. How can the poor countries receive, accommodate, and feed these new human beings and provide them with work? In the present state of our knowledge, uncontrolled population growth is a powerful factor of impoverishment in poor countries.

LOSS OR REJECTION OF CULTURAL IDENTITY

Loss of community structures in Peru

In the old days, we Indians used to live longer than we do today because we drank less, we had enough to eat, and when the harvest was bad there was food which had been stored and was distributed to those who needed it. The Spanish destroyed this system and even after independence, the Creoles who were still the masters of the country continued to exploit the land which they had stolen, using Indian labour under terrible working conditions. Today we have to reconstruct everything starting from scratch.

The leader of the Indian community of Cuyo Grande in Peru recalled the disappearance of Indian populations through massacres, suicides, and epidemics. The social architecture of the Indian world has collapsed. Some systems of production and particularly the farming system for working community plots or collective work on the land of one peasant are also vestiges of the Inca world.

The rural community, or *ayllu*, was based on the primitive family ties which unite its members. The economic structures were characterized by two principles — reciprocity and redistribution — guaranteed by the local chiefs, whose role was considerable. The distribution of land was made according to a simple rule: one-third for the state's requirements, one-third for the needs of the religious community, the last third being left at the disposal of the community. The Andean peasants thought of their far distant past, of their lost and sometimes forgotten customs, not only with nostalgia but also with a new desire to find inspiration for the future.

Mario Tapia, agronomist in charge of several development projects in Peru, described to us the most obvious reason for the difficulties facing organizations dealing with rural development projects in the Andes: the loss of Indian cultural identity.

The deep traces which centuries of alienation by the colonial machinery have left on the mentalities of the Indian peasants in the Andes are not yet effaced. Independence in the last century did not help the Indian population, oppressed by the Spanish Conquest. On the contrary, only the direct descendants of the Spanish *conquistadores* have benefited. They threw off the yoke of Spanish rule in order to be able to exploit the Indian land for their sole benefit, without having to pay dues to the Spanish crown. And to the alienation of the Indian population is added an obscure feeling of fear, difficult to combat. The first decades following independence saw massive deportations of Indians to the mines, condemned to hard labour for the benefit of the Spanish colonialists, the destruction of families and of community structures created by the Incas, and the challenge to a complex but well-balanced social system.

The main feature of the Indian is perhaps his vast ancestral memory. For him, the Conquest was yesterday. The collapse of his universe belongs to his immediate past. Distrusted to this day by the ruling classes in Peru, Indian society in the Andes survives withdrawn within itself, maintaining a fragile balance which is under constant threat. Agrarian reform has facilitated the distribution of plots of land of one to three hectares to heads of Indian families. However, Indian communities now have to reinvent an agricultural system, a community way of life, a development path. It is not certain that the communities will manage to achieve this alone. But the day will come when the formidable dynamism, now dormant in Indian society, will have to explode.

Loss of cultural identity in the Philippines

At an international conference organized by UNESCO, the Third World countries complained that the Western 'cultural' industries were speading their values to the detriment of the national cultures of the countries coveting such values. They quote the example of advertising, which persuades people suffering from malnutrition to consume soft drinks rather than milk. Western television, radio, and other media are the agents of the cultural erosion of the Third World.

'The cultural imperialism of Western media tries to control people's minds. It is not aimed at one field of action only, but tends to dominate attitudes and beliefs,' a spokesman of the Philippine government said in the magazine *Today* in August 1982. The advertisements on Philippine television channels are mainly for foreign goods (cigarettes, alcohol, food products, etc.) and these are presented in a context more appropriate to the Western world than the Eastern. Like many television companies, the Philippine TV channels adapt their advertising to the seasons of the year and a few days before Christmas, advertisements for coffee are set in mountain landscapes, with snow, sledges, and fur blankets. This is no doubt extremely well suited to a Swiss public, much less so to that of the Philippines.

Advertising interests are against decrees aimed at controlling advertising of such products as tobacco and medicines. The advertisers are aiming at the rich and they are not concerned about the effects of such campaigns on poor consumers. The members of the Commission on Advertising are criticized for 'consorting with foreign interests, to the detriment of national development requirements and cultural identity'.

Philippine agencies, which produce two-thirds of all domestic advertising, generally send their executives abroad for training so that they will come back with American-style techniques. It works well. Local advertising leads to an ever-increasing number of people consuming imported goods. 'The colonial ideology of mass marketing is centred around foreign-sounding labels, on drinks or toothpaste, jeans or deodorants.' Thanks to this, American firms have tripled their exports to the Philippines. A journalist says, 'The Filipino has the mentality of a white man in the body of an Asian.'

Perhaps we might close with A. R. Magno, professor of political science, who says, 'Ethnic genocide kills the souls and assassinates the intelligence of 70% of the masses in the Philippines who are below the poverty line'.[1]

Rejection of tradition in Africa

Some countries in the South have managed to take from Western culture what they need and integrate this in their own culture; others, in the desire to copy the Western model, lose their own identity without the new habits having taken root properly. This type of quasi-assimilation is in fact a loss of cultural identity.

In most countries visited, people wear American-style clothes (denims, T-shirts, etc.), listen to Western music, follow Western fashions. Young Africans, in particular, disregard tribal values and discipline in favour of urban culture centred on the transistor radio and Coca Cola. In the name of progress, Africa is gradually giving up its rites, customs, traditions, everything which in each country went to make up the social structures and codified behaviour patterns and social relationships. What is left of the Bantu traditions in East Africa? Just forty years ago, Kenyatta lamented the loss of religious rites and sacred traditions. 'It is not surprising that there isn't enough rain. The young generation is turning away from Ngai (God),' he said. 'Relations with the ancestors are breaking down.'

In general, the customs of African tribes were such that man was able to live in harmony with his environment. 'Africa has social injustices, a caste system, young people exploited by their elders, poverty and alienation following on the slave trade, then on the colonial system and its consequences. Given the shortage of goods and the lack of appropriate technologies, it is easy to see how and why Africa has been reduced to inventing systems of myths and rites, whose therapeutic function of appeasement and consolation cannot be denied.'[2]

Not all regions or tribes have given up their customs and there is a certain 'traditional' Africa resisting Westernization for the time being; nevertheless, there are many Africans who are living rootless in their own countries. Some tribes are resisting the process in more or less precarious conditions, such as the Dogon in

---

[1] Review Who.
[2] L.V. Thomas, The Anthropology of Death

Mali or the Masai in Kenya, who live in reserves and become tourist attractions. Others, such as the mysterious Dorobo, who according to tradition were the sole inhabitants of Kenya when Diogenes the Greek made his voyage in the first century AD, have had to move on. Defeated by the Masai, their lands stolen from them by the Kikuyu, and in some cases exterminated, they are apparently no more than a few hundred, likely to disappear entirely from the face of the earth.

Furthermore, the increasingly difficult plight of farmers who have left their land, not only because of drought but also due to extension of crops or speculation on land prices, forces them to migrate to the cities and to change their life-style. The change for them is then as radical as if the had left their country. A particularly African phenomenon is the rejection of food traditions.

> Just fifteen years ago the staple foodstuff in Nigeria, as everywhere else in West Africa, was millet in the north, the number one tropical cereal, and manioc in the south. Once oil revenues allowed wheat to be purchased from Europe, bread, considered until then as a European — hence desirable — luxury, made a widespread appearance in eating habits. Gigantic flour mills, vast industrial bakeries, were built. Some people were able to accumulate vast fortunes. Now bread has become the staple diet of more than half the population and thousands of tons of wheat are imported from the countries of the North. Production of food crops such as millet and manioc are falling year by year. At the present time, while foreign countries continue to buy Nigerian oil, bread has not yet become an expensive food item. With bread and dried fish, a worker can make a meal. If he earns 100 naira a month, that makes 10,000 kobos. A loaf and dried fish cost him 50 to 60 kobos.

A Belgian agronomist goes on to say:

> Now the Nigerian wants to eat bread and more bread, but from this initial desire, the desire for other European food products is born. After bread, won't he want to have beef? Over 80% of beef has to be imported and it costs 35–40 naira/kg. And then the ingredients which accompany it, for example mustard which goes for 45 and even 60 nairas/kg. So more and more has to be imported, accordingly more oil has to be sold. One day it will blow up.

A Nigerian film director remarks: 'We are building palaces which we don't know how to manage and cars which we can't repair. We are attracted by all that glitters, we are the slaves of other civilizations.'

For some ethnologists, scientists, or economists, traditional

Africa south of the Sahara is already a 'fossil' continent, without resources, industry, culture, and will not survive beyond the year 2000. Many Africans are becoming increasingly aware that tribal life was the source of traditions, of social and spiritual values. 'In the traditional society in which we live,' said Kenyan legislator Eddah Gachukia, 'it is urgent and necessary to establish an effective system of relations with our children.'

The confrontation between Asian societies and the Western world of technology, communications, leisure activities, has without doubt been brutal, at least so far. It is true that young people have difficulty in resisting the behavioural and value changes which are transmitted by cinema and television films. However, Asian societies are founded on multisecular cultures and philosophies which, over the course of their troubled histories, have given them a tremendous capacity for digesting everything new from the West, without losing the vital characteristics of their traditional values.

CORRUPTION: PROFITEERS AND PIRATES

In rural communities there are all kinds of people who try to take advantage of poverty, ignorance, and the weakness of the villagers. They are to be found in a wide range of social categories.

The young Thai woman in charge of the project looks 15 years old, but in fact she is 32. In the village of Law Gel, in the north-east of the country, she describes the difficulties the peasants face there. 'We get little support from the civil servants, who are a little jealous of the dynamism of our organization (the Thai NGO PDA), of its rapid intervention, efficiency, popularity, which they contrast with their own difficulties in working and being accepted in the villages.'

She goes on to say: 'The worst are the middlemen who buy the produce in the villages cheaply and sell it at a very high price. They exploit the peasants.'

At Ayanapura, in the Madurai region in the south of India, the head of the project, Mr Lingam, says: 'We give the villagers advice on marketing. When prices fall, I advise them to wait a month and to store the goods. If they need money, it can be lent to them. There is a constant threat of exploitation by middlemen who harass and pressure them: "Sell quickly, the prices are going to fall next week, you've still got time." To beat them we would need a parallel sales organization.'

The Lamido of R. in Cameroun is a traditional chief who rules on a hereditary basis. The central authorities in Yaoundé recognize him as the district chief, and therefore as the obligatory intermediary between villagers and the local sub-prefecture. There is no doubt that the power system of the Lamido arises from 'clientism' or cronyism. Apart from the fact that his brothers hold positions of considerable responsibility (one is head of the co-operative, the other is Imam in the mosque), the Lamido receives a tithe from the farmers (one-tenth of the millet harvest), keeps part for himself and redistributes some to his favourites in times of scarcity. He can speculate on food crops because the tithe enables him to create stocks at harvest time.

The Lamido willingly answered our questions:

> Thanks to the victory of my great-uncle, my father's uncle, over the Peuhls (the Foulbés), he became undisputed head of the Moundang. My father, who died seven years ago, was Lamido after his uncle. I succeeded my father and the central government of Yaoundé recognized me as traditional chief as well as administrative chief of the district.
>
> What are your obligations?
>
> Since I represent civil authority, I am the guarantor of respect for the State's authority.
>
> Do you have any legal powers?
>
> Of course, but I only intervene in a conflict between two people if the Lawan and the village council cannot resolve it. If the parties do not accept my decision, which is rare, then they can go through the normal legal procedure in court, but that would cost them a lot of money.
>
> On what basis do you have legal powers?
>
> First of all because I am Lamido, and also because I am Hadj: I have made the pilgrimage to Mecca. I am a Muslim, as was my father, who was converted to Islam in 1922. Before that he was an animist.
>
> Do you have any religious powers?
>
> Only wisdom, because I am Hadj, but I appoint the Imam, that is to say the man in charge of the mosque, who teaches the Koran. Right now one of my brothers is Imam.
>
> When you have to solve legal problems, do you seek help in Koranic law?
>
> Of course, sometimes there is more wisdom in the Koran that in the laws of men.

What role do you play in the economic life of the district, and villages?

I can force those who have stored too much in their houses and who want to keep everything for themselves to sell to those who have not been able to build up stocks.

Are you yourself able to store?

Of course.

How do you feel about the presence of the Volontaires du Progrès (volunteer workers) in Gaban?

I think they are doing a very good job. Everyone who wishes to come and help the peasants is welcome.

At this point in the conversation, a brother of the Lamido came in and he was introduced to us as the Managing Director of the Board of Directors of an agricultural co-operative set up in the district.

Why has a co-operative been set up?

The peasants had to organize themselves to face problems together.

Who was behind setting up the co-operative?

I was.

How many farmers are members of the co-operative so far?

Only about thirty because we have to convince farmers of their interest in belonging and that takes time.

How does one become a member of the co-operative?

(The brother answers) The Saré head, that is to say the farmer head of family, pays 100,000 francs CFA (2,000 French francs) which entitles him to a share. He can do this in several payments.

What is done with the money collected?

The co-operative builds up millet stocks during the harvest and millet is sold to the peasants during the drought.

Only to the members of the co-operative or to all peasants?

(No answer)

At what price, or rather how much above the purchase price?

(No answer)

At 100,000 francs CFA, the shares are expensive. Surely only rich farmers can become members of the co-operative?

(The brother) All farmers ought to become rich.

Has the co-operative already started working? Is it also going to help to modernize farming methods?

It's starting now. If possible, it is going to try to be modern.
Do the central authorities in Yaoundé, the Ministry of
Agriculture, agree with setting up the co-operative?
Of course!

It appears that a caste of rich farmers more or less related to the
Lamido and to his family, will be the main beneficiaries of the 'co-
operative' operation, through speculation on millet.

In fact, this seems to be a modern way of perpetuating the feudal
system. The talks that we had with the Secretary General of the
Ministry of Agriculture and with the Director for Community
Development in Cameroun gave us to understand that the present
government authorities are in favour of the 'co-operative' solution
in rural areas. However, between Yaoundé and Lara there are
1,500 kms of dirt tracks and an unknown number of middlemen,
and what may be ideal on paper in an office in the capital could
well become a new aberration in the field, if the project or
operation gets out of hand.

In Nigeria Alhaji (Muslims who have made the pilgrimage to
Mecca) and the chiefs (a title which in the context of a village
community confers the right to participate in decision-making)
form a vital network within the ruling classes. However, it is
important to note that the Alhaji and the chiefs, because they
always belong to one of the ruling classes, have direct access at all
times to the corridors of power. Practically all commercial or
industrial firms in Nigeria, once they get beyond a certain size,
have at the head of their board of directors or as general manager
an Alhaji or a chief, not so much for their competence as for their
influence. Even those which were formerly European and have
now been Nigerianized, recruit a chief, an Alhaji or both or several
of them, since they constitute power in the State and it is
impossible to do business if they are not included in the deal. This
means that they are either very well paid or they get large
handouts. They are continually adding to their fortunes and are
thus able to increase their clientele constantly. When their services
are solicited they always agree, but they expect the community
which has approached them to give them something in return: for
example, the community gives up its right to a piece of land where
a large firm is going to build a factory, or where the State wants to
build a road or barracks. All managers are fully aware that the
crony systems are well developed and that it is better to deal with
them than to criticize them.

In Cajueiro (Brazil), where a rural community is living on land belonging to the Bahian municipality of Feira de Santana, the sub-prefect owns a *fazenda* of several hundred hectares where he carries out multiple cropping and stock-raising. The countryside around Cajueiro is a wide valley surrounded by gently undulating hills which have rocky outcrops, granite with a low quartz content, crumbling on the surface and eroded by the prevailing north-east wind. Rainwater runs down them, washing the fertile topsoil into the valley. Theoretically, wells would have to be drilled to a depth of 40–50 metres half-way up the hills to find water. By contrast, in the valley bed, the accumulation of feldspar marl, combined with the alluvium from the rio, has created a thick layer of earth which is all the more fertile since the groundwater table is only three metres down. The sub-prefect's *fazenda* covers the whole valley, whereas the farmers' small plots of land are situated on the hillside. The prefect refuses to grant permission for the construction of a system of wells, with water elevation devices and canalization on the *fazenda*, although such a system would enable the small farmers to have at least sufficient water for the family and community gardens.

Not far from Jikhira in West Bengal there is a large hospital. Doctors refuse to work so far from town and for a small salary. If one of them actually does agree to do so, he only holds out for a few weeks. Either that or he comes back once a week, to accept patients for his private practice. This case may appear minor, but it means that a whole region is deprived of medical assistance.

In the Philippines corruption is rife. At all levels of power, from the government right down to the mayors of the villages, those in positions of authority hope to take advantage of aid and to impose their own law. Those living in the countryside are particularly vulnerable and it is not uncommon for them to be exploited by junior army and police chiefs who take advantage of their credulity and of their fear. 'The Philippine army sells drugs, marijuana, amphetamines, to children. When the army discovers a stock of these, it sells them instead of destroying them.' Bureaucrats in the civil service, like middlemen, large landowners, and banks, often form a powerful united front to maintain the status quo which favours their privileges. They do not look favourably on any farmer organization determined to improve their lot, because any progress for the poorest in the community will be against their own interests.

In Zaire, the traditional chiefs have established a hierarchy which works to their advantage and from which it is difficult to escape:

The *salongo*, the compulsory unpaid day of work once a week which is demanded of the villagers by the authorities for the upkeep of roads and administrative buildings, is frequently misused by the traditional chiefs, who make the farmers work in their fields. When a villager refuses to do this work he is accused of rebelling against authority and must pay a fine, which in many cases represents part of his livestock. The villagers, who are the victims of the state officials (civil servants as well as police or security forces), as well as of traditional chiefs, do not dare to oppose them.

We had a problem at the beginning with a traditional chief, a Mwami (king) who was against development because he wanted the peasants to remain his serfs. He came and threatened us. He's a powerful man with his own army and he refused permission to set up the co-operative, claiming that he alone had the monopoly for marketing agricultural produce in his territory ...

The Jopaje (association of young people) helps us to free ourselves from the tyranny of our chiefs. We used to be arrested all the time, they made us pay fines, took our goats and chickens for the slightest reason. Now we are more free. You can combat arid land, drought, and floods, rebuild after earthquakes. But all that is nothing in comparison with what we have to do to protect ourselves from the corruption of civil servants, the greed of large landowners, pillaging from middlemen who get rich at our expense. But we're not going to let it go on like that any more.

In Mali, a co-ordinating committee was set up to facilitate emergency action by NGOs among victims of drought who, in addition, are subjected to speculation 'which knows no bounds. Every day new food stocks are coming to light for sale.'

There is the same kind of speculation on foodstuffs in Cameroun, with consequences as tragic as in Mali. In December 1983, when the white millet was harvested, the farmers who were still in debt from the previous year because of insufficient harvests, had to sell their millet for 80 francs a bag (about 5 cents a pound). In June 1984 in Lara, the millet was sold back to the peasants at 340 francs a bag (20 cents a pound); by 2 July in Maroua, millet reached 25 cents a pound. In order to pay this huge difference, the farmer either has to go deeper into debt or leave the village to live in the town or go to work for Camriz or Socucam,[1] living in camps, with

---

[1] State controlled companies for the production of rice and sugar respectively.

a salary of 240 francs a month cutting sugar cane. Either that, or he gives up producing millet to produce cotton, thereby reducing even further the amount of food crops. In Gaban, in the space of one year, the area devoted to cotton growing has increased by almost 30%, to the detriment of red and white millet.

From country to country, we have noted the existence of these networks of profiteers and sometimes of pirates, who divert financial aid or emergency food aid sent by the richest countries. Corruption is a factor to be found everywhere, but its ravages are always most serious when it hits the poorest.

What is new is that farmers are becoming aware that this problem constitutes one of the major obstacles to development and that such profiteering and pillaging can only lead to increased poverty. What is also new is that they are no longer prepared to accept blindly a situation of which they are always the victims.

PART THREE

CHAPTER 6
Factors of Development

A NEW AWARENESS

Farmers are perfectly aware of the vicious cycle of poverty oppressing them and of the unfailing of abundance which works for the landowners.

In a Philippines village:

> Since they have high incomes, the landowners can develop their physical and intellectual capacities. They are able to send their children to the best schools. We, the landless poor, are unable to provide an education for our children. We are forced to take them out of school early so that they can work full time, or send them as domestic help to the houses of the landowners. The sons of the landowner become political leaders. Our children remain penniless, uneducated, and are considered worthless. Is it really God who is responsible for our condition?

The poverty phenomenon in a country such as Brazil, which ironically is considered to be in the full swing of development, typifies of the complexity of the problem which many poor countries are experiencing. Below are some symptomatic facts.

In 1983 the area in Brazil under sugar cane increased by 9%, but more than 50 million Brazilians are suffering from malnutrition with less than 1,600 calories a day (25 million in the urban population and 23 million in the nordeste alone). 35 million children under the age of 16, whose families are unable to feed them, try to earn a few cruzeiros every day to live, by begging, by doing a job — any job, illegal if necessary — and by committing petty crimes. Five million have been completely abandoned and live as best they can, in the villages, the *favelas*, and even in the town centres.

As Dr Fernando Nobreja, President of the Brazilian Pediatric Society, said at the Second Brazilian Congress on Nutrition in October 1984:

> The Brazilian economy is concentrated in the hands of a few groups, and Government policy is exclusively aimed at foreign currency-

producing agriculture; these are extremely serious factors which in the last four years have led to an alarming development of malnutrition. Today 80% of the population in the nordeste is hit by malnutrition and unborn children are affected if the pregnant mother is malnourished. In the nordeste there are 10 million men, women, and children suffering from irreparable brain damage as a result of malnutrition, which makes them practically incapable of looking after themselves.

A social worker in João Pessoa quotes a professor of medicine at the State University of Paraiba: 'In one generation, the average height of the peasants of Sertao has diminished by several centimetres. Today it is only 149 cms, i.e. one centimetre less than the average height of pygmies.' Another woman social worker confirms: 'During the course of 1983, for the town of Fortaleza alone, slightly more than 5,000 children between the ages of 1 and 5 years were abandoned by their families, and have gone blind due to lack of vitamins and malnutrition.'

The Secretary for Agriculture in the state of Céara in Brazil at a plenary session of the State Parliament, which consists mainly of large landowners, declared: 'The state of Céara is confronted by social upheavals, with almost the entire rural population dying of hunger and thirst, and the resulting infant mortality rate is unacceptable; in a country which calls itself rich and which has such potential and accumulated wealth at its disposal, 250 children out of a thousand die before the age of one year, whereas the normal figure for infant mortality ought to be 20 per thousand. Of the survivors, the majority suffer from irreparable brain damage.'

Even if the increasing sophistication of mechanized agriculture enables Brazil one day both to be self-sufficient in food products and to export agricultural produce to bring in foreign currency, this will be done at the cost of the suffering and death of millions of individuals. The figures speak for themselves and the truth cannot be denied: Brazil is the fifth largest manufacturer and seller of arms in the world.

The number of countries suffering from food shortage is decreasing every year. Between 1966 and 1968, out of the 118 poorest countries, only 36 had a sufficient calorie count per head. In 1970 the figure rose to 44, and in 1976 it reached 52. By 1980, 62 countries considered poor had reached the threshold of food stability. Nevertheless, although there is progress, the number of people with insufficient resources, underfed, badly cared for, without education, is in the order of 2 billion, that is to say 40% of humanity.[1]

> Until recent years, and even now this is still the case for the majority, Nigerian farmers worked the land in an extremely intelligent fashion, in perfect harmony with their environment. However, since agro-industry has started to invade the countryside, many farmers have lost their land; with the improvement of the road network consumer goods have arrived thanks to the oil revenues, but something has come unstuck. Now it is possible to see that whole areas which used to be very rich have become poor all of a sudden.

There are 500 million people in the world suffering from hunger or malnutrition. Half the active population is unemployed or under-employed. This underemployment concerns both the rural population, which is still increasing despite rural migration, and the population crowded into the shanty towns which is increasing at an annual rate of 10–12%. This poverty, far from improving, is going to worsen for most developing countries. Their overall growth rate, which was 4.8% in the seventies, now stands at 1.9%. All these factors of impoverishment are better understood nowadays by the rural population.

This condition need not be ineluctable, but it is the reality against which we can and must fight. Awareness of all the factors of impoverishment can slowly but surely change the behaviour of the rural population; and this change will be one of the major factors of development.

WHAT ARE FACTORS OF DEVELOPMENT?

In Chapter 4 we described two contradictory phenomena which we have observed, without exception, in all the countries visited in the course of this study:

> impoverishment, of which we analysed the most striking factors as they appeared in the course of interviews with villagers.

> the spread of development projects which are the manifestation of a vast movement, of which it is difficult to assess the scale, distinguish the direction, measure the efficiency, let alone understand the promises it holds forth.

In order to have a well-ordered view of these projects, we propose to start from the needs they are trying to meet. We shall

[1] FAO figures

see that, whatever the climate, soil types, socio-political environment, and cultural traditions, the development process — extending from satisfying man's basic needs to enabling him to do this
himself and thus improve his lot — is the same in practically all
cases, even if the different stages do not take place in the same
order.

To clarify the process, we propose to distinguish between two
main stages:

> the factors which combine to satisfy villagers' basic needs and
> enable them to pull out of absolute poverty;

> the factors which make villagers aware of their situation and
> empower them to act.

---

1. SATISFY IMMEDIATE BASIC NEEDS

WATER
— *drinking water*
— *rainwater reservoirs*
— *wells*
— *small-scale irrigation*
● *reservoirs*   food, crops, health
● *small dams*
— *protection against water (floods,
erosion, transmission of disease)*

FOOD
— *vegetable gardens*
— *market gardening*
— *orchards*   war against malnutrition,
— *cereal crops*   scarcity, famine
— *livestock*
— *fish-farming*

BASIC HEALTH AND HYGIENE

---

2. AWAKENING AND EMPOWERING VILLAGE GROUPS

1. SOCIAL/GROUP ORGANIZATION
   — *involving the neglected*
   — *democratic decision-making and leadership*
   — *legal recognition*
   — *relations with the other parties: leaders, administration, financial institutions*
   — *training leaders and educators, and preparing them for project management*

2. MANAGING AND IMPROVING PRODUCTION (The role of women)
   — *Agriculture*
     ● seed selection
     ● improved land use
     ● reclamation of arid or fallow land
     ● crop diversification
   — *Livestock*
     ● stock improvement
     ● stock diversification
   — *Small industry and crafts*

3. LEARNING ABOUT AND PROTECTING THE ENVIRONMENT
   — *energy resources*
   — *reforestation*

4. IMPROVED USE OF LOCAL RESOURCES
   — *food crops*
   — *appropriate technologies*

5. HEALTH AND HYGIENE
   — *health care*
   — *sanitation*
   — *better housing*
   — *immunization and preventive medicine*
   — *maternal and child care*
   — *nutrition*

6. ACTIVE PARTICIPATION IN THE DEVELOPMENT PROCESS
   — *market mechanisms*
   — *savings*
   — *credit*
   — *investment*

7. CONTROLLING POPULATION GROWTH

8. EDUCATION FOR DEVELOPMENT
   — *children*
   — *adults*

9. KNOWING AND EXERCISING ONE'S RIGHTS

Transforming factors of impoverishment into factors of development is what is at stake in the daily life of villagers in the poor countries. The factors of impoverishment can discourage them and lead them to revolt. In a tense international climate, where national egoism tends to harden, movements of hope, solidarity, cooperation supported by volunteer organizations and NGOs (from both the South and the North), contradict — at least partly, but vigorously — this tendency towards despair, and their very extensiveness is a sign of hope worthy of attention.

These movements, which by their daily action in the field, working miracles, making arid land fertile, giving life to children and hope to peasants, are not only a sign of confidence in the future; we are seeing the beginning of a crusade by two billion peasants for their daily food and for their dignity.

Before analysing the capacity of NGOs to respond to the basic needs of these villagers, to make them aware of their situation and to help them take action, it is appropriate to examine the complex world which these organizations form. It to this observation of the NGO phenomenon, vital if we are to understand their history, nature, and mechanisms, that the next chapter is devoted.

CHAPTER 7
NGOs: A New World Phenomenon

Governments and international organizations, confronted by the multitude of factors which influence the impoverishment or improvement of the daily life of two billion peasants, often feel impotent, that the situation is beyond their power. Their monolithic structures — heavy and often bureaucratic — are unable to adapt to the multi-faceted and complex reality in order to reach the poorest villages, down to the poorest families in the most isolated areas.

In the countries of the North, as in those of the South, it is remarkable that in such apparently dead-end situations, the determination of a handful of men and women manages to set things moving. In the most hopeless cases, there is always a small percentage of the population who think that there is something to be done. In Brazil there is a song that goes: 'If you dream alone, it's only a dream, but when you dream together, it's the dawn of reality.'

In the Philippines, farmer Many Ruben in his rice paddy says:

> Our experience has made things clearer: we can no longer sit back and wait for a Messiah or a Saviour. We can only count on ourselves. Of course we know that Jesus Christ did the one thing reasonable: have faith in the people so that they will have faith in themselves. Only the well organized rich people can use the government as their instrument. Most of us, isolated from each other, are so disorganized that, for us, the government is not an instrument but a master. It's not a democracy that we have, but a demon-crazy. Now there is only one thing left for us to do, and that is to recognize that we are inferior to the rich, in terms of economic and political power, but that one thing goes in our favour: our numbers. That is not enough; we have to give quality to our numbers by organization. If each farmer acts alone, he cannot fight efficiently for his rights. It is only when we have overcome our isolation and become unified that we shall become strong.

NEW AGENTS OF DEVELOPMENT

Non-governmental organizations are of course no new phenomenon in the North. Groups of individuals sharing common interests, professional, scientific, humanitarian, philanthropic, and many others, organize themselves around their interests to exchange information, share experience, or initiate activities in common. Such bodies may be strictly local or nation-wide but during the last century, a large number have sprung up which are international in scope (INGOs) and they have become important agents of international co-operation, often reinforcing, complementing, criticizing, or extending the efforts of inter-governmental bodies which, although more powerful and more adequately financed, are frequently bureaucratic, subject to political constraints, and hence less able to move as rapidly and freely as the NGOs.

The last two decades have witnessed a remarkable growth of NGO activity in relation to the development needs of the Third World and it is with these that we are concerned here. Although we recognize the existence and importance of NGOs in many other fields, we shall for the sake of brevity use the general term NGO essentially in relation to those involved in Third World development and especially in rural development.

There is a multitude of private organizations in the world — non-profit-making, volunteer associations, informal groups — working for development on a smaller or larger scale, who express faith in the group and the desire to unite to be efficient. In spite of their innumerable denominations, we shall put them all under the heading of NGO. These NGOs have varying structures, and so far no one has been able to say how many of them there are, nor how many really work. Frequently nothing is known about their history, their transformation, the evolution of the NGO phenomenon in the world, and the causes of its emergence.

What is their share in total aid to poor countries, in financial resources, transfer of know-how and appropriate technologies? How much of the rural population benefits from their action, directly or indirectly? In other words, in definitive terms, what force or what alibi do these organizations represent for development of the Third World?

This study begins to answer some of these questions.

DEFINITION

The term NGO, non-governmental organization, usually seems the most appropriate, even if it is not perfect. It is in fact an expression invented by the United Nations: Article 71 of the United Nations Charter, in giving a mandate to the Economic and Social Council to set up relations with NGOs, opened the way to the adoption of similar relations with other organizations. It was a *de facto* recognition of non-governmental organizations, i.e. those resulting from private initiative: in this they differ both from inter-governmental organizations, set up by governments, and from sovereign states, to whom in principle they owe neither their creation nor their financing. The bodies then recognized must have an international structure, i.e. they have to represent associations belonging to several countries: the Economic and Social Council of the United Nations thus considers NGOs as 'International organizations which have not been set up by inter-governmental agreements'.

Very rapidly, practice has moved away from the generally accepted legal notion of NGO to adopt a definition such as the one advocated by the French sociologist Marcel Merle: 'By NGO is meant any group, association, or movement set up in a durable fashion by private persons belonging to different countries for the pursuit of non-profit-making aims.' It is sad that this definition is narrow and negative, stating what NGOs are not, and does not take account of their true nature. Some organizations have refused to adopt this definition and prefer to be considered private voluntary agencies or organizations. Moreover, in the United States, foundations such as the Rockefeller Fund or Ford Foundation play an important part in supporting rural development programmes in the Third World.

Regardless of the term used to designate them, NGOs are represented at international conferences, recognized by most governments and international institutions. The great majority of NGOs prefer the term even though it may gloss over diverse and complex realities, as we shall see later. Therefore, in the interest of clarity and simplicity, we shall use it here.

QUANTIFYING NGO IMPACT

Work carried out in 1981 at the OECD Development Centre in Paris and subsequently updated by us shows that in industrialized countries there are currently 2,087 NGOs which are directly concerned by or involved in development issues. The geographical breakdown is:

Western Europe	1,356
North America	630
Japan	101

The common aim of these NGOs is to promote economic and social development in the Third World, although there are enormous differences in their approaches. Some work directly in poor countries, others co-operate with groups in Third World countries, while yet others work to inform or influence public opinion in their own countries as to the development issues and problems encountered in the Third World. Some NGOs devote special efforts to working with groups in urban areas, in slums or depressed areas. Given the thrust of this study, we are particularly concerned with NGOs involved in rural development, in areas such as agriculture, livestock, health, education, job training, organization, credit management.

The attempt to identify and quantify NGOs in developing countries comes up against several obstacles:

the phenomenon is fairly recent, except in a very few countries such as India, Bangladesh, or Indonesia, where the first attempts were in the sixties.

the phenomenon is fluid and in full evolution. The present flourishing of all sorts of groups within village communities, either as an outgrowth of a Northern NGO or as a result of local initiatives, is the sign of a profound change on the part of the rural population. However diverse these groups may be, whether they be in Bolivia, Zaire, or Sri Lanka, they do not hesitate to call themselves NGOs, because this is the magic word which unlocks the door of the vast international financing network, from which they hope to benefit.

However, we can begin to indicate, for large groups and for certain countries, the magnitude of the phenomenon.

In Asia, the movement in general has existed since the sixties and there are many organizations. There are several thousand NGOs in the Philippines (52 million inhabitants); in Bangladesh (100 million inhabitants); in India 7,000 (for 750 million inhabitants). More than 1,000 are registered in Thailand (for 50 million inhabitants), but only around 200 to 300 of these seem to be really active: as few as a hundred of them have full-time staff and activities directly in the field. In Indonesia, 277 NGOs were counted for a population of 180 million.

In Africa the phenomenon is even more recent than in Asia, and in most of the countries visited the number of NGOs is not well known if at all. In Kenya there are 370 NGOs, but there were only 100 five years ago (for 18 million inhabitants in 1984). It is difficult to give the precise number of NGOs in Nigeria, but according to different sources there are reckoned to be 650. Practically all of them are local NGOs, i.e. associations or groups which are entirely controlled by Nigerians, even if the financing is still assured, for the most part, by NGOs in the North. If we take into account the criteria by which these NGOs are defined, we find, as everywhere else in the world:

NGOs created on European initiative which started up with money from the North and which have gradually managed to obtain Nigerian financing, or which have become sufficiently independent to dispense with aid.

NGOs resulting from local initiatives which needed or still need aid from the countries of the North. To an increasing extent, these NGOs, particularly when they are dealing with large populations, become para-governmental organizations, with the Nigerian state as their main sponsor, or a company with majority Nigerian holdings.

It appears from many of our sources of information that there are still few NGOs able to live off their own resources; in other words, few projects can be realized without regular financial or material assistance. The figure may well be something like a few dozen out of 650 (for 100 million inhabitants). Those NGOs or projects which are today independent, or about to become so, are those which benefited from an enormous amount of financial assistance at the outset. In most cases, the aid came from oil companies.

It is estimated that there are 112 NGOs in Cameroun, 23 in Togo. For Burkina Faso, Mali, and Zaire, despite lively activity on the part of Northern and Southern NGOs, it has not been possible to obtain even an approximate figure of the number of NGOs working in the field. In Egypt there is a very limited number of

NGOs, all initiated by Coptic Christian minorities, and so the NGO phenomenon is marginal.

In Latin America, in contrast, the abundance of NGOs is similar to that seen in Asia. In the last six years, 2,500 NGOs have seen the light of day in an area which includes Bolivia, Ecuador, Peru, and Brazil. The Mexicans estimate that there are over a hundred NGOs active in their country (for a population of 80 million inhabitants). In Ecuador there are about 300 (for a population of 8.5 million), 227 for Bolivia (population 6.5 million), 380 in Peru (population 19 million), 24 in Colombia (population 30 million).

This type of quantitative approach is difficult to carry out and it can be criticized on three counts:

> the figures are known for some countries, estimated or unknown for others, and they never reflect the real dimension of the NGOs nor their sphere of intervention, let alone their efficiency.

> it is not always easy to obtain an exact breakdown of NGOs specializing in rural development, those active in purely urban areas, suburban areas, and shanty towns, and those that are multi-vocational.

> in a certain number of countries, NGOs or volunteer groups have opted for a confidential or even clandestine existence, because their action is rejected by the government in power or they are threatened with being taken over by the public authorities.

NGOs are extremely diverse, as Peruvian sociologist Mario Padron points out.

> In Peru we can easily say that there are 380 non-governmental organizations, associations, or private centres working in the field of rural development, apart from local churches, religious groups, and other charity organizations. I am talking specifically about organizations which have an institutional structure, legal status, and which receive aid from abroad. Of these, something like 30%, despite the fact that they satisfy these criteria, limit themselves merely to surviving, without any precise orientation or the means for taking effective action: their role is not clearly defined. The other 70% do serious work. And of these I would say that only some, that's to say something like 60 to 80, can be considered as organizations trying to design and implement alternative development strategies. And they do this with the least favoured sections of the population, the marginal

sectors, in clearly defined activities and with concrete results. The phenomenon of the rise of these organizations in Peru is very specific to the country, although there is a similar tendency in other countries in the Third World.

The economist Fausto Jordan, former Minister of Agriculture in Ecuador, explains his attitude towards NGOs:

> I have no absolute criteria by which to judge NGO actions. It seems to me that a *sine qua non* for NGO work is good knowledge and experience in the rural environment first of all, and of the country and the specific conditions of rural development. There are different ways of interpreting more than 400 years of history in the rural milieu. But you have to know it. You must also remain broad-minded and pay close attention to what the men and women in the countryside say. They are the best experts in rural development.
>
> There are Ecuadorean NGOs which have been working for 20 years in this sector, which they know intimately. FEPP, CESA, and the CAAP (Andean Centre for Population Action) benefit from considerable commitment on the financial and moral levels from the large international NGOs such as Misereor, Brot für die Welt, Oxfam, Care, etc.
>
> Other groups are present in the field also, working on small, sometimes short-lived projects, almost all of them claiming a left-wing ideology — I call them the romantics. Their goal is a rather confused consciousness-raising and a mostly theoretical self-sufficiency. The systematic anti-government diatribes of some of these organizations — such as Terra Nova — is rarely the result of rigorous analysis of the reality of the 'class struggle' in Ecuador or of a good knowledge of men and of the land. They are frequently the plaything of political agitators, and do not offer any real development alternatives.

Asked whether he discerned differences in NGOs according to their countries of origin or approaches to the problems of rural development, he replied:

> In general, I think that most Ecuadorean NGOs take care to diversify the sources of funding from foreign NGOs in order to maintain greater independence. It must also be said that most NGOs from the North, working in Ecuador, are serious in their approach and have a good knowledge of the terrain, because they take care to consult with and base their work on Ecuadorean teams.
>
> Europeans, the Dutch, Swiss, and Germans in particular, seem to me to have a more clearly defined personality and often more original approaches in their development programmes. European NGOs show

great maturity and a desire for independence which does not exclude co-operation with national institutions.

The American groups don't seem to me as free and innovative, because the American Government promotes its bilateral programmes and technical assistance on a State-to-State basis. In the Ministry we have had Peace Corps volunteers who were absolutely outstanding, others who were less so. I think that this policy does some harm to the initiatives of American NGOs. On the other hand, as I have already indicated, there is a whole constellation of groups, individuals, and organizations (highly respectable in the USA) who are practising a form of assistance or aid to development which is quite frankly reprehensible. Under cover of evangelism, they bring ideologies and behaviour patterns which are totally foreign to the Latin American milieu. Moreover, these intrusions of cultural (and economic) imperialism obey the classical process of 'divide and conquer' whether it be markets or souls.

Closer observation will enable us to distinguish:

the NGO which is involved in one project and which was set up to carry through this one project.

the local NGO which exists in one village or group of villages.

the provincial NGO which extends its action over a province or a state (for example Gujarat in India).

the national NGO, covering a whole country

International NGOs, those which are active in several different countries, existed until recently only in the countries of the North. They are the result of increasing awareness of the problems involved.

HISTORY OF THE NGO MOVEMENT IN THE NORTH

To understand the present-day phenomenon, we need to examine past trends, each of which has left its traces behind. Four successive streams of thought have inspired action for the countries of the Third World and in favour of development.

The missionary pioneers

Even before the colonial era, the countries of Africa, Latin America, and Asia were targets for church missionaries, Catholic and Protestant. The presence of the churches and their desire to help the poorest sectors of the population led to a vast movement of hospital and school building, opening of dispensaries, reception centres and emergency assistance services.

Action for poor countries was born of religious philosophy; the attitude to development within the Roman Catholic Church is based on definitive statements dating back to the time of independence from former colonial powers, in particular the encyclicals 'Pacem in Terris' (1963) and 'Populorum Progressio' (1967). This philosophy is based on the idea that every human being has rights and duties. Man is the subject, foundation, and finality of social life; he is the sole agent of social life; he is the sole actor, agent, and architect of his own development.

In recent works, Vincent Cosmao outlines the permanence of man's place at the heart of development, at the same time as the 'reversal of the development problem': henceforth it will be the people of poor countries who wish to become developed, who will organize themselves according to their own way of thinking in order to do so.

> After the era of aid and of technology transfer, after that of questioning the system or of the implementation of a new economic international order, it is today the actors or subjects of development who appear centre-stage, in practice as in theory. Henceforth, it becomes clear once more that there is only development of man and by man.[1]

Ethical currents

Talk of ethics in an international context may appear to be a challenge: morality would seem to have little place in relations between states. Without doubt, the ethical dimension is present in the thinking of certain specialists in international relations. However, in an inter-governmental world society where the use of force, though prohibited by law, is widespread daily practice, the share of ethics is perforce limited. Nation states make up a unique type of society which imposes its standards on its members and yet tolerates the use of armed force. As long as international society retains this hybrid and, in a sense, contradictory character, the morality of international action will also be equivocal.

NGOs manage to escape from this logic. To the extent that the solidarity which inspires them escapes the ascendancy of governments, they have established with the populations of the Third

---

[1] Vincent Cosmao, *Un monde en développement?* p. 11. (A developing world?), Editions Ouvrières, Paris, 1984.

World relations which attach great importance to moral preoccupations. Poverty in the Third World imposes a moral duty of co-operation. The awareness of this duty sometimes takes on elementary, sentimental, rather than rational, forms. The rich owe assistance and reparation to the poor. Sometimes it appears as a condition for international peace, or as an imperative of human solidarity.

Political thinking and economic theory

Political stances exercise a certain influence on the language of NGOs: there are in fact militants who find their natural expression in Third World development philosophy, and it is appropriate to examine the influence of the various currents of thought present in the field of politics. Thus it would be possible in Europe, for example, to highlight the presence of Marxist, Socialist, Christian Democrat, or liberal currents. Nationalist and Trotskyite currents, it seems, are the only ones not to appear among the proponents of NGO action in Third World Countries.

Most associations affirm their apolitical character, which leads to the search for consensus in order to efface ideological difference. However, there is one theme, which as a result of its universal character is adopted by all NGOs; this is the ideology of human rights, singularly reinforced by the repeated statements, in many places and on many occasions, of Pope John Paul II.

Economic thought on development is divided into two major currents. The first, illustrated by Walt Rostow, states that underdevelopment can be defined as a simple delay in growth. This was the leading trend at the time awareness of underdevelopment began to dawn. The Marshall Plan enabled the reconstruction of Europe; a similar policy was to assist the development of the Third World. This current inspired international development co-operation policies, and also the action of international organizations. NGOs were persuaded to go along with this development assistance policy in the first stage of their action; this is the case in particular of the NGOs which participated in the War on Hunger Committees, set up by government initiatives on the occasion of the campaign against hunger launched by FAO in 1960.

In the second current of thinking, underdevelopment is not just retarded growth: it is a structural phenomenon, linked to the emergence of a certain number of dominant economies which profit by the exploitation of underdeveloped countries. The phenomenon takes place through disintegration of the economy and society in poor countries: part of the economy and society is outward-looking, integrated into the world market, while the traditional economic and social structures are inhibited and become marginalized. This analysis leads to a critical view of the world economic order which results in underdevelopment, and is therefore often qualified as 'radical'. This description is only partly applicable. No doubt Third World ideology has radicalized analysis during the sixties; according to a Marxist analysis of imperialism, guerilla warfare, national liberation struggles, and the 'foco' theory of Che Guevara have been exalted.[1]

However, another source of this current of thinking springs from non-Marxist authors (François Perroux, Gunnar Myrdal, Raoul Prebish) and we should therefore not be surprised that it has exerted its influence far beyond Marxist circles. At the present time, this is the current which inspires the development doctrines of many NGOs.

Although it is possible to carry over 'ideology' into currents of thinking, it can nevertheless be seen that there are no common sources of inspiration. Each association, each organization, has its own terms of reference and almost the same could be said of each militant.

DEVELOPMENT OF THIRD WORLD NGOS

Third World NGOs are often the settling place of currents of thought which have more or less filtered through from NGOs from industrialized nations during co-operative efforts or in the course of working relationships. Though they are historically younger, NGOs in poor countries are sociologically more diverse. In Africa, for example, where community traditions are still very much alive, the councils of wise men, women's groups, family and tribal structures, religious groups, and water syndicates scarcely need to take on a modern institutional form in order to exist or function. But once dialogue with outside parties such as foreign NGO partners becomes necessary — within a given aid or development project for example — groups tend to assume the appearance, name, and behaviour of NGOs. This is also the case

[1] Gérard Chaliand, *Mythes révolutionnaires du Tiers Monde, guérillas et socialisme* (Revolutionary Myths of the Third World, Guerilla Warfare and Socialism), Le Seuil, Paris, 1976.

when groups undertake to produce and market their crops in different, more scientific ways.

NGOs also provide a way for women or minority groups to affirm their existence and rights in societies which tend to neglect, mistrust, or reject them. Many of these groups are very pragmatic and mostly concerned with protecting their rights and immediate survival. They have rarely given thought to long-term development strategies. Above all, they are suspicious of attempts to control them from outside. Like farmers in Ireland, Missouri, the Mezzogiorno, and the Auvergne, these peasant groups are generally wary of government, civil servants, and rapid change. They want time to reflect on the issues that affect them in order to make informed choices. They want to improve their living conditions and the future of their children.

The expression of awareness born at the Bandoeng conference of non-aligned nations in 1956 still has a political influence on the intellectual elites and leaders of the Third World, but it is hardly the galvanizing force pushing rural villagers to organize themselves into NGOs or grassroots organizations.

Different types of Third World NGOs

We have seen a series of examples which show how NGOs and village groups spring up.

NGOs set up by organizations from the industrialized nations generally remain independent. This is the case with most church-inspired groups. Organizations such as Caritas are generally based in Catholic parishes or dioceses which in turn give birth to hundreds of active village and community groups throughout the Third World.

Many NGOs owe their existence to more or less chance encounters or circumstances. In Turin in 1968, Professor R. Giovanni Ermiglia, at the age of 65, reflected on his bachelor life, his career as a professor of philosophy, and was struck by the thought that he had not really been of much use to humanity as a whole. He set off on his travels and for the first time in his life went to India because he had been very attracted by the example of Gandhi. There he met one of the leaders of the Sarvodaya Gandhi Movement, Mr S. Jaganathan, who suggested that he tour south India and offered one of his young assistants, S. Loganathan, to accompany him.

The region was a wasteland, the misery of the people in the

villages was overwhelming. On the last evening before their departure, Giovanni Ermiglia took out a substantial sum of money and urged Loganathan to start doing something. One of the farmers to whom they had said during the day, 'something must be done', had looked at them as if they were mad.

Six months later, Giovanni came back with more money from his savings; Loganathan took him by scooter to the village and he saw a small green patch. With the money given to him, the farmer had been able to dig a well and start a vegetable garden. People came from all around to look at the miracle. Giovanni realized that the little green patch could be the beginning of something big, but he was alone. Consequently he turned to an Italian NGO, Movimento Sviluppo et Pace. Accordingly, between 1969 and 1976, ten Sarva Seva farms were launched. In 1978 there were 16 in five districts of Tamil Nadu, covering 79,187 acres, benefiting 364 families. At this stage he decided to set up a national organization, which became the Association for Sarva Seva Farms (ASSEFA). In 1984 ASSEFA was active in eight states of India.

In Peru, Mario Padron, head of the research-oriented Centro de Estudios y Promoción del Desarollo (DESCO), tells us of the different causes which led to the creation of these groups.

One of these was the concern, born with the arrival of the military government of Velasco, in power in 1968–70, to link the popular classes to a vast reform programme backed up by specialists and intellectuals. However, this process was interrupted in 1976 with the arrival of a new regime which dismissed the civil servants and professionals who were working to promote economic development for the benefit of the marginalized groups. More than 3,000 civil servants and project workers were dismissed. These measures primarily affected the people who were working to help set up popular organizations.

The second explanation for the extraordinary development of NGOs in Peru is to be found in the very dynamism of the people's organizations, which, despite the retreat of the government, have remained alive and active. Since the end of the Velasco era, there has been a fantastic growth of grassroots organizations, agricultural co-operatives, rural or fishing communities, and local neighbourhood associations.

There is also a whole range of self-managed groups which are the driving force behind popular movements. They have taken over the role formerly played exclusively by trade unions and workers' movements. This trend continues despite the fact that more than 40% of the population of working age is unemployed and only 20% of the active population is unionized. Gradually, as these organizations have grown up, they have called in professionals for advice and help in organizing their work.

Thus, NGOs have given thought and direction to their policies in order to be able to offer advice, help popular sectors in their organizational efforts, design education programmes, and even participate directly in solving technical problems, such as identifying sources of credit for farmers, one of the tasks which the Peasant Federation of Peru recently entrusted to NGO experts specializing in rural development. The Federation assigned to a development research centre the study and design of an alternative agrarian programme. This was a somewhat sophisticated and specialized task which required a fairly high level of professional qualification.

In Africa, many NGOs have been set up by local intellectuals in an effort to develop their own villages. In some cases, even large multinational corporations have promoted the creation of NGOs. This was the case in Nigeria where the Shell Petroleum Development Company helped set up Imo State, a rural development NGO which subsequently became totally independent of the company.

Since 1975, Shell has financed and promoted wide-ranging development efforts which have benefited over 63,000 rural Nigerians. This activity continues in all the Nigerian states where the company is working, especially around sites of oil production, research, and exploration. When our team visited the Uboma clan community project in Imo State, they also had the opportunity of meeting other NGOs which were set up by local associations and peasant groups. Conceived and managed exclusively by local villagers, these associations are authentic local NGOs.

Their funding comes partly from the oil companies, from European or North American NGOs, and from the Nigerian government, which hopes in this way to maintain a degree of control over them. Agents or representatives of the government are always entitled to sit on the managing committees or governing boards of these organizations. However, government control can also be exercised without direct intervention or presence among the management of an NGO. Whether in primarily Christian- or Muslim-dominated areas, local leaders — chiefs or Alhajis — act more or less as government proxies or watchdogs to make certain that the interests of Lagos come before those of local constituencies.

It is clear that although NGOs originated in industrialized countries and their history is considerably longer than that of their cousins in the developing world, they have not always had a very sophisticated notion of what constitutes constructive development co-operation. Inevitably both professional incompetence and ignorance of Third World cultures and socio-political realities among some Northern NGOs have been perpetuated by a number of NGOs in poor countries, which have modelled their organizations on Western ideas often unsuited to their own needs and circumstances. As a result there have been misunderstandings beween NGOs from opposite ends of the world. In some areas, as we shall see in Ecuador, these differences have not always been overcome to the benefit of rural populations.

CHAPTER 8
NGOs in the Field

THE NORTH–SOUTH MISUNDERSTANDING

It appears that there are over a hundred international NGOs operating in Ecuador. Everywhere in Quito our team heard the same criticism: foreign organizations seem to be in competition for the 'market' of aid to the local rural population. Ecuadoreans reproach them with lack of co-ordination, duplication of effort, and a certain mistrust of government which stems, no doubt, from the implications of some of these NGOs' actions — ranging from criticism of the exploitation of peasants to prosyletizing in rural areas for foreign religious sects. One of the leaders of an Italian volunteer organization complained that the seven Italian NGOs working in Ecuador had never in ten years managed to sit down together and reach some kind of agreement on a common approach to the policies and principles that should guide their actions in support of the marginalized groups with which they are involved.

There is considerable confusion in Ecuador concerning the aims and actions of foreign NGOs involved in development projects, or who are co-financing projects with Ecuadorean NGOs. Mistrust was eloquently expressed in interviews with many rural villagers encountered by our team. Villagers claimed they were being bombarded with aid and assistance projects from abroad (and from the Ecudorean government). The leader of one Indian community in the Andean Cotopaxi province, not far from Quito, strongly expressed his views regarding foreign groups that land in their communities. His position, which was widely shared by members of local Indian and peasant groups, also applied to Ecuadorean NGO and government development initiatives.

> They want to impose their way of seeing things on us. With good intentions and the best will in the world, these people think they are doing good, but they go against us and do not understand our way of life and our traditions. Often they want to try out their solutions on us. And then they bring in money and that's when the problems begin, because once money comes into the matter, you start to get differences

of opinion within the community, jealousies, conflicts. The experts come along with projects for piping water which we have to carry out collectively in our traditional work gangs, the *mingas*, when what we are clamouring for is paths and roads to give access to the market so that we can sell our produce and buy basic commodities. And when the water finally comes, our children start to get ill. The water was cleaner when our women went up the mountain to collect it from the streams.

Generally the Ecuadorean organizations most critical of foreign NGO action in the rural milieu were Indian and peasant groups and federations which were opposed to attempts to integrate rural populations into the economic mainstream. These organizations suspected some NGOs of trying to infiltrate them and of consciously or unwittingly working to subordinate rural populations to the authority of the government and dominant economic groups.

Foreign NGOs, as well as local organizations, have to proceed with caution in a troubled political environment where the hypersensitivity of groups and the desire in some quarters to reap the benefits of NGO action are fairly widespread. The role of certain foreign groups, especially those connected with religious sects such as the Instituto Linguistico de Verano (the Latin American offshoot of the 50-year-old North American missionary group concerned with the 'cultural and linguistic' mission of translating the Bible into indigenous languages and which has been banned in Ecuador), complicates the task of NGOs concerned exclusively with economic and social development and reduces their credibility.

Among the criticisms and charges levelled against foreign NGOs were those of the leaders of Ecuarunari, the federation of Ecuadorean indigenous peoples' organizations.

> We are fighting for the complete expulsion of the Institute Linguistico de Verano and are demanding the application of Decree 1150 which mandated the expulsion. We also want World Vision, the Plan Padrino, and other sectarian NGOs expelled. These groups use the pretext of projects, loans, and education and other bait to destroy our culture and undermine our organization. Foreign religious groups are dividing and abusing Indian communities. The funds which NGOs give us sow discord and divide our communities.

Our team visited a village where the only visible result of the action of the US foster-parent scheme Plan Padrino were the plastic cups and spoons which had been distributed to the children. Mothers in this community told of how they had been given boxes of baby food for their infants, but they complained that after eating it their babies began to suffer from diarrhoea and enteritis. They preferred to breast-feed their babies since the only water they had to mix with the baby food given by the Plan Padrino was infested with parasites. They described with humour how the American missionaries had arrived on foot in the village, immaculate in suits and ties, in this area of the Andes at over 3,500 metres altitude, accessible only to four-wheel-drive vehicles after a long drive on dusty tracks. The missionaries spoke to the women in perfect Quechua and, after distributing Bibles in their native tongue, offered the children plastic cutlery and dishes.

Similar criticisms of NGOs were made by peasant federations such as UROCAL (Regional Union of Peasant Organizations of the Coastal Provinces), UNASAY (Azuay Province), as well as in Quito, the capital.

> We do not want to be shamefully dependent on the projects of foreign organizations. We know the solution to our problems will never be in begging for crumbs from aid organizations ... although some of these groups express good intentions, we have had the bad experience that many communities and peasant groups seem to think that they must behave in such a way in order to be given a development project to solve our problems, without having understood why we are social outcasts. We know that in some cases money coming from abroad is accompanied by paternalistic attitudes, or still worse by the manipulation of our resources to the benefit of economic interests of the rich countries. We are fed up with people coming to help us with the idea of imposing approaches on us which are not at all suitable and end up dividing us. The gringos come and present us with a tractor. But when we ask for land to use this tractor on, they treat us like Communists. Many organizations which supposedly work for us in Quito and here, look forward to the money from abroad to make sure they get good salaries, cars, and a social position whereas we only get a small amount to build a community shop which will remain empty because we don't have enough money to work our land or to buy from wholesalers in the towns the necessary products at a reasonable price. We are forced to go and work in Quito and Guayaquil, as peons, leaving our families in order to survive.

There are practically no foreign NGOs working in the field in Bolivia. Isolated development actions are carried out by organizations such as USAID or CICDA from France. In Bolivia, as in practically all the countries of Latin America, it is the local NGOs which have taken rural development problems in hand. The United States is present to a certain extent, through the churches and North American Protestant groups. However, many people we spoke to were distrustful of these groups which have often been accused of working in collusion with the CIA. North American research institutes are accused of working for the benefit of 'gringo' companies, mainly large oil companies. But it is difficult to distinguish between fact and fantasy in the statements of the people to whom we spoke.

As far as Bolivia — recently returned to democracy — is concerned, the political equilibrium is still extremely fragile; it is certain that during the years of dictatorship, North American organizations working for development were not necessarily innocent. These black years have left bitter memories among many Bolivian intellectuals concerned with development. But what also remains from this sombre period is an extreme distrust of initiatives from outside the country. This mistrust is to be felt above all among trade union leaders of Peasant Centrale of the Bolivian Workers Confederation (COB), who are trying to control rural development initiatives and to manage funds from foreign NGOs. Among these people, the fear of seeing the gringo setting himself up in the country in force provoked a certain type of nationalism. Although these misunderstandings are less and less frequent, they do still persist.

Experience in the field, the failures and the difficulties encountered, sometimes a new balance of power resulting from the emergence of Third World NGOs, rapidly led the NGOs from both hemispheres to evolve together. This evolution, confirmed by the emergence of NGOs on the international scene, has made them more visible; and while they are taken more seriously, they are subjected to more criticism.

To understand this evolution, we shall examine successively the development of relations between NGOs, the transformations which have taken place in the relations between NGOs and governments, and lastly the tendency of Third World NGOs to look for ways of becoming financially independent.

TOWARDS BETTER CO-ORDINATION

In recent years NGOs have been characterized by a certain confusion in their language, reciprocal ignorance of one another's

activities, a certain feeling of competition, and lack of communication between them, even when groups from industrialized
countries and the Third World were involved side by side in a
given country.

The disparate nature of their efforts, frequently inefficient and
wasteful, the desire of governments and of international and
financial institutions to avoid having to negotiate with too many
partners at once, have all prompted NGOs to move towards
combined effort and participation in national or regional co-
ordination commitees, even if at times somewhat reluctantly.
Thus, since 1982, there is an NGO Liaison Committee within the
European Community, which represents most NGOs from member countries. The same trend can be observed in individual
European countries, Canada, and most other developed countries
where co-ordinating bodies and working sessions enable NGO
leaders to define a common language and exchange experience.
This co-ordination is generally within each of these countries, but
with more difficulty between them.

The situation in some African countries illustrates the wide
differences in NGO co-ordination. Inter-NGO relations in
Burkina Faso seem still to be in the initial stages. 'There is a
definite lack of co-ordination between NGOs. They act in a
disparate fashion; they are in competition, not only with government services, but also with each other.' As a result, each individual microproject is an end in itself, rather than being part of
an overall development policy. 'It would be desirable to group the
NGOs into one such body to prevent them from competing within
the same sectors.' Such a body exists in Burkina Faso (SPONG —
Permanent Secretariat for NGOs), but is apparently fairly inefficient. 'It has never managed to do much more than carry out a
post hoc listing of projects undertaken.'

In Mali about twenty NGOs work together on a larger-scale
development project concerning a whole region. Local NGOs
furthermore made a joint intervention at the conference of donors
held in Mali in December 1982, and this necessitated prior consultation on their part. This joint approach became all the more
obvious in January 1984 with the creation of the CCAV/ONG
(Coordinating Committee for NGO Emergency Actions).

In Zaire, NGOs do work together, but they are afraid of State
intervention and tend to work under cover of the churches and
through different umbrella associations. CODEZA (Committee

for the Development of Zaire), is one such association launched by one NGO (AIDR) and the Catholic Church, and includes Protestant and Kibanguistes NGOs; however it did not succeed, no doubt because the NGOs were careful to not attract too much publicity. As a result, in Zaire the right hand does not know what the left hand is doing.

Elsewhere, NGOs have been united for several years, either at the request of governments who wished to have only one partner to deal with, or at the request of donors, for the same reasons, or yet again voluntarily, in order to act together. Among the African countries examined, Togo seems to be the most advanced from the point of view of organizing NGOs. Apart from the creation in 1976 of a common think-tank, the Congat, NGOs in Togo for the last few years have had Congat/Service at their disposal. This is an assistance structure which works as a consultancy or technical adviser for NGOs who wish to avail themselves of its project research, administrative procedures, financing research, distribution of finances, co-ordination of action of several NGOs, advice, and so on. Congat has staff competent in different fields, and assures NGO relations with government and outside partners. It cannot be said that the level of co-operation between Togolese NGOs is very advanced, but at least they have got to know one another and through the intermediary of Congat and Congat/Service they do communicate with each other.

Congat organizes training sessions and seminars for its members and invites counterpart bodies from neighbouring countries to attend. Thus in March 1984 in addition to Togolese NGOs, there were also one representative from Congad (NGO group from Senegal — twenty NGOs, half from the North, half local), one representative from CFRAR of the Ivory Coast (Centre for Training and Research in Rural Education), and one representative of the Mali Association for Research Action and Development, as well as several representatives from Gercoop (Group for Study and Research on Co-operatives) from Benin.

A joint structure covering some NGOs in Kenya was set up in 1981 under the name of Kengo. One of its leaders, Stewart Marwick, says:

> In January 1981 there was a meeting of the founding members (six to eight NGOs) and after a little advertising, their number increased. We had the idea of having an exhibition of NGOs in Kenya in June 1981, two months before a major United Nations conference was to be held

in Nairobi, the idea being to have a get-together. We were hoping for 30 organizations; 65 came to the conference and for the exhibition. The organizations did not have any networks, did not know each other. At the exhibition, braziers, mills, windmills were presented. Twenty-five countries participated with high technology products. Sixty-one NGOs exhibited only very simple objects, for immediate use. The crowds thronged to the exhibition. The Secretary-General of the United Nations was very impressed. He came several times. It was such a success that we set up Kengo. The name was provisional, but it has stuck. The new Minister for the Environment has taken an interest in NGOs. He said, 'OK, go ahead, and if you need any help, just say.' In the beginning we had to proceed with great care in order not to tread on the toes of any of the leaders. Now there is co-operation.

Kengo is financed through European co-operation (for example the West German GTZ) and USAID. The American Government has large-scale projects in Kenya (Kenya available energy project).

There was competition between NGOs (the Kenyans are competitive people), but competition does not facilitate work. People easily understood the importance of working together. There were many meetings, reports. There are Church-inspired NGOs in Kengo. In Kenya it is impossible to work without the churches; it is really a paradise for the different religions. The amount of work carried out by missionaries is considerable. Before, they were there solely for evangelism, now their attitude has changed. They have effected a kind of revolution.

Kengo is a legally established association, set up in 1982. Its present policy is to maintain co-ordination and exchange of information between the NGOs of Kenya with regard to new energy sources and community development. As a national NGO, Kengo plays the role of catalyst by planning, initiating, and co-ordinating NGO projects concerning renewable energy sources and community development. It promotes projects by supplying technical assistance and organizing training programmes, and offers NGOs direct material assistance, transfer of information, programme co-ordination, training, and technical assistance. It has close relations with the Kenyan government and research institutions.

In Ecuador, where 40–50 per cent of the population belongs to minority ethnic groups, familiarity with indigenous organizations, which play a major role in the country both as pressure groups and as agents of development, is obviously necessary. Most of them are grouped under the Ecuarunari movement (Runacunapac

Riccharimui, or Awakening of the Ecuadorean Indian in Quechua). Founded with church support, Ecuarunari is primarily concerned with preserving Indian culture, promoting and setting up development projects for the benefit of the various indigenous peoples representing more than four million people, mainly from the Quechua, Shuar, Huaorani, Secoya, Siona, Tetete, Cofane, and Zaparo 'nations'.

The pivotal role played by the Catholic Church in inspiring and supporting development action in Ecuador, as well as in most Latin American countries, encourages, if not formal institutional co-ordination, continual information exchange between NGOs and other groups, and also limits the dispersion seen elsewhere. In contrast, the working links between NGOs and the different rural organizations (in particular FENOP, the National Federation of Peasant Organiztions, which brings together most of the major organizations of rural Ecuador) stimulates a real exchange of communication and experience between them.

In Latin America there are three levels of co-ordination which appear to be particularly significant:

The Organization of American States officially recognizes most NGOs working in the region. The OAS publishes an NGO directory and periodically invites NGOs to participate in meetings on specific issues to present their points of view.

The Economic Commission for Latin America within the United Nations plays a role similar to that of the OAS as a forum and offers NGOs the chance to express themselves. In the case of ECLA, as with the OAS, this situation did not come about spontaneously, but is the result of the NGO struggle to become true partners of these two organizations, and to play a real pressure-group role within them.

The Episcopal Conference of Latin America co-ordinates Catholic action to encourage development on the regional level. Since in most cases the Catholic Church is present in parishes, basic communities, priests, and lay people working with NGOs, CELAM quite naturally assumes the role of communications centre and of driving force behind development activities and social improvement schemes.

Turning to Asia, there are broadly three groups of NGOs in Thailand: the largest ones need increased amounts of funds to expand and also more technical training; a second group are active, but have not reached a sufficient level of internal management, or of use of human and financial resources, to start up projects; the smallest recently created NGOs have potential, but still have to be built up. These NGOs are very isolated from one another, are often not aware of each other's existence, and rarely communicate.

Efforts have been under way in recent years to overcome this lack of communication. International networks have been set up to promote personal contacts and the exchange of information among NGOs. Centres in Switzerland such as IRED (Innovations and Networks for Development) in Geneva and IFDA (International Foundation for Another Development) in Nyon play an important part in ensuing world-wide circulation of information on NGO work and development. Through the meetings they organize and their publications, these groups promote the dissemination of information on development projects, new technologies, and general issues regarding the Third World and economic development. They also stimulate the creation of regional networks in which they seek to involve local leaders.

Particular attention is given to the exchange of information between developing countries — the 'South–South dialogue' — another important facet of NGO activity around the world. These exchanges are increasing rapidly, no doubt because they help individual NGOs overcome their isolation through congresses and conferences. A number of regional and international get-togethers have enabled hundreds of NGOs world-wide to meet and compare mutual experience, for example, joint meeting of Latin American and European NGOs in Santiago, Chile, in 1983, international meetings in the same year in Rome among Third World, European, and Canadian NGOs and in New Delhi on Community Development, the regional meeting of African NGOs in Togo in 1984, and a large conference organized by OECD in Paris in February 1985 to enable NGOs from the Third World to sit down with donor groups and NGOs from the industrialized North. These meetings help to expand NGOs' global view of their activities and the issues of development that they share, and also promote a better understanding of the differences and similarities of these organizations. NGOs are given the opportunity of comparing notes as well as of reviewing the political, technical, and financial obstacles they may encounter. Such exchanges encourage progress in development while at the same time they cement the solidarity of a movement which is making a profound impact on the rural Third World.

RELATIONS WITH AUTHORITIES

NGOs from industrialized countries are well represented in Africa as a result of pressing economic and climatic problems there, which even before the drought of recent years required international aid, whether governmental or private. Once installed, sometimes for an emergency problem, the NGOs have generally remained in the country and their impact at the present time is not negligible. It is therefore not surprising that local authorities are eager to find out what NGOs represent and to gauge their power and influence. 'NGOs represent 8 billion francs CFA, so it is necessary to know where the money comes from and where it goes' (leader in Burkina Faso).

It should be stressed that the change that can be seen in relations between NGOs and authorities is attributable as much to the authorities as to NGOs themselves. The first stage of relations is generally characterized rather by avoidance than contact. In most cases, there are no special regulations or policies governing NGO activities. This is the case in Zaire and in Burkina Faso, although the situation is different in each of these countries, and other nations in the Third World present a broad spectrum of NGO-government relations.

Zaire

In Zaire the government professes a certain well-meaning neutrality towards NGOs. 'The government of Zaire has great difficulty in managing its large-scale projects. In these circumstances, how could it be conscious of and control "small-scale" NGO projects? Nevertheless, it is not unaware of them and does encourage their actions, providing moral support, and granting authorizations and sometimes even plots of land.' Occasionally the government delegates its responsibilities to an NGO. 'Last year, Marshall Mobutu recognized the inability of the government to provide health training and passed on responsibility for this area to NGOs.'

The key word in Zaire seems to be 'live and let live — in hiding.' NGOs are very reluctant to operate in the open for fear of government repression. They can only work in the shadow of the officially condoned, powerful church groups. They can organize their activities in this manner since there is no government service to regulate private associations. 'If a group wishes to obtain the status of a non-profit association it has to wait for two years until permission is granted by the Office of the President, sole authority in this area.'

Many NGOs short-circuit government attempts to control their activities and funding by working under cover of non-profit groups such as the Catholic Church, since churches generally easily obtain this status. 'It could be said that as a general rule NGOs place themselves under a bishop's mantle and they are integrated, in one form or an other, into the action carried out by churches. New NGOs therefore seek the protection of a bishop, otherwise the Government will try to catch them. Here, above all you must keep a low profile, otherwise the Government comes down on you and imposes taxes and licences.'

If in a country like Zaire NGOs manage to work by avoiding government interference, the same does not apply at the local level.

> Projects have no chance of succeeding unless they have received local approval. It should be borne in mind that any project or development action which has not received the blessing of local authorities, albeit informal, has no future. The civil service would block the project immediately and discourage its promoters. You have to get the interest of the most important man, the District Commissioner.

In general, relations between NGOs and local authorities are not the best, owing to lack of mutual understanding and awareness of one another's motives. In the course of this study an inquiry was carried out among local authorities and NGOs to find out their respective points of view and expectations: it clearly showed a lack of mutual trust and acceptance. In regions where action was taken subsequent to this study, relations have improved.

Burkina Faso
Here the situation can be summed up by saying that NGOs often do as they please, or as they are allowed to. In the absence of clear guidelines or a precise government policy with regard to NGO activity, these organizations are relatively free to act. 'NGOs act in a disorganized fashion and often without informing the authorities. We do not know what is being done in the villages' (Prefect of Ouagadougou). They generally pay lip-service to the major options as defined by the authorities, but their action in the field depends exclusively on their own assessment of the local situation. NGOs often compete with government services at the local level and with Burkina Faso's regional development agency, the Organization for Regional Development (ORD). In the field, NGOs and

ORDs apparently have friendly relations, with no problems, even if each of them has different methods. In fact, they watch each other like hawks and there is basically keen competition, often to the advantage of NGOs which have greater financial resources and possibilities of intervention than ORDs. When an NGO arrives in a village, it sets up its own village group, alongside that of the ORD, and this is not always beneficial to the villagers.

NGOs' independence and disregard for official policy are not to the government's liking and a new bureau directly attached to the President's office was recently set up. 'The National Revolutionary Council has understood that the NGOs can achieve a lot, on condition that their efforts are guided and co-ordinated. NGOs have to be integrated into our Development Plan. The various NGO activities have to be standardized' (Minister of Equipment).

> In concrete terms, our working method will be to influence the geographical implantation of NGOs and their activities. The monitoring unit will define the exact place and nature of activities for NGOs wishing to act in the field. We define the geographical area for NGOs. Given their specialization, we grant them a sphere of activity. We do not wish to be coercive, and hope, on the contrary, to preserve the freedom of NGOs because it is synonymous with flexibility and efficiency. (Director of the Bureau for Monitoring NGOs)

It appears therefore that, after having given a great deal of freedom to NGOs — perhaps too much — the government of Burkina Faso wishes to control them more closely, despite the claims of liberalism by the Director of this NGO Bureau. However it must be recognized that the dispersion of NGOs, their independence, the competition between them, often prevents them from being as effective as they could be in meeting the needs of those whom they are supposed to help.

Mali
Although many NGOs work in Mali, few of them are of purely Malian origin. The primary reason for this is the desire on the part of the government to control popular initiatives: it is suspicious of any activity that goes on outside the dominant, officially supported party and its own organizations. While the Keito regime generally accepts foreign NGOs, it has serious reservations about authorizing independent Malian groups. Therefore, foreign NGOs, which employ permanent staff in the hundreds as well as many volunteer

expatriates, constitute the main source of NGO-supported development activity in the country.

However, in recent years the government has somewhat softened its attitude towards local NGOs. In December 1982 it invited several local groups to take part in a donors' conference and called for greater participation in rural development through grassroots initiatives at village level. Further proof of goodwill was given when the government decided to reactivate the village *tons* or councils, officially recognizing them so that they could administer development projects in rural areas. In return, NGOs were urged not to ignore the existence of national development committees which the government set up to promote decentralization. To emphasize its change of heart towards NGOs, the Ministry of Economic Planning was entrusted with co-ordinating NGO activities in order to set up guidelines for them.

The Mali government is not so much opposed to NGOs or their vital work as anxious to control their activities and not to be outflanked by them. The authorities seek in particular to keep tabs on NGO activities, which has not always been the case. They are also determined that the focus of NGO activity remain the village and that these groups work in conjunction with and under the guidance of the local *tons.*

If in the past the government of Mali has shown mistrust towards NGOs, it can be said that they were repaid in kind. NGOs rarely informed authorities of their activities, either because it was not necessary for their work or because the government had not turned out to be as co-operative as expected, or yet again because NGOs were afraid of having their freedom restricted, or even of being forced to work under the thumb of officials who are not always qualified.

Unlike neighbouring Burkina Faso, the government of Mali does not seem to need to keep a tight rein on NGOs, but after having let things drift, it appears that it wishes to take control of matters.

Togo
In 1976, NGOs in Togo formed a council, the Congat, set up under the auspices of the Ministry of Economic Planning and Administrative Reform, and in 1983 an agreement was signed between Congat and the Togolese government. Recently, the Ministry of Economic Planning called on NGOs to work actively

towards the success of its programmes in five priority areas — agriculture, village water supplies, rural crafts, food storage, and rural road infrastructure.

Forced to adopt austerity measures, the Togolese government has had to cut by two-thirds the budget it had earmarked for rural development in its third five-year plan. It apparently thought it could rely on NGOs to help provide funding for its programmes in this sector. However, given the authoritarian tendencies of the Togolese leadership, there is good reason to view this offer of 'co-operation' as a ploy on the part of the regime to exploit and control NGOs in that country.

Those in charge of Togolese NGOs are well aware of the fact: 'There ought to be a law concerning NGOs so that the government cannot put a hand on them.'

All the same, thanks to formal co-operation, NGOs are able to work more easily. 'Before the agreement, NGOs in fact were not really able to work. Civil servants did not take their efforts into account'. But personal problems always have to be reckoned with: 'Informal co-ordination works better than official co-ordination'; and NGOs do not always work very freely: 'Directors for social affairs want to take over all the problems of the region, although they are often not competent.'

One representative from the Ministry of Economic Planning who was attending a Congat seminar (along with representatives from other Ministries) recognized that the aims of Congat conform with the overall Government strategy for rural development, and recalled that waste of funds at the disposal of NGOs must be avoided. He congratulated Congat for not letting up in its efforts since it was created in 1976. Our team in West Africa was not in a position to determine whether Congat was set up on the initiative, or at least at the request, of the government, but there are grounds for thinking so; Congat documents show that 'on the eve of the third five-year development plan, designed as a plan to promote the masses, NGOs, both confessional and lay, Togolese and foreign, legally installed in Togo, met to analyse their activities and evaluate their efficiency. This joint reflection resulted in the setting up of a permanent structure responsible for standardizing and co-ordinating NGO activities.'

Cameroun

Cameroun is in a no less catastrophic economic situation than its neighbours, but until recently it was generally cited as a model of good management and political stability. The government maintains good relations with most NGOs: although it has not instituted formal co-operation with them, it has yet to come into conflict with them. According to most NGOs working in Cameroun, the government generally favours their actions. 'The Ministry of Agriculture is perfectly in favour of grassroots initiatives set up in response to villagers' needs. The development of our country must take place gradually, without brutally overwhelming customs and age-old farming practices. Sustainable development can only be assured in Cameroun if there is popular participation at village level. Traditions and customs must be respected, and at the same time put to good use.'

The Directorate for Community Development (in the Ministry of Agriculture), whose aim is to address the socio-cultural aspects of rural development and to promote the role of women, was also 'very much in favour of NGO activities'. NGO projects, whether local or foreign, are generally given the support of the Ministry of Agriculture. However the situation in each region depends on the attitude of local civil servants.

At district level an NGO in the north must develop relations with the Lamido. On the village level, in order for an NGO and its workers to be able to operate they have to be authorized by the Lawan (village chief), the Djoro (neighbourhood chiefs), and by the Marabout (the leader of a Muslim organization). If everything gets off to a good start, then relations are harmonious. The problems, which could arise later, come from State companies (cotton, rice, and sugar), which may come into conflict with NGOs on fundamental issues — extension of cash crops to the detriment of food crops, for example. Furthermore, education (literacy programmes) dispensed by NGOs to workers in some of these industries may make them less docile to employers' authority.

The type of relations, or absence of relations, which we have just observed between NGOs, whether from the North or from the South, and governments in five countries in West Africa, gives a fairly accurate picture of what exists and of the tendencies which are becoming apparent, even if it varies somewhat from country to country in Africa and in other regions of the world. In Nigeria and Indonesia, governments hope to use NGOs and to control them, by carrying out what some of our interviewees have called 'infiltration' of NGO governing boards.

Nigeria
One NGO worker in Nigeria explained the government point of
view:

> The equilibrium of the country is completely artificial. Christians and
> Muslims do not fight, but suspicion remains. At the present time, the
> head of government and those in high places in government are
> Muslims. This seems to be a guarantee against Communism. But all the
> same thousands of Muslim villagers in the north-east were killed last
> spring and their villages burnt to the ground because the Marabouts
> revolted against the central government. And the government is always
> suspicious of anyone or anything foreign, whether volunteers from
> European humanitarian associations or simply money destined for
> organizations such as ours.

What becomes apparent is the manifest desire of the military
government to Nigerianize all outside private initiative, whether
charitable or profit-making. What this means in simple terms is
stated clearly in an interview we had with the Director of Public
Relations of the Shell Petroleum Development Company in Port
Harcourt, who told us that any foreigner is *a priori* suspected of
acting against the interests of Nigeria and, as far as possible, his
activities must be supervised by a Nigerian counterpart. And, if it
is feasible, he should be quickly be replaced by a Nigerian.

> The rest of Africa is jealous of us because we have oil, hence money.
> Europe, Russia, America, would like to get our oil cheaper. Or make
> business deals here, behind our backs and to our detriment with as
> much profit as possible. We truly have to defend ourselves, and we do
> this with the only weapons at our disposal, numbers and time. There
> are so many more of us here than Europeans, so we can control them.
> No doubt in a few years we shall be able to replace them in all areas.

As far as NGOs are concerned, whether they be managed by lay
people or by missionaries, the situation is the same.

> We are suspect, whatever we do. Local authorities, as well as federal
> authorities, imagine at all times that we are acting against the interests
> of Nigeria, and above all that private European development organ-
> izations, or those for health or education, are only instruments for
> getting money out of the country.

Kenya
In Kenya, the government is very open with regard to NGOs.
They must be regularly declared, but they are not subjected to any
control, to the extent that they really are working for development.

Two NGOs have been dissolved by the government, one because it was financed by South Africa, a country with which Kenya does not have diplomatic relations, and the other because, under cover of education, it was in fact a political organization.

Most NGOs in Kenya were started up on the initiative of Catholic or Protestant church groups. The Ministry of Social Affairs is entrusted with controlling the different NGOs' activities and is responsible for listing them. Some NGOs get more than 50 per cent of their funding from the government. NGOs are registered either with the Attorney General's Office, and as such are not allowed to make any profits, or with the Ministry of Co-operatives. These co-operatives are allowed to make profits (most women's groups in rural areas belong to this category).

Asia

The NGO movement in Bangladesh is very structured and entirely run by Bengalis. There is convergence of opinion among NGOs and they work together with the government to promote land reform and in the pharmaceutical industry. NGOs maintain an ongoing dialogue with the Government and are not without influence in the development of national policy, at least in some areas which concern their sectors of activity.

In the Philippines, NGOs exist officially and do not have any problems in their relations with the government. However, difficulties frequently arise in relations with local governments in villages and regions. Development, in the eyes of the local authorities, mayors, chiefs of police, is sometimes suspect and can spread a spirit of independence among farmers and a certain freedom of judgement which some authorities might consider pernicious. The whole system based on corruption is implicitly being criticized by people who are incorruptible. They have to be got rid of. 'Got rid of' means imprisoning or executing Irish or Filipino priests, NGO educators. Some of these priests have had to go underground to escape such treatment.

The Thai government has expressed increasing interest in co-operating with NGOs. This is confirmed by the fact that the Ministry of the Interior has defined an official policy in support of NGOs and many government agencies have begun working closely with them. Nevertheless, there is also a temptation within the government not to let NGOs have free rein. The tax laws do nothing to encourage donations to NGOs and the government tries to obtain international aid for its own agencies rather than for local NGOs.

The government of India has shown neither interest nor hostility towards NGOs. It appears that the government has yet to define a policy concerning them and that any problems arising have only been at the level of the various states where they operate. Government programmes to fight poverty are multiplying. The largest of them, the Integrated Rural Development Programme, is often accused of favouring the better off farmers and above all of filling the pockets of civil servants. The Communist Government in West Bengal has carried out a genuine land reform, by distributing to the share-croppers title deeds for the lands they were working. Indian NGOs which work in this state for the most part receive a positive welcome and support from the public authorities. In the case of Seva Sangh Samiti, the irrigation and drainage project and the integrated development project which accompanies it (in the field of malnutrition, education, forestation, etc.) would not have been possible without the co-operation which this NGO has established with the Bengali government, the presidents of the panchayats (municipal assemblies), the villages concerned by the project, the various political parties, and the banks.

In the state of Tamil Nadu in the south of India, the expansion strategy of ASSEFA is promoted through the support of municipal and regional authorities and by constant negotiations with banks to obtain loans.

South America
In the Andean countries, relations between NGOs and Government reproduce fairly well the cases observed in West Africa. In some cases there is co-operation, and state conventions mandate certain NGOs to work for integrated rural development. In other cases, NGOs are legally recognized. Some of these, as in Peru or in Bolivia, tend to set themselves up as a counter-force to the disintegration of the state or its absence.

Some governments have banned NGOs or are opposed to them because of their concept of development or because the NGOs accuse them of favouring powerful multinational companies. When an outright ban is not possible, government action sometimes consists of trying to infiltrate organizations or to buy off their leaders. In some areas, although the NGO is not officially banned, there is government opposition and an attempt to control what is happening at local level. Governments are also frequently opposed to NGOs inspired by 'dangerous' left-wing ideologies.

In Mexico, the government maintains a good degree of control over NGOs and limits their activities as well as their initiatives. Although some foreign NGOs are present at project level, the few small-scale development initiatives which are not within the direct purview of government organizations or parastate institutions are carried out by local NGOs and groups which are often either unofficial or forced to operate without official status or approval — they work at the edge of legality.

> The work of NGOs in Mexico in the rural sector and in particular with indigenous communities or refugee groups, for example in Chiapas, is often hampered by the bureaucracy of the Mexican state, not to mention resistance by local feudal chieftains, or *caciques*. Foreign NGOs are always suspected of intruding, if not directly spying. Even church activities are subject to government control. In Mexico the state is omnipresent in a labyrinth of administrations which go beyond their role of supporting marginalized groups to exercise a veritable monopoly of activities in the field of rural development.

Despite the great disparity in the situations NGOs face, the following observations can be made. First of all, most of the governments concerned do not have an official policy line with regard to NGOs. They generally approach the issue on a case-by case basis, or in terms of each regime's interests. At the local level, village or provincial authorities generally have greater authority and relations take on a different aspect. There are obvious reasons for this. Central government is further away and day-to-day decisions are the responsibility of local government which is often jealous of its prerogatives and authority. Nor can personal relations between NGO staff and village notables or authorities be neglected — they often have a determining effect on the success or failure of a project. Red tape or corruption can seriously jeopardize an NGO's task at local level. Another important factor is the competition between project personnel and local authorities in terms of project implementation and decision-making. Local authorities and civil servants do not always look kindly upon those who run counter to their wishes or authority.

Local and foreign NGOs are not generally subjected to the same type of treatment, and often do not share common approaches. Foreign NGOs are more independent in many ways, while local groups have to pay more attention to government directives and are more obedient because they are more vulnerable. The absence of relations between NGOs and governments generates mistrust on both sides, and can lead to conflict situations, as does any lack of communication at whatever level it may be.

At times NGOs have deliberately ignored governments or kept them at arm's length, so that the latter are now taking measures concerning them which may be excessive. As always, the swing of the pendulum has gone too far in the opposite direction; the more independent NGOs have been in the past, the less they are now or will become in the future. It must not be forgotten that for years many NGOs behaved as if governments did not exist, when they were not in outright opposition to them. While not attempting to debate the merits of such an attitude, we would stress that it is not abnormal for a government, whatever its faults or shortcomings, to react when it is being criticized.

It can be foreseen that governments, having understood the financial advantages represented by NGO presence in their countries, and having tied them up legally, will take over their activities in favour of their own policy. Unless of course the industrialized nations, which furnish the major part of funding, intervene on their behalf, as seems already to have been the case. Americans are re-examining problems between NGOs and governments. Recently in Senegal, USAID called together all the NGOs and declared, 'We have six million dollars, and it's for NGOs. Government organizations have had their chance and now it's time to give NGOs a chance to do the development work!' (Quoting an NGO representative at Congat seminar in Senegal.)

'SELLING' A PROJECT

Development projects in Third World areas are sometimes indiscriminately funded by NGOs from industrialized countries which do not bother asking pertinent questions but simply hand out the money as though for an emergency aid programme. 'Before, they used to give you money, if they liked your looks,' one NGO worker remarked. However, many NGOs face difficult problems in securing funding for a programme or for their activities in general. This need of financial support has two consequences — one positive, the other double-edged.

The first consequence is that groups are forced to organize their work, analysing it carefully before launching themselves full-scale. They must precisely delineate each aim and step in a project before soliciting funds from donors. Frequently, the rigour of their presentation is to their advantage.

> The people who have the money now don't want to finance just any old project. We have to get organized to present coherent schemes. We have heard of large projects which didn't have any draft budget, any end-of-year statement, and donor agencies threatened to cut off funding if they didn't maintain proper bookkeeping.

The second, more unhappy consequence, is that some people, having mastered the mechanics of fund-raising, create false projects and use the money for personal gain. 'All too often co-operation is synonymous with duping. "Advanced" Zaireans set up a co-operative with a little money, pocket the profits once it starts to succeed and then disappear.' A former minister set up a fictitious village group which existed only on paper and which in fact was created merely to grab the subsidies being offered.

In the course of some field visits our teams came up against a few such 'alibi projects' where part of the money, hard to estimate, was used for personal purposes. But this situation was extremely rare. In fact, for some time now, donors have tended to be more parsimonious with their funds and demand more than a well-articulated project before they loosen the purse strings. There is greater control and more regular evaluations are carried out in accordance with more serious criteria, including some variables which strongly resemble cost-benefit analyses.

This situation, which has the unquestionable merit of distin-guishing between legitimate NGO activities and ill-conceived or inappropriate efforts, also forces groups to confront the problem of self-reliance. In some cases this can produce a negative effect, for NGOs are forced to devote a considerable amount of time and effort to administrative tasks totally extraneous to the actual implementation of a project.

TOWARDS GREATER FINANCIAL INDEPENDENCE

The tendency of project leaders in the field is to move towards financial independence wherever possible, in order to ensure greater freedom. After depending for a long time on foreign NGOs for project funding, many Third World NGOs and expatriate project workers are eager to diversify their sources of funding: instead of looking for financing which would cover all expenditure, they seek a variety of different donors for specific activities. Moreover, it should be pointed out that there is a similar tendency among donors, who tend less and less to finance an entire project, but only part of one, so as to be able to act in several areas simultaneously.

Once NGOs have diversified their funding and their projects begin to produce palpable results, they start to reduce external financing to a minimum and operate on their own income. Jopaje (Young People's Association) in Zaire is two-thirds self-financed. It sells agricultural products in a shop they operate in Jomba, in order to combat speculation in food-stuffs by village chiefs. They also own a mill and are active in animal husbandry. PDA (Thailand) has undertaken a certain number of profitable activities and intends to set up a company whose profits will make it less dependent on external financial assistance. 'It is as if the Ford Foundation owned the Ford Motor Company,' says its General Secretary, Michai Viravaidya.

This subject was particularly at the centre of NGO preoccupations during the Congat meeting in Lomé.

The churches have stopped thinking about self-financing and they have managed to do it.

Self-sufficiency doesn't mean closing in on yourself, we who are the poorest groups. Even the most developed countries build bridges between themselves to finance new technologies, which are extremely expensive.

NGOs have to be placed in an 'entrepreneurial' situation, which doesn't mean turning them into businesses, but it is an attitude, a question of methodology, management.

Being non-profit-making does not mean not accumulating capital which can be reinvested.

Generally NGOs of both the North and the South have moved into a new phase in their activities; it is no longer a question of grants, of free aid. All sums of money are lent, and have to be reimbursed. Whenever a villager is given poultry to start up a poultry farm, seeds to sow new crops, or equipment, this must be repaid in money or in kind.

CHAPTER 9

The Significance of NGO Activity around the World

As suggested by the early missionary zeal which inspired the activities of many groups from the industrialized countries, NGOs were initially engaged in charitable activities, providing emergency assistance, food aid, and medical care.

In the case of wars and natural disasters such as drought, floods, and earthquakes, NGOs would frequently collect clothes, medicine, and food in order to provide relief to victims. They are now present in Ethiopia and Central America as they were formerly involved in Biafra and Bangladesh. Their flexibility, speed of intervention, and the dedication of volunteer workers have been recognized alike by government and international organizations, which now promptly call on them whenever the need arises in an area of the Third World.

However, many NGOs are not content to limit themselves to this type of intervention. Their leaders are all too aware of the limits of emergency aid. Indispensable in times of catastrophe, it addresses the consequences of problems but never attacks the root causes of hunger and poverty which in many Third World countries are not the exception but the rule. The question, then, is whether emergency aid is not ultimately self-defeating. People receiving this type of assistance often tend to become 'charity cases' and remain incapable of taking matters in hand themselves. When an emergency aid programme ends, local populations are often left with feelings of frustration and abandonment. Many NGOs believe that once emergency measures have been taken the roots of underdevelopment should be addressed — the real battle only begins then.

Consequently, most European and North American NGOs have moved towards long-range development work involving education and training, assistance in developing farming techniques, and the provision of health care in rural areas.

In the second stage of this process, a multitude of dispersed actions designed to meet individual needs are undertaken in a variety of areas, including health, agriculture, and education, without however there being any guiding concept of development. These efforts are generally welcomed by Third World populations who benefit from them without having any real say in the matter or participating in the decision-making process. The results of our documentary survey of 227 development projects were particularly enlightening with regard to this trend towards greater emphasis on integrated programmes. The overwhelming majority of the projects studied — 251 in all — were geared to responding to development needs in a variety of different sectors including agriculture, water, health, and development education, while only 26 projects all told were purely aid or assistance programmes.

The African historian Joseph Ki-Zerbo recently drew an interesting parallel regarding the intervention of foreign NGOs in Africa.

> These organizations should not identify the success of one small-scale endeavour with the overall redemption of an African country. Far from it. It would be tantamount to limiting one's view of Michelangelo's fresco of the Creation of man to the beard of God or Adam's toe. Nor must NGOs get stuck in lofty global principles or macro-economic hocus-pocus. They have to come down from Sinai to earth and study the real options before the Tables of the Law are drawn up. And this is a matter of constant dialogue with those whom a project is to benefit.

FROM MICROPROJECTS TO INTEGRATED DEVELOPMENT PROGRAMMES

A Scottish proverb with a twist: 'Many wee things, in many wee places, by many wee people can change the face of the world.'

Let us return for a moment to the microproject, the ancestor — all things being relative — of today's projects, and to the evolution which led an agency such as Secours Catholique (French Caritas) to start out with a package of microprojects, then move on to overall development activities. Nicole Rivet, who is in charge of microprojects, relates the initial requirement: 'Ask our friends in African Caritas, what can we do with you? What do you want?'

> Gradually the first requests started to come in. To have more to eat, we shall have to farm better on larger areas of land, replace the traditional *daba* with ploughs and oxen, or more frequently with donkeys, such as these 'nice little donkeys from Ouahigouya', which for many people for a long time were to constitute the typical microproject.

However, in order to use it, this type of harnessed ploughing had to be learned and for that there had to be some building materials to put up small rural training centres in the bush. Teachers and educators were necessary.

In order to have water to drink without having to go for miles and miles, wells were necessary, and so on.

All these answers came in pell-mell and we had to quantify them clearly and cost them in discussion with the people in charge in Africa. After presenting the needs and requests of one sector, an African team added the following remark, very typical of that time: 'But is that what you want?' It took time for the Africans to realize that their projects really became the projects of Secours Catholique, their priorities, its priorities.

In these microprojects many people could only see their smallness. It must not be forgotten that this smallness is that of the microbe: in a suitable terrain mocroprojects can multiply.

Among important dates in the history of microprojects, the first Indian microprojects in 1966 should be noted, then the Haitians in 1971, and the abandonment of the geographical limits to action by Secours Catholique. The governing board asked only that priority be given to the poorest countries or to neglected regions or sectors of countries having achieved a certain economic take-off; it asked above all that microprojects retain their educational value.

A small Indian village in the throes of famine did not hesitate to ask those who were about to receive a goat for milking to give back to the local Committee a female kid so that it could be handed over to another family. After Haiti came Africa and Latin America: Peru, Ecuador, Brazil, Honduras, Chile, Nicaragua, and so on. Through the Christian community development project, Haiti helped us understand the importance of motivation in setting up and implementing a development project. Thanks to Haiti, it is possible to see on a vast scale how to move from one microproject to launching a whole series of microprojects.

The 50,000th microproject is part of plans for the construction of a small dam in Baskouré in Burkina Fasco. Mr Kyelem, Father Lazare, and their team have managed to convince Secours Catholique that it was possible to use large pieces of machinery in their programme of microprojects. To restore the groundwater table, to provide water to the inhabitants of four villages in one sector, a dam had to be built across the valley, and the whole population concerned was prepared to get down to work. However, this herculean task had to be carried out during the dry season and without the help of machines it was really not possible to undertake and complete the work before the rains, which in one second could annihilate everything not completed. Thus machines were used, but they did not merely complement the work of man. The small people in the Baskouré sector which had already had occasion to realize many microprojects themselves, were able to retain control of their dam project. They were not crushed by technology, which remained in the service of man. The Baskouré dam, only recently completed, was achieved by microprojects of the Caritas team from Koupéla, with the help of bulldozers from Caritas Nationale.

It can also be seen that aid, frequently donated to individuals at the outset, is now directed to entire communities, and that requests for funds to purchase equipment (capital goods, building materials), are increasingly giving way to requests for training (study sessions, payment of teachers' wages), since microprojects now only indirectly provide material progress and increasingly use local resources, thanks to very motivated and well-trained educators.

Thus, inspired by the reality of the villages, gradually identifying the basic needs on the basis of a given problem in the fields of agriculture, health, and education, NGOs have moved away from individual projects towards integrated development programmes.

However, owing to limited material and human resources, all problems cannot be addressed simultaneously. Priorities must be set within an overall development plan. This is the trend among most of the more recent development projects to be set up, while in the past project workers were often obliged by force of circumstances, or because they came up against a particular problem, to add other facets to their programmes.

Project integration can take place on two levels. First, at the level of agricultural production, for example on a farm where food crops and stock-raising are combined to ensure local food self-sufficiency or at least a degree of food autonomy. This first step can logically lead to the production of small surpluses which can be sold once a family's basic food needs have been satisfied. This process can help a family or group achieve a certain amount of economic progress.

Manolo farms three hectares of land which he rents. He has been married for the past 30 years and has thirteen children. A Philippines NGO sponsored a month's training for Manolo in Japan where he learned how to farm organically, using intercropping techniques. He learned how on two hectares he could farm rice and get two harvests each year while he grew five rows of garlic and green beans, tapioca, and tomatoes during the dry season, as well as set up a fish-farm using waste material from the farm. He also found out how to raise enough chicken and pork to feed his family and sell in the market, as well as how to use water plants for compost fertilizer and to feed the chickens. Most of the farmers in Manolo's district are now beginning to adopt the farming techniques Manolo learned in Japan, although on much smaller plots and with much smaller families.

The second level on which project integration can be achieved is within a single field of endeavour, such as agriculture, health and education, or in integrated projects which cover several essential areas together.

It is interesting to observe that, of the three continents visited, Latin America had the greatest number of projects or programmes covering several areas of development. Besides the truly integrated projects, according to our definition there were a number of other possible combinations in which a single project embraced two or three areas within its term of reference. The three disciplines or areas of concern frequently encountered together were, of course, agriculture, health, and education. Next in importance were agriculture and economics, agriculture and skills training, and health and agriculture. In Asia, two out of three projects are concerned with more than two different fields of activity at once, generally agriculture associated with either health or training and education. In Africa, most projects tended to be concentrated in a single area of endeavour. Half of the projects visited there were purely agricultural in nature. Of the 93 projects visited in nineteen countries, 60 were concerned with more than one area of activity, and many were multifaceted.

These observations show that NGOs are truly moving towards a greater diversification of development activity and there is a growing recognition of the importance of integrating each aspect of economic and social life within the context of a given project.

By becoming aware of the need for sustained dialogue with project beneficiaries, NGOs have entered a third phase of their evolution. At this stage, they have firmly committed themselves to working with organized local groups, at village or national level in the developing country which is participating in a given programme. This also implies overall agreement on the concepts governing the development project. From now on, development must be designed for a local population in the light of its needs, and using local resources, in three different forms: self-reliant development, alongside the reshaping of international economic relations; community development, which stresses the idea of participation of local populations in their own development; eco-development, which advocates sustainable development practices that enhance the natural and human environment, rather than destroying it.

A policy of co-operation based on dialogue, on the initiative of groups from the poor countries, is one of the characteristic principles of the change which is taking place. However there are other novel characteristics of this fundamental change and reordering of development strategies.

In fact, the NGO phenomenon itself is evolving rapidly, enriched every day by the appearance of new ideas and organizations. The flexibility and informality of these organizations, which by their very nature remain militant associations rather than administrators watched over by the bureaucracy, explains their surprising ability to evolve and the rapidity with which they can adapt.

FROM DEVELOPMENT WORK TO DEFENCE OF HUMAN RIGHTS

Third World NGOs have not undergone a process of evolution identical to that of their counterparts in the industrialized world. Most of them started their work directly at the third stage of the process described above, with development.

They realized that development was not just a battle against poor land, archaic habits, or natural disasters, but that they must also attack the factors of impoverishment that inhibit development. The fight against underdevelopment has taken on a new dimension in India, Bangladesh, and Latin America as local NGOs struggle against corruption in government bureaucracies, the dishonesty of middlemen, the abuses of large landowners, and all 'profiteers and pirates' whose actions block development. This vast movement among Third World associations has gradually turned into a struggle to defend basic civil rights.

Following a conflict with the management of the Canadian NGO with which she worked, a young volunteer worker left the Bangladesh Rural Advancement Committee. Most of her employees decided to go with her, and so a new Bengali organization was born, Nijera Kori, run today entirely by Bengalis. The director, a young Bengali woman, Kushi Kabir, ensures that the main thrust of the NGO's activities remain the defence of the rights of landless peasants. This struggle is articulated in terms of overall development policy rather than being confined to a political or moral issue, and Nijera Kori is careful not to set itself up as a political party. Yet it is still criticized in some quarters for digging up conflicts uselessly without trying to solve concrete cases.

In the town of Narchi, with the support of the French organization Frères des Hommes, Nijera Kori has set up a training centre for landless peasants in which 230 groups from 77 villages throughout the country have been trained. These groups learn about their rights — the right to organize, the right to farm unused government land, the right to decent wages, the right to due process of law, and equal rights for women. In addition, they are encouraged to learn how to save and use a group savings account. Training in animal husbandry is also available in conjunction with a government programme.

All in all, Nijera Kori works in 50 districts and runs more than 1,800 community groups with a national staff of a little over 100 workers. After an initial phase of rapid development, the organization now hopes to consolidate its work, widening its following among women's groups and landless peasants. However, it is not trying to push these groups into forming their own co-operatives.

> They have to begin by learning how to manage their money and simple problem-solving on an individual basis. Since here in Bangladesh our society is still centred on individual effort — the banking system, the market economy, and the political system — you have to be very strong to resist the accepted norm and uphold the community spirit.

Kushi Kabir believes that groups of destitute villagers throughout Bangladesh can be helped. In order to do so, Bengali NGOs will have to become a true grassroots movements mobilizing women, landless peasants, and all marginalized groups to form a genuine pressure group.

In Madaripur, the Bengali Legal Aid association provides free legal assistance to poor people. Set up in 1978 by a group of young lawyers, it helps uneducated and illiterate rural villagers, among other marginalized groups, to exercise their legal rights. The Association helps people fulfil government requirements and even pleads for them in court when necessary, although it prefers to reach out-of-court settlements whenever possible in order to reduce costs and secure rights for disadvantaged groups without coming into direct conflict with local interests.

The cases are varied and reflect the social and economic problems particular to a traditional society where Moslem and Hindu cultures coexist, sometimes precariously:

destitute woman with children, abandoned by her husband with no available means of survival;

a second wife taken by a husband without the consent of the first wife as required by law (polygamy is in fact fairly infrequent);

disputes over land left vacant by poor Hindus who fled the country after 1965;

dowry problems (very frequent), battered wives, etc.

The Legal Aid Association is located in a simple ramshackle office in the middle of the village. People come in and out all day for advice, including the staff of many local NGOs seeking advice in cases affecting people from the rural areas where they work. In this way the Association participates in the development process of the surrounding rural areas. It is staffed on a voluntary basis by fifteen lawyers who work in shifts in order to ensure that there is always someone available for consultations. This type of organization is now fairly widespread in Bangladesh.

In the Philippines, many of the large NGOs work to defend the legal rights of rural villagers. They even act on behalf of villagers who do not belong to any development organization.

In India, Ramesh Nandwana from Rajasthan decided to work for one of the first rural development NGOs — Seva Mandir in Udaipur — when he finished his studies. At first he helped out in adult literacy programmes and in the campaign to combat the effects of the drought. After several years he realized that if rural populations were to become self-reliant, they would need legal assistance. He went back to university to study law and now works to defend peasants' interests and teaches them to make full use of their rights. He managed to talk other young professionals into setting up the Tribal Area Legal Aid and Entitlement Centre (TALAEC), which eventually merged with his own Rajasthan Legal Support and Social Action Centre. This is only one example of the many ways in which legal aid and action in defence of peasants' rights are spreading throughout India.

In Thailand several organizations are working to defend human rights in rural areas. To name a few: the Co-ordinating Group for Religion in Society, set up in 1976, has contributed considerably to denouncing police abuse and to promoting dialogue on development strategies inspired by Buddhism as well as offering legal aid to rural villagers; the Commission for Peace and Justice, set up in 1977 under the auspices of the Episcopal Council, works on behalf of rural populations which have migrated to the cities; the Federation of Farmers and Peasants of Thailand was set up in November 1974 to defend landless peasants. Many of its leaders, struggling to uphold land reform and to combat corruption, have been murdered by right-wing extremists.

In Brazil, the first NGO specifically aimed at defending the rights of the rural poor was set up in 1976. The Centro de Defesa Dos Direitos Humanos — Assessoria e Educacãon Popular, was originally created as a service of the Catholic diocese of the north-eastern city of João Pessoa, on the initiative of Archbishop José Maria Pirés (widely known as 'Don Pélé' because he was the first black bishop in Brazil). The Centro has struggled to uphold the rights of poor and landless peasants in a very sensitive political context, where the military dictatorship and corrupt landlords are in a position to impose their power on the rural poor. The main task of the Centro has been to defend the peasants against political repression. Since the end of military dictatorship, the Centro's work continues, for abuses still go on and have tended to increase locally with the prospect of possible nation-wide land reform.

The essential task is to provide legal aid and assistance to peasants who are trying to remain on the land or to affirm their right to farm and settle unused plots. Its staff are aware that by helping people to prepare their requests and file them with local government and legal authorities they are merely helping the rural poor stay in a position of inferiority. They are trying to overcome this paternalistic approach and help peasants learn how to become self-reliant by handling these tasks by themselves. To prepare them, the Centro offers extensive education and training courses to rural villagers regarding their rights and the steps they need to take to protect their interests.

Until 1979 the Centro remained part of the pastoral work of the Church in the state of Paraíba. Since 1980 it has been a legal, non-profit-making lay organization which is officially recognized by the municipality of João Pessoa where it is based.

In Brazil, the total income of five per cent of the wealthiest people is equivalent to the total income of 80 per cent of the population. Five million Brazilians have absolutely no means of support. Seventeen million Brazilian workers receive no social security cover whatsoever. Every minute a child dies of disease or hunger while 86% of the surviving children suffer from chronic malnutrition.

The work of the Centro can be placed in the context of the fight for land reform. The leaders of the land reform movement have carefully analysed the social and economic problems of rural Brazil, covering all regions, in the light of rural migration brought on by the unrestrained growth of urban centres and the pressures faced by poor peasants in rural areas. Moreover, they are perfectly aware of the fact that the implementation and application of land reform in Brazil ultimately depends on the technocrats in Brasilia. It is absolutely necessary, according to the staff of the Centro and other members of Brazilian NGOs, that small farmers and landless peasants be closely linked in this reform, that they become the prime partners in the process. It is only by anchoring these small farmers and peasants to the land and by giving them the means to farm it better — by promoting collective forms of production and improving productivity — that enough food will be produced domestically to feed both the rural and urban populations. Then, and then only, will Brazil no longer need to import most of its basic food products at prohibitive costs. The country's debt burden will be decreased as well as its dependency on foreign suppliers.

However, nowadays, a lawyer from the Centro told us, 'The struggle for land reform starts with an uphill battle to prevent the rural population from leaving the land or being forced off it. This struggle is a constant threat to those who amass fortunes by extending the land area they use for farming agrofood crops for export.'

The rural area in which the Centro works extends to over 40 municipalities but its direct area of intervention is within 22 'municipios' around João Pessoa, representing 1,100 families, or approximately 8,000 people. Every week, each of the 22 municipios is visited by workers from the Centro who provide legal advice on specific cases or help farmers' representatives (three for each municipio) organize information meetings to introduce training sessions.

The objectives of this activity in rural areas were explained by the co-ordinator of the Centro:

To encourage small farmers to occupy and farm unused land, by explaining the legal steps they need to take to stay on the land; to indicate how the lawyers of the Centro will defend these 'new farmers'; to strengthen group and community structures so that each informed individual can help enlighten the entire community and then act in concert with others if any member of the community is threatened or is involved in a conflict; and to draw up joint programmes with the communities in order to improve the environment and to increase agricultural production.

To conclude, let us quote from a letter sent by seventeen small farmers from the state of Paraíba to the President of Brazil and to other senior officials.

> ... This letter is to inform you of what is happening to us here. We are farmers on land near Muçangana, on the Salamago farm, and no one knows at the present time to whom this land belongs.
>
> Since we have already been expelled from another estate and we cannot remain without shelter, becoming vagabonds, we have decided to make our home on this unoccupied piece of land.
>
> We had been occupying this land for five years when a man called Manuel Oleira da Costa arrived. He settled on our land to work it and to plant sugar cane on it, ordering us to leave. We are prepared to fight to stay here because we do not want to die and we do not want to go away as our children would die of hunger. Our right to use this land is guaranteed by the Federal land law that says that any farmer settled on a piece of land has a right to work that land and to stay there.
>
> We ask you Excellencies to take the necessary action.
>
> Cruz de Espirito Santo, 5 October 1981.
>
> Signed: S. S. da Silva, J. S. dos Santos, A. O. Bonto, M. S. de Amarel, L. L. da Silva, M. V. dos Santos, A. A. da Silva, A. A. da Silva, J. E. da Silva, J. I . da Silva, L. M. Bento, N. F. da Silva, J. F. da Araújo, M. V. Filno, M. S. de Conceiçao, S. M. de Conceiçao, M. do Carmo Pereira.

The trend among NGOs to move in defence of human rights is undoubtedly the begining of a major movement. Third World NGOs will increasingly be drawn to this type of action when they are confronted with the abuses of power exercised by large landowners and officials. For the rural poor in many Third World countries, legal action often represents the only hope of removing obstacles to the right to development caused by bureaucratic inertia, abuse of power, and widespread corruption. The new awareness that it is possible to act in defence of human rights through the legal system may lead to the NGOs of the South becoming a powerful lobby group, and this may well be a vital step in their future evolution.

CHAPTER 10

Accountability

A NEW DESIRE TO EVALUATE RESULTS

Another sign of the increasing maturity of NGOs can be seen in the systematic evaluations which they are now carrying out, underscored by the creation in Brussels of an evaluation service within the European Commission. Though there are still discussions and disagreements on the criteria to be used and on the definition of the indicators, it is encouraging to observe in this regard the highly responsible behaviour of NGOs of the North, such as OXFAM or CEBEMO. It is an encouraging development because, up to now, NGOs tended to neglect economic factors, cost-benefit analysis, and other financial measurement tools in favour of sociological and cultural criteria for evaluating the success and impact of their operations. Project assessment in terms of profitability, pay-back on investment, and other economic indicators was often considered too business-oriented, inadequate to account for the 'human' dimension of projects, and even, for some, a capitalistic anomaly. However, the sheer volume of money passing through the hands of NGOs, the desire to eliminate waste and to appear in the eyes of the international funding institutions, as well as those of individual and government donors, credible and worthy of confidence, has prompted most organisations to overcome any reluctance to confirm their presence as accountable partners on the international development scene.

A certain number of facts highlight this trend. In recent years, the media and governments have started to take seriously the importance of the NGO phenomenon and its world-wide dimension. Television and the press in general have given wide exposure to NGOs, naming them as such, explaining their activities, and at times illustrating their achievements. This is a first step in the recognition of their role in development, after a long period in which emergency aid or rescue operations were all that was shown or covered.

The NGO press in the developed world, also an associative

endeavour, is aimed at gaining the support of individual donors by informing them of work in progress and achievements, if not actually providing a critical point of view. These small publications — often in-house bulletins — are distributed in thousands if not millions, and end up kindling a spirit of solidarity and making the affluent aware of how the poor of the Third World live. They regularly report on the progress of development projects under way, contributing largely to the creation of a certain image in the public eye of the NGO movement and its efficiency.

This new awareness is also reflected by the status which many international and government bodies have officially granted NGOs by recognizing them and setting up liaison services with them. The position of the World Bank with regard to NGOs is particularly noteworthy in view of the fact that the Bank has long been the very symbol and instrument of international development policy, even though it has now become the object of severe criticism, even by its own management. This is how, since 1982, the World Bank envisions the co-operation that it would like to carry out with NGOs.

NGOs often have a first-hand knowledge of local institutions and the socio-cultural milieu in which they work and can therefore be of precious assistance in project design. In general, it is easier for them than for officials or consultants to make contact with the population of areas covered by projects, since they are fully up-to-date on the local situation, possess great administrative flexibility, and can draw upon a whole network of members, correspondents, and affiliates at community or village level.

NGOs can often promote and implement inexpensive appropriate technologies and help local populations adapt to new life-styles or new working methods. NGOs can often rely on extra resources to enable them to finance activities parallel to the main project, aimed at the same target population, or to meet unforeseen needs which have arisen during the execution of the project. NGOs often act as pioneers in development, in particular when they take on pilot projects likely to be repeated elsewhere. NGOs have low expenditures: their resources for the major part come from voluntary contributions and they are often staffed by volunteers. In any event, they do not engage in profit-making ventures. On the other hand they sometimes have at their disposal specific technical knowledge difficult to find in the commercial sector.

In recent years, the Bank and NGOs have worked together on several occasions. In 1980, the Bank made concerted efforts to increase operational co-operation with NGOs. It encouraged its staff to look for suitable occasions for such co-operation and to bring these to the attention of governments and concerned institutions in borrowing countries. The exchange of information with NGOs developed, and sectoral seminars were organized with the participation of major NGOs.

In 1981, at the request of several NGOs, a Bank–NGO committee was set up, responsible in particular for increasing co-operation and for evaluating mutual efficiency. Institutions such as the World Bank, and more recently the Inter-American Development Bank and the European Community, not to speak of governments from industrialized countries, now consider NGOs in a favourable light, although this is not without some ulterior motives.

In fact they realize, without always admitting it, that their former policy of development co-operation has only rarely achieved its goals, and that in poor countries these failures have led to disillusionment and bitterness, even when the responsibility was shared. Governments in the industrialized North know full well that the economic mechanisms and consequences resulting from the oil crisis are beyond their control, compounded by changes in the world economy since 1974. When one of the leaders of an international financial institution was asked whether after all it would not be wiser and more efficient to pass on to the NGOs the main tasks of development, he replied, 'These are organizations of militants — generous, dynamic militants — who are happy to make do with low salaries ...' The temptation to reduce the level of commitment by this means is all the stronger since many Western countries, while affirming the priority of development aid, are increasingly absorbed by their own financial problems and by unemployment. As can be seen, the NGOs of the North take advantage of the authority delegated to them to occupy a vacuum and to give full rein to their dynamism.

In the Third World countries, the civil service, relied upon by Governments as the principal machinery for economic and social development,[1] is either breaking down or slowly asphyxiating. Its lack of credibility makes it the main target of the new policies being implemented, for better or worse, under pressure from the IMF and the World Bank. Bureaucratic inertia, combined with corruption, leaves the field open to non-governmental activities.

[1] cf. Lalau-Keraly and Rouillé d'Orfeuil: 'Pour une redéfinition des espaces de coopération gouvernementaux et non-gouvernementaux' (Report. Paris, June 1983).

This combination of the crisis in international co-operation and political or administrative blockages to development, confers on the NGOs of the North and the South a responsibility which they had not foreseen and for which they have not always been prepared.

PRIVATE SOURCES OF FUNDING

Most NGOs and voluntary organizations call on public generosity for their funds, each one turning to the constituency from which it derives support for its 'clientele'. Thus Catholic agencies with the support of bishops regularly solicit financial contributions from the faithful.

The presentation of actual projects to be set up, of successful operations financed with the help of a parish, have gradually created additional enticements by giving donors a clear view of the use made of funds collected. This type of funding, destined for specific projects, has contributed to developing a more acute sense among donors of their solidarity with Third World countries, while at the same time contributing to a better understanding of the situation and needs of these countries.

If we consider OECD member countries as a whole, the volume of private grants financed by NGOs from their own resources in 1977 was in the order of $1.5 billion, that is to say, 0.03% of the combined GNP for all these countries. This figure represents almost one-tenth of the public effort for development aid. In 1980 the volume of private grants reached $2,248 billion, in 1981, $1,962 billion, and it rose again to $2,317 billion in 1982 and $2,356 billion in 1983. The major donors of private aid among the countries belonging to the Development Assistance Committee in 1970 were the United States, Germany, and Canada.

In 1983, the countries with the highest figure for private contributions as a percentage of GNP were Norway and the Netherlands (0.08), Sweden (0.07), Germany (0.05), followed some distance behind by the United States, Canada, and Belgium (0.04), then by Finland and New Zealand (0.03), by Australia, Austria, Denmark, and the United Kingdom (0.02), then by France (0.01). It can be seen that although private contributions increased 60% between 1977 and 1980, there has been a certain tailing off. A report published by the Development Assistance Committee in January 1985 pointed out that the mobilization by NGOs of resources from private donors had ceased to be a dynamic element in project financing. Alongside this slowing down of the resources from private sources, there is a comparable tendency in official contributions from the countries on the Development Assistance Committee.

PUBLIC SOURCES OF FUNDING

The level of public funding has fallen from 4.9% of total overseas development aid in 1981 to 4.6% in 1983. An analysis by country of this aid figure shows that between 1981 and 1983 public aid increased considerably in Canada (from 104 to 125 billion US dollars), in Australia, (from 10 to 18 billion), in Switzerland (from 91 to 98 billion), in Germany (from 170 to 177 billion), and relatively little in the United States (from 568 to 595 billion dollars). On the other hand, there is a downward tendency in Scandinavia and from the European Community. There are few elements to explain these variations between 1981 and 1983 or the differences observed between countries.

DIRECT CONTRIBUTIONS TO THIRD WORLD NGOS

The OECD figures give an idea of the amount of funding collected by NGOs, from both governments and private sources. However, the diversity of their aims, including regular food aid and emergency aid, does not allow us to identify with certainty among these sums of money, the exact amount devoted by NGOs to development activities.

A very clear evolution has been taking place since 1979 in the way in which these funds are distributed. In the beginning the NGOs of the North found that they were entrusted with almost all funds destined to support activities of Third World NGOs. There were only two exceptions to this rule: Canada had already organized CIDA as an agency for co-operation with the major international NGOs present in developing countries, while Norway directly supported its National Council of NGOs involved in the Sudan. Since then, a certain number of industrialized countries such as Denmark, France, Germany, the Netherlands, Sweden, Switzerland, and the United States have been funding Third World NGOs directly. The amount of this direct financial support increased between 1980 and 1983 from 10 to 39.3 million dollars. It has thus quadrupled in value, although these sums still represent only a very small part of overall financial aid ($1,139 million in 1980, rising to $1,276 million in 1983). These figures do not take into account direct aid provided by the United Nations Development Programme, or other international agencies.

QUANTIFYING BENEFICIARIES OF NGO ACTIVITY

Despite the efforts already made to improve understanding of the different uses made of these funds, much still remains to be done, on the part of both governments and international institutions and NGOs to ensure that the accounting procedures show just how the money is spent. Such information is vital for anyone who wishes to study systematically the cost-benefit ratio of NGOs in development.

Although progress is still to be made in overall understanding of the destination of investments for development handled by NGOs, other means of approaching a multiple and complex reality will have to be found, bearing in mind that these sums of money, which appear insignificant in the countries of the North, are considerable in developing countries. When observing these phenomena, we must never lose sight of this difference of scale. In the same vein we must frequently abandon Western criteria when comparing and evaluating extremely divergent social and cultural situations.

At the present time there are no means of accurately assessing just how many farmers, how many villages, directly or indirectly benefit from NGO activities in developing countries. Neither governments nor NGOs themselves have global figures in this area. This is all the more regrettable in that the number of beneficiaries of NGO rural development activities constitutes an essential factor in measuring the cost-effectiveness of this type of activity.

It is not possible to make an estimate on the basis of the projects presented by the NGOs of the North, because any one project may at different times receive the support from several NGOs and hence appear on several occasions in their respective reports. Thus we are obliged to confine ourselves to a limited series of direct observations which permit only cautious interpretation and are perforce subject to criticism.

Dating projects
The vast majority of NGO projects we visited were started in 1970 and particularly in 1973 and 1974 and flourished simultaneously in Asia, Africa, and Latin America. The action of Bina Swadaya in Indonesia was set up in 1958 by a farmers' organization. Mention should also be made of the efforts made in India in the sixties in the spirit of the Sarvodaya Movement of Gandhi and as a tentative answer to the desire of Nehru for village development, in parallel with the vigorous industrialization policy which he initiated following Independence.

However, most of the projects analysed are less than 15 years old, and the vast majority have existed for little more than a decade. This observation has two consequences: these experiences are still too young to have reached the threshold of maturity, a factor which must be taken into account when analysing them, particularly since the pace of rural areas is set by the seasons and the weather which also substantially affect development in towns and industry; consequently the experiences are still too fragile to be able to draw any concrete lessons from them, since the duration of a project could modify its significance and scope.

Project origin
What is the origin of a project? The answer is simple and the variations are limited. Before becoming a structural or organizational problem, first and foremost it is a question of human beings. We shall give examples of the seven categories of initiatives observed:

individual initiative: Father Dominique Pire, who received the Nobel Peace Prize, in Tombouctou (Ile de la Paix–Island of Peace); Father Verspieren in Mali (Aqua Viva); a Thai economist, Mechai (Population and Development Association); a young doctor in Indonesia (PPSE, Panitya Pembangnnan Social Ekonomi); the architect Alvaro Perilla in Colombia (CDDES, Cooperative Multiactiva de Desarollo Social); the retired water engineer Jean Louis Chlecq (GARY, co-operative of rural craftsmen) in Burkina Faso.

meetings/encounters, often by chance: the Italian Giovanni Ermiglia and the Indian S. Loganathan (ASSEFA); Bernard Léda Ouedraogo of Burkina Faso and the Frenchman Bernard Lecomte (Nam groups and 6-S associations in Burkina Faso, Senegal, Mali, etc.).

group initiative: women's groups in Kenya (women's association in Kibwezi); Christian groups in Ecuador (Peasant Union in Azuay); retired civil servants and missionaries (Niou Project in Burkina Faso).

parish or Christian community initiative: hundreds of cases could be mentioned in Africa, Asia, and Latin America.

initiative of an NGO from the North

initiative of research institutes; the Inter-American Institute for Co-operation in Agriculture in Peru in liaison with the universities of Cuzco, Puno, and Ayacucho; the Centre for Rural Studies in the Andes-Bartolomé de las Casas, founded by Father Guido Delran in Cuzco (Peru); INADES (National Institute for Economic and African Development); the Asian Development Forum; all examples of research institutes which became operational.

government initiatives: for example the commitment of CARE, the American NGO, from 1976 onwards on the initiative of the Indonesian government, or at the request of the Egyptian government for assistance to fishing communities in the Aswan region.

MOTIVATION: PRIORITY TO THE POOREST

To convey the motivation, the driving force, behind these various creators — some in industrialized societies would say, these entrepreneurs — nothing can replace the direct contact of interviews, examples of the experiences collected during the many meetings in the course of our study. In Cuenca, we spoke to Alberto and Carmeline, officers of the local section of the Ecuadorean Indian Peasant Confederation (Ecuarunari).

How was this project started?
Alberto: We started in 1970 after the Vatican Councils, through the Christian revolution. After the changes which took place in the Church and the importance which was given to the poor, we started to fight, to mobilize ourselves, to commit ourselves and to help each other. We took the blinkers from our eyes by studying the Bible, holding meetings, making visits, singing and celebration, and by our work in the *mingas* (collective work). This is what we have been doing for six years.
Foreign priests or Ecuadoreans?
Alberto: Ecuadorean priests from this province, even this parish, using

the catechism classes. Afterwards, other priests came who didn't agree
with the progressive ones and they changed everything. But we didn't
want to go back to the old system. We all refused to change, our eyes
had been opened, no one could close them ever again. We continued to
study the word of God among ourselves and to work; we remained
united and have continued to make progress despite opposition from
backward-thinking priests. We included all the farmers of Turi,
Acchayacu, Baños, of all the surrounding villages, we were not alone,
we continued to organize ourselves like brothers. It was wonderful.
That was before the problems came, before the jealousy and dissen-
sion. At that time we had only our goodwill and our unity, we prayed
and we sang, we met in the small chapel nearby. We asked ourselves,
'How did communities live in the time of Jesus Christ?' We would
have meetings of 50 to 60 people and made a collection to help our sick
brethren, or those in need, or we would help each other tilling the land
of the small plots, or helping with the harvest. We reintroduced the
mingas, and more *mingas*. And then we discussed pooling our
resources, our land. The 'padres' did not say anything to us. It was we
who thought that we could truly live our Christianity in this way.
Then we saw that there were some priests who said one thing and
others said the contrary. We asked the bishop: 'Monsignor, you say
one thing, but the priests say something else and the nuns something
else again. What must we believe?' Then we were accused of being
evangelists, which here is worse than being called a communist.
Carmeline: We were even called Marxists, agitators.
Alberto: The priests had controlled us for centuries because they had
the monopoly on the Good Word. We had realized that we were able
ourselves to understand the teachings of Christ. Then we started to do
our own baptisms and marriages. We said the prayers and sang the
hymns according to our traditions. And then, we men had a tradition
in holidays and community meals, we ate among ourselves, and it was
only afterwards that the women joined us. We said that this was not
good, that we should share everything, so we invited the women to
come to the table with us. From that time, we decided that women
would be our equals. The women worked even harder than us. We
continued to struggle to overcome everything which was preventing us
from making progress.
And it was your mother who bequeathed the land to you for the
community, on condition that you unite and that you organize a
training centre for the Indians?
Alberto: Yes, we built a community house, organized the farmers'
union of Azuay and later the people from the FEPP came to help us.

In Kenya, Jeanna Molo, leader of the Women's Association of
Kandito in the province of Nyanza, tells of their beginnings:

We founded the association in October 1982. Our aim in setting up the association was the following: simply we wanted to find the means of getting the things we needed.

We were five mothers who got together to think about our needs. Mrs Omanya from Nairobi was with us. She advised us to form a group, to unite our efforts with much mutual love and respect. Before actually forming the group, she introduced us to a woman who showed us how to grow vegetables. That was in August 1979. That man over there gave us land for the vegetable garden. We grow cabbages, spinach, tomatoes, beans, and sunflowers.

Mrs Omanya looked for money to help us and we got some. We were given goats and were shown how to raise them, look after them. We also had the assistance of a veterinary surgeon and we now know how to inoculate the goats ourselves and we know the medical doses. Before, we didn't know that goats had to be dipped, now we know that and dip them once a week. The vet also showed us how to cut the goats' hooves. We didn't know how to do that and now we cut their hooves. The vet also showed us how to look after the kids. With goats, you have to wait one week before starting to milk them and even at that only for a few minutes to leave milk for the kid. When there's a lot of vegetation, you get two glasses of milk from each goat. That's what we get from our local goats. Goat milk is excellent for children suffering from kwashiorkor. They get much better after drinking goat milk for a week.

If we want to recruit new members in our association, we have to go into the houses and talk personally to the women. It is very important. Mrs Omanya taught us that and we are very grateful to her. Several women have got to know each other through the group. The final objective of the women is to set up a centre for child care.

From the beginning, NGOs have been preoccupied with the poorest people and the projects undertaken on their behalf were almost always the main priority. The influence of the churches is certainly not without importance but, overall, this desire to do something to help the poorest has its source in inspired choices of those in charge of NGOs. Because their vocation was to attack the factors of impoverishment, they devoted themselves to development. Although not always aware of the existence of the spiral of poverty, nor of its magnitude, they set up projects for society's misfits, those excluded from the development process, but also for the victims of development, for whom many regions in the Third World constitute a gigantic graveyard. The present study shows that such projects can be directed towards excluded or marginalized groups such as the untouchables (Harijans) in

India or the lepers of Ossiomo in Nigeria, and to considerable effect.

To analyse the role of the NGOs we will now examine successively the two stages in what we have called the development process outlined in Chapter 6: the factors which combine to satisfy villagers' basic needs and enable them to escape the zone of absolute poverty, negating the factors of impoverishment, and the factors which enable villagers to take initiatives to improve their living conditions. We shall examine the capacity of NGOs to reduce the factors of impoverishment by providing for the immediate basic needs of the villagers, then to empower them to act. We shall then consider the external obstacles they encounter, obstacles which sometimes come from the NGOs themselves, and the limitations on their activities.

PART FOUR

CHAPTER 11

Can NGOs Limit the Factors of Impoverishment?

To confront the eight factors isolated in Chapter 5 as being at the root of the implacable process of impoverishment can result in a sense of anguish or impotence, as if faced by an impending cyclone or earthquake. Let us examine these factors one by one, to determine to what extent NGOs, however vulnerable or fragile, are in a position to affect them.

POLITICAL INSTABILITY

Although NGOs would not seem particularly well equipped to deal with political circumstances, there are two ways in which they can indirectly influence or even oppose them. In some areas, through their struggle against the abuse of power by officials or bureaucrats, they uphold the rights of the rural poor. In these cases NGOs may even themselves become factors of political instability by the very fact that they undermine the power of authoritarian regimes and repressive systems in the hope that a more just and democratic system will eventually prevail. In the long term these very NGOs may be promoting future political stability, since they are helping to reduce poverty in some areas by helping the poor to organize and to assume responsibility for their own development. These rural groups are destined to become productive and to contribute to the economic growth and stability of the nation. They might even become the future middle classes in areas where until now only poverty and misery have been known. Through these collective experiments people learn how to live and work together democratically and eventually become fully-fledged citizens and empowered members of the community.

INDEBTEDNESS

The burden of debt, and the heavy sacrifices that it entails, often seriously compromising the futures of most poor countries, does not appear to be an area which NGOs can effectively influence. However, they can in perceptible ways slow down the process of indebtedness since they are capable of creating factors of development. They help villagers learn how to utilize local resources, thus reducing reliance on imported goods and technologies. They also play a part in encouraging thrift and savings in rural areas, and this can have an impact on the level of indebtedness. Although modest in appearance their role can be farreaching in the long term.

MISUSE OF LAND

In this area NGOs have more than proved their efficiency through programmes of reforestation, soil conservation, use of environmentally safe fertilizers and insecticides, improved seed selection, and irrigation. They have shown that these efforts can be successful, although we have yet to see how they can be fostered throughout rural areas in the Third World.

MISAPPROPRIATION OF LAND

Pressure on peasants to leave their land or surrender it to others is above all a political problem. In this crucial area only a concerted effort at governmental level can help stem abuses and encourage a fairer and more productive distribution of land, giving priority to food crops for the domestic market. The contribution of NGOs in this particular area is mostly negligible but certainly not nonexistent. Their support of villagers' resistance to unjust land policies and the part they often play in shaping public opinion can have a positive impact and can force governments to take necessary action. Realistic land reform is a *sine qua non* of lasting rural development in Latin America and in some areas of Asia.

UNCONTROLLED MIGRATION

The displacement of rural populations by large-scale development projects is a matter which concerns the political and social choices of governments. However, NGOs might effectively work with governments to help establish resettlement areas where displaced groups could find sufficient farmland and improved living conditions. The problem with such an approach might be that governments would be encouraged to implement programmes of this kind even when they were not absolutely necessary.

Rural migration is not merely an economic phenomenon brought on by poor villagers' search for the means of survival in cities or other areas, it is also a social problem caused by the irresistible attraction that cities exert on the rural young. At this point no one is capable of determining whether the migration of rural populations to the cities will be as lasting and extensive in developing countries as it once was in the industrialized North. In some rural areas of the Third World, as in industrialized countries, people are beginning to return to the land. But now the villages lack the appropriate structures and facilities to respond to the new needs of its erstwhile inhabitants — entertainment, cultural and educational facilities, and so on. Until now NGOs have been mainly concerned with the basic needs of returning populations. They have not given enough thought to the challenge of providing incentives and activities in villages for younger groups.

UNCONTROLLED POPULATION GROWTH

Family planning is a priority area of concern for some NGOs, particularly in Thailand (PDA) where it has been quite successful. In many instances work in this important area is carried on in a subtle and non-obtrusive manner, for example in the context of health and hygiene programmes for women. The prospects for success of NGO programmes in this area mostly depend on the traditions, religious beliefs, and cultural values of the peoples with which they work.

In most cases NGOs tend to shy away from this problem, either because they are not convinced it is a major cause of impoverishment or because they are afraid of incurring the hostility of village groups, and they have have thus not been sufficiently attentive to the expectations of women. Without going so far as to suggest a general drive for contraception, the needs of women in terms of education and information often remain without an adequate response from NGOs. Only in scattered instances have NGOs proved to be efficient in this sensitive area. Perhaps they have not given it the thought and attention it truly deserves.

LOSS OR REJECTION OF CULTURAL IDENTITY

Many villagers are cruelly aware of the brutal effects of the generation gap as they see their young people withdraw from them, preferring to imitate Western life-styles rather than conform to the patterns of tradition. The rejection of traditional customs and values deprives the group of its fundamental cohesiveness and the individual of his sense of belonging. While a new value system has yet to emerge, many young villagers continue to strive for what is merely a caricature of Western life-styles without actually having the means of attaining them. India is one of the few countries where ancestral values and traditional cultures have blended harmoniously with the modern world; but, like other developing countries, India is still held back by certain rites and traditions that are more regressive than forward-looking. A typical example of these is the dowry which an Indian father must be able to provide for his daughter, when she marries — it may take years to amass these often enormous sums of money.

Sri Veerandra Hegade, head of the famous south Indian Dharmasthala Sanctuary, has tried to solve this problem in the context of the integrated development programme he has set up. He explained how each year he organizes mass weddings for 400 to 500 young couples. The cost of the bridal saris as well as the expenses of the wedding feast are covered by the sanctuary. This giant community celebration allows the young couples to experience a sense of unity regardless of their different backgrounds and the various sects to which they belong.

A number of NGOs are aware of this problem and in some projects they are attempting to preserve or reinstate threatened cultural values, but these experiments tend to be exceptions, especially in Africa. Since NGOs are often confronted with the brutal consequences of the loss of cultural identity, they certainly would do well to find means of dealing with it without turning their backs on the modern world. It is up to NGOs to find a new balance in this area, and the villagers themselves ultimately must imagine and integrate cultural models that are at once respectful of the old and open to the new.

CORRUPTION

In many instances corruption, in its various manifestations, is part of a cultural and historical pattern, and it is therefore sometimes difficult to expect governments to intervene, all the more so because the State is often the main agent and perpetuator of corruption through its bureaucracies. This issue undoubtedly calls for special attention since many Westerners, out of ignorance, tend to react judgementally without taking the trouble to look beyond appearances at the multiple and complex ramifications of this problem. If the perverse effects of corruption are to be eliminated, its social and economic causes as well as its subtle psychological mechanisms must be properly understood. But whether the origins of this phenomenon are recent or linked to earlier historical or cultural events, it still acts as a formidable obstacle to development in the Third World and must be attacked if progress is to be achieved.

Although NGOs often work diligently to eliminate the symptoms of poverty, they are not always conscious of its true dimensions and are frequently unaware of the spiralling effect of the factors of impoverishment. In other words, NGOs are not always cognizant of the complex web of interrelated factors which contribute to the rapid spread of poverty in the Third World. It is only by recognizing and fighting these multiple factors of impoverishment that NGOs, thanks to their dynamic capabilities and openness, can hope to strengthen the rural poor in their efforts to overcome the forces of regression and oppression.

In the perspective of a new approach to development, the reduction of these factors of impoverishment constitutes a top priority for NGOs and requires of them greater efforts to understand and control their multiple manifestations. They must realize that even if they can only play a secondary part in addressing the issues of political instability, indebtedness, land reform, migration, and corruption, they are still in a position to provide decisive answers to the problems posed by the misuse of the earth and its resources, the control of population growth, and the emergence of a system of values which, without rejecting the past, takes into account the realities of the present.

SELF-HELP: AN IMPOSSIBLE GOAL?

'Aren't NGOs engaged in a seemingly impossible undertaking — trying to change the way of thinking and behaviour of the rural poor?'

The idea that the poor are themselves ultimately responsible for the backwardness and lack of progress in rural areas of the Third World is not only fairly widely accepted in Western nations but also reflects a prevalent trend of thinking among the ruling elite of the developing world.

On the other hand, a growing number of people reject this contention and vigorously refute it. Filipino peasant Tio Badding angrily retorts to his unseen detractors:

> They say we're poor because we're lazy, but have they ever seen us sitting down to our breakfast? If they had seen what we have for breakfast and were obliged to eat the same thing every morning, they would go crazy if someone said they were lazy. Think of the long and back-breaking hours we spend in the field from dawn to dusk, under the burning sun or pouring rain, just to stay alive. This is the life we lead in the sugar-cane fields, where even our pregnant women work ten to twelve hours a day cutting and carrying for a daily wage of less than 55 cents. Enough of this nonsense about laziness!

Another Filipino villager, Mang Pedring, remembers:

> One day I went with a group of villagers to visit the model farm set up by the government and some landowners. They showed us everything in the hope that we would adopt the modern production techniques they use. I was very impressed by all that I saw and kept asking questions about the cost of the irrigation pumps, the fertilizers, pesticides, herbicides, and all the rest. I also noted that they used a type of netting to prevent birds from eating the crops. When the owner of the land I farm asked me a week afterwards if I was not tempted by the modern methods I had seen at Santa Barbara he reminded me that I was poor because I was 'resistant' to change. I replied, 'How could I possibly afford to buy special netting to protect the seeds and crops if I can't even afford to buy mosquito nets for my own children?' Since then I have been haunted by his accusation that I resisted change. They would be very happy to see us change superficially but they emphatically reject the very change that our ancestors have demanded for centuries: they have done everything they can to prevent us from owning our own land.

Philémon Engongomo Tina, local official in the rural village of N'Koteng in Cameroun, declares:

> No! They certainly are not individualistic. Every peasant thinks 'If I only had more money, I would buy a bike,' or 'When I get rich, I am going to take a second, third, fourth wife.'
> But by himself a peasant in our country can never get rich. He works

more or less and he earns more or less money, but he stays poor if he works on his own. The people here know that a peasant belongs to a clan. Each village is a group of peasants who in fact belong to different clans. Like the Europeans I have lived among for many years, I too believed that a peasant group is merely a group of peasants. Well that's not quite the case, I think we still have a lot to learn from the peasants about development.

To admit that rural people have a special part to play that should be recognized is a relatively new phenomenon around the world, and we heard it expressed time after time in the areas visited.

Mang Igui from the Philippines:

> The nation could be compared to a tree. A tree has several parts. What people see is of course the visible parts: the green leaves, the branches, the thick trunk, the flowers, and the fruit which looks delicious. These are the most apparent aspects of our society: the politicians, the priests, the doctors ... But do they really represent the more important part?
>
> In the case of the tree the most important parts are invisible or hidden. They are buried in the earth, beneath the mud. One never notices them, they are not considered important — I mean the roots. If someone were to cut the branches, the leaves, the flowers, the tree would continue to bud and grow, perhaps even better if it were properly pruned. But if you dig up the roots and sever them, the entire tree will die. The peasants are like the roots of a tree. They are the roots of the nation. If you want the country to be strong you have to allow the peasants to be strong.

This awareness of the role of peasants is accompanied by the feeling that nothing will come of their lives if they fail to take the initiative. Of course, they need help, knowledge, but first of all they have to organize. Philémon Engongomo Tina responded willingly to our questions:

> Learning about development is above all a matter of willingness, courage, and the commitment of villagers to the welfare of their community. While the appropriate tools exist insects and disease continue to destroy crops, and somehow the villages still manage to survive. Men, women, and children go on living and dying. Who really cares about them? Now thanks to our Bureau de Promotion Collective[1] villagers can get together to consider and discuss the problems they encounter from day to day.
>
> Yes, but with traditional approaches what real solutions can be applied?

[1] A local Camerounian NGO.

There is no solution to the death of an old villager. He was old and he had lived his life for better or worse. But there must be a solution to prevent the death of a child. It has not yet begun to live. It must live. It can't be sent to live in France or in America, it must live here.

It does not live because there are development problems. It is up to us to learn from those who know what can be done and to teach others. First of all, the villagers must learn to help each other as quickly as possible. And even the volunteers and the church can learn, if they are attentive to what the villagers are saying. A single villager will be reluctant to speak. Our organization collects this information at the grassroots level in each community, in each village: it takes note of their needs as well as of the significant events in the lives of the villagers and in each community. This information is made available to other communities so that they can learn from it; it is also communicated to the Volontaires du Progrès who in turn consider it in the light of their own experience and then we sit down with them and try to find solutions.

And once the solution is found, what happens then?

Well, then we publish this new information according to the needs of each community and to help problem-solving. This is done in meetings with village educators and through our bulletin.

Which educators?

The very same villagers. The Bureau trains the village educators as well as the others, with the help of organizations such as the National Institute of Social Development, the Camerounian Red Cross, the Canadian World University Service, and the French Volontaires du Progrès.

In order to get things moving one must first of all organize and then avoid becoming dependent on others, in other words, cultivate self-reliance. These are the key words which galvanize energies and enthuse villagers from the high Andes to the tropical savannahs and deserts — even if there are still people who lag behind or prefer to get drunk, as in all human societies.

Thanks to better communication, by word of mouth or otherwise, with or without the written word, NGOs, village associations, or informal groups spread the word and the work of the barefoot revolution. These NGOs owe their existence and *raison d'être* to their struggle to bring about change and progress in the rural world.

First and foremost come basic needs, food, water, health, and hygiene. Then the villagers must become aware of their resources and be given the opportunity to act. We will be following this process from the ground up from village or community initiatives supported by a network of Northern NGOs to the hundreds of small-scale projects pioneered by the newly emerging local NGOs. The development of NGOs throughout the Third World does not necessarily signal a retreat of the Northern private agencies, but it points to a shift of responsibilities and a change in the terms of North–South co-operation which highlights the dramatic increase of local initiatives. Many encouraging examples of this trend are beginning to surface.

For one south Indian farmer, 'Two meals a day instead of one every two or three days is a step in the right direction.' In the tiny rural village of Melapatty Rasimangalam in the Rudukotad district, Thira Velayutham answers our questions while he milks a cow.

I belong to one of fifteen families that live on a Bhoodan estate of 3,377 acres donated by a generous man. He gave the land to the Bhoodan Movement in 1960, but we were not in a position to farm the land. We didn't know how to farm and finally the Board took back the land. Then they heard that we were ready to start work. The ASSEFA Association had helped train us to develop the farm using modern methods.

Our first priority was to find adequate water resources. We dug a well enabling us to irrigate twelve acres. But that was only enough for six families and the Bhoodan board, which had given us 42,000 rupees, could not allot us more funding. Then I went to the Rural Development Agency which referred us to one of the government banks. We finally managed to get a loan so that we could dig a second well.

As you see, we have improved our situation here, but not enough as yet, and now we are planning to request more loans to start raising poultry and sheep and for other projects that we shall agree on together for the future. For although the loans are individual, it's the community of fifteen families that manages the farm and takes decisions. And despite the fact that these families belong to four of the lowest castes, we are able to work together and co-operate. Now you can see why we eat twice a day instead of once every two or three days.

Egypt's Coptic Evangelical Organization for Social Services (CEOSS) works with the poorest segment of the population. Villagers in the communities of Assiout and Itsa in Upper Egypt appreciate the progress that has been achieved thanks to the sensitive approach of this NGO. Many are grateful that thanks to CEOSS their sight has been restored following cataract operations, for which they pay only five Egyptian pounds instead of the normal fee of at least 40 pounds for the operation. One villager who had been blind for four years told us that he had given up hope when he went to ask the CEOSS ophthalmologist for his help. The doctor removed his cataracts for a fifth of the normal cost, and now the man can see.

Another man, a tailor, had lost his sight in one eye and only had partial vision in the other. Now, with glasses, he can see wherever he goes and with a second pair he can continue his work. A young woman who had been childless for seven years was treated by the CEOSS volunteer doctors and finally gave birth to a healthy baby. She was able to purchase medicine at a co-operative pharmacy at a third of the normal cost, thanks to subsidies provided by the organization.

A 24-year-old peasant was able to learn how to read and write thanks to the literacy programme.

'What did your neighbours say?'

'I don't care what they say.'

A young woman who had just learned how to read and write. 'Knowledge is light! A woman who knows how to read and write can be a better mother to her children than if she is illiterate.'

Another young woman who attended the literacy programme has now become a volunteer educator and one of the village leaders. She is attending classes organized by CEOSS on village leadership:

> Now I am teaching people how to read, I visit the women in their homes and encourage them to organize group meetings. Even though I am married, my husband does not object since I get up before he does to take care of my domestic duties before I go out. I've learned a lot from these meetings between men and women; they've given me new insights. Before, I was shy, I never dared speak in front of men. Now I believe that as women we have an important part to play in the life of the community. We have to help one another; men don't have a monopoly on serving God and helping others.
>
> I don't want to have more than three children. What's important is to give them a good education and a good start in life.
>
> I have become a volunteer educator in the literacy programme, in Bible study, and in the young women's groups of the Orthodox Church. I've attended several training sessions for leaders at Assiout and at Itsa. I've learned how important it is to serve others, and how to think for myself. I've cast off my old habits, my superstitions and belief in magic and in spells, visiting the graves, and so on ...
>
> When CEOSS announced in its newsletter that a sewing programme was being set up for the women of the village, I wrote to the CEOSS

office and someone came to visit me to see if I was really genuinely interested. I was accepted. I attended classes with eight other women from various villages for two months at the CEOSS centre at Minia. This programme involved classes in theory and practical exercises. When I passed the exams, CEOSS helped me acquire a sewing machine at a discount. I couldn't have learned this in my village since none of the women know how to use patterns or take measurements and use sewing machines. In any event, I would never have been able to learn all I have in only two months. A sewing machine enables me to bring in extra cash and allows me to help other people in the village. I can supply them with clothes fairly quickly, the workmanship is good, and the price is reasonable.

Many moving testimonials like this one have been collected throughout the Third World. The question is, are these enthusiastic success stories recounting the struggles of villagers merely 'the trees that hide the forest' or the promise of the forest to come? We must never lose sight of the real challenge, which concerns the quality of life and the very survival of two billion people who live in poverty in rural areas of our planet. As we pointed out earlier, it really is a matter of survival. Do NGOs have a real impact on the factors of impoverishment? Can they effectively rescue these populations from conditions of dire poverty? Can they significantly contribute to creating real factors of development?

CHAPTER 12

Can NGOs Create Factors of Development?

Generally, an NGO's main activities are geared to meeting basic needs. This type of endeavour could be called 'primary development'. The most immediate needs are dealt with first — for example, a well is dug — and then a training or education programme is set up.

However, the opposite approach is also found: an NGO works in a village or region 'in depth' for several years, encouraging the community members to analyse their development problems and then proposing solutions to the problems which the people themselves have identified. The approach generally depends on the situation of the village or region concerned. In almost all the projects visited, attending to the basic needs of villagers ultimately leads them to a better understanding of their situation and prompts them to engage in activities to foster their own development.

The 'consciousness-raising' method which seeks generally to involve villagers in identifying their own problems and empowering the people themselves to resolve them, if it is to be lasting and efficient must be followed up by concrete and appropriate action. But even if villagers have become conscious of their problems and of possible solutions, of their rights and possible courses concerning specific areas, it does not always follow that they have the means at their disposal to tackle the situation. If the concerned NGO is not able at this point to provide concrete assistance to the people, by lending them money, supplying materials, seed, technical advice, and so on, matters become bogged down and the project begins to vegetate. This was the case in several of the projects visited.

> Our efforts in terms of time and money invested to create a dynamic community will yield but fragile results if they do not lead to concrete achievements and tangible results which can be economically measured.

Let us briefly review the two major categories of needs that were outlined in Chapter 6.

Basic needs. These are essentially water and food, along with basic health care and hygiene, enabling the population to overcome malnutrition, hunger and famine.

Awakening and empowering village groups. Once basic needs have been properly understood and addressed, the process of economic and social development can begin. In the initial stage of a project the fundamental task of the NGO is to encourage villagers to understand the need for participation and identification of realistic goals for the group or community. The following list ranks in order of importance the fundamental steps which must be taken if the beneficiaries of the project are to achieve a clear understanding of the development process and the means to ensure significant progress.

1. Organizing or reactivating the group.
2. Understanding the need for education.
3. Learning about primary health care and hygiene.
4. Learning to control population growth.
5. Learning to use local resources and protect the environment.
6. Learning how to produce more and of better quality.
7. Learning how to participate actively in the development process.

The analysis of the 93 projects visited shows how NGOs can help address these various needs.

ATTENDING TO BASIC NEEDS

Of the 93 projects, 63 focused on one or both of the two basic needs: water and food supplies.

Water

Fifty projects involved improving existing water supplies by purification, or providing water supplies from new sources, by digging wells, constructing small dams and reservoirs, or boxing or capping of springs or streams which were piped (using gravity) into villages to supply stand-pipes or community taps. In some cases, windmills and other types of pumps were installed.

In 32 instances small irrigation systems were set up using existing water supplies or by building rainwater catchment tanks. In several projects, rainwater catchment devices employed primitive local technologies under the supervision of project leaders or the villagers themselves. In Kenya rainwater collection tanks were made out of wooden frames covered with a mixture of mud and brush or cement. These tanks were generally earth-coloured and blended nicely with the natural surroundings. A similar type of tank was seen in Thailand, although the technologies used were somewhat different. In some cases tanks made of metal or corrugated iron were used. They proved to be somewhat more obtrusive and subject to rust.

In other areas, boreholes were used for water supplies. The major problem encountered with these is evaporation, although underground water supplies are not seriously depleted thanks to seepage of rainwater. Small water reservoirs and damming of small rivers and streams provided judicious solutions to local needs in many cases. Small dams have the added advantage of contributing to soil conservation by limiting land erosion caused by run-off of rainwater. The soil deposits collected can serve to increase arable land areas.

The use of trickle-and-drop irrigation systems coupled with ditches and ridges was helpful in extending areas of cultivation and in controlling erosion. One innovative approach observed was the use of weirs — wire cages filled with stones — to control the flow of small rivers or streams. The sediment gradually collects in these weirs, making them impermeable to water and allowing maximum efficiency in diverting water for irrigating crops. This method, widely used in West Africa, was practised by an NGO in Burkina Faso, and in Colombia, similar small dams were made of piles of plastic bags filled with clay and then covered with a thin layer of cement.

Only ten of the projects visited provided adequate protection against erosion caused by rainwater run-off on unstable or sharply sloping terrain. In Peru, one group had carried out the planting of 18,000 eucalyptus trees over a three-year period on slopes with an incline of 30–40°. Here a marked improvement in land conservation was observed and the 'spill-down' effect of acidic high-altitude soils had been partly arrested. Similar programmes were encountered in the Philippines, Kenya, Indonesia, and Burkina Faso.

Food

Food production and supply was a problem of major concern in 52 of the projects visited. A variety of crops and agricultural production systems were applied to increase and diversify food production and supply, including cultivation of individual, school, and community vegetable gardens, grain farming, and keeping of small livestock (poultry, goats, pigs, rabbits, and guinea-pigs). Bee-keeping was also found to provide a good source of income from the sale of honey and beeswax. It has the advantage of requiring only modest capital outlay and it is ideally suited to areas where land is scarce or farming and keeping of livestock are difficult or impossible and has proved to be a good source of supplementary income in areas of Kenya where the tsetse fly decimates cattle herds. The same holds true in some regions of Peru where 'the present social and economic context makes it impossible to organize production of grain crops owing to the scarcity of land and the lack of capital for the poorer small farmers.'

Fish-farming, by stocking and breeding in existing ponds, swamps, and rivers, or the excavation by villagers of small reservoirs or artificial lakes, can provide a good source of protein and income (*Tilapia*, among other genera, has been bred with success in man-made lakes). Although fish-farming is not very widely practised in the projects seen. it has been successful in Indonesia, Thailand, Bangladesh, Kenya, Egypt, and the Philippines; it was rarely observed in Latin America, and no examples were found in West Africa.

These 'primary development' schemes provide an excellent opportunity for mobilizing groups in village or community undertakings. Although the digging of a well can be accomplished with or without the participation of the concerned population groups, it can also become the focal point of a common undertaking, enabling villagers to take an active part in planning, organizing, and executing the work themselves, thus setting the stage for more ambitious future development schemes.

Communal or collective farming is another sound basis for organizing or reactivating group initiatives, since it implies sharing the responsibilities and the product among the entire participating group. Excavation of artificial lakes for fish-farming is also a convenient means of mobilizing a group since an undertaking of this scale requires manpower and collective effort.

However, motivating a group to work together harmoniously is not always an easy undertaking:

> What took the most time was finding the young farmers to take charge of the project. The village chiefs wanted to impose members of their families in order to increase their power and influence. The agronomist

wanted all the villagers to elect the fifteen or twenty people who would manage the farm. The entire process took almost a year, with regular meetings nearly every week.

AWAKENING AND EMPOWERING VILLAGE GROUPS

'Getting people to stand on their own two feet' is the way one NGO project leader described the fundamental goal of his action in the community where he was working, and this expression seems to fit most of the efforts we observed. Inducing villagers to become self-reliant is the basic characteristic of all NGO action to promote rural development. The process starts by encouraging villagers to begin by thinking through the problems they are confronted with and then helps them to find appropriate solutions. This approach can be successful only if the villagers are allowed to assume responsibility for their own development; no other agent can take their place in this essential task.

> We begin by informal discussion in groups in which the entire community is represented — elders, young people, village leaders, and the most marginal elements — and in the process they are not even really aware that they are being 'taught' something.

> What is most important at this point is 'consciousness-raising'. We have to organize meetings and discussion groups to make villagers aware of their problems, to urge them to think for themselves. One approach is to ask them, 'If you had five children, how would you provide for them?' or, 'What happens when the population grows while the available land stays the same?'

> The challenge is very clear. Rural development is first and foremost a matter which concerns the villagers themselves. They have to become the agents of the rebirth of agriculture in the Andean highlands or in the semi-tropical Amazonian regions. But we are also trying to awaken their critical faculties through our training programmes, so that the peasants will not be content with passively accepting without thought what politicians would have them believe.

> It is up to us to awaken the rural poor so that they will be able to make informed choices regarding their future, so that they will not be merely manipulated by some higher authority which decides what is 'good' for them and then forces them to do it.

Most of the activities considered here were instrumental in opening

the eyes of the rural poor. Many villagers throughout the nineteen countries visited acknowledged this:
'We were in the dark before.'
'We didn't know we were capable of doing all this.'
'Before, we were like sheep.'
The NGO approach which depends on full participation by the beneficiaries of projects is a complete reversal of the strategies formerly applied by most private, governmental, or international development agencies. Many groups, however, continue to force aid and assistance programmes on villagers, making them the recipients of development aid rather than fully-fledged development agents responsible for their own choices and destiny.

> There is an extraordinary proliferation of organizations offering aid and assistance programmes to the rural poor or to groups of peasants who have migrated to the cities. Certainly there is justification for offering help to people who have been struck by natural disaster, but the continuation and spread of this kind of assistance eventually handicaps people to the point that they become incapable of fending for themselves.
>
> In the Bolivian highlands there are hundreds of Indian communities which receive direct food aid from private international agencies, or are given grants in kind or money. This system transforms these peasant communities into institutionalized beggars.

Some programmes which were set up with humanitarian objectives have unpredicted consequences. The North American 'Plan Padrino' encourages groups or individuals in the USA to 'adopt a starving Third World child' by sending regular contributions of about $20 a month to a child they will probably never meet. In Bolivia, for example, the child receives what amounts to about 360,000 pesos, or three times the monthly salary of an engineer in La Paz, the capital. With this amount of money the child's family is no longer concerned with 'development' and it reduces food production to meet the barest needs, since it now has more than enough to get along without much effort.

Organizing or reactivating the group
Social and group organization is the initial task of NGOs or individuals intent on ensuring that villagers attain a greater level of self-determination. This type of activity can take on numerous forms according to the groups and individuals involved. It is not merely a matter of assembling people in a classroom (when one is

available), in church, on the village square, or under a banyan tree, to set group dynamics into motion or help people understand their collective interests. It is a long and patient process, involving weeks, if not months or even years, of painstaking effort.

> Building a group requires the patience of Job and the care with which Penelope wove her tapestry. What has taken patient planning, investment of financial and human resources, and a great deal of effort to set up so that each villager becomes involved, can be easily demolished for a variety of reasons.
>
> When village life was centred on the weekly market, people met regularly and exchanged goods and information in a communal spirit, there was real social cohesion. But when land reform was instituted and each person began to act out of self-interest, community ties were broken and took years to mend. If villagers as a group are not involved in determining and fashioning their own development process, nothing can be done to help them. You can't force them against their will to act in their own interest.

No one should be left out. Organizing the group means above all not overlooking anyone. Each and every member of a community must be included so that development efforts involve everyone.

THE ROLE OF WOMEN IN RURAL DEVELOPMENT

In Africa, as in most societies in which knowledge and traditions are transmitted orally, women have a special relationship to the earth. They are holders of unwritten titles to the land and decide on its uses. They are also principally responsible for its cultivation in traditional agriculture. In Latin America too, where Indian communities represent a majority of the rural population, the strict division of labour between men and women and the fact that women provide for the basic needs of the family conditions the very nature of life in rural communities. The loss of cultural identity and sense of a common destiny and purpose in these traditional societies can only be regained by restoring women to their traditional position as partners in all aspects of the life of the family and the community.

It is necessary to involve women in development projects, taking care not to exclude them from the very tasks which tradition and culture designate as being specifically theirs. In a number of projects considered here there is a lack of understanding of the specific role and attributes of women in a developing society. However, some organizations, particularly in Latin America, have successfully incorporated women's programmes in the planning and implementation of development strategies.

> The social role of women must be restored within the communities. In our work here at La Granja, men and women are considered as equals. The same holds true for activities outside, in the surrounding communities, where we encourage the villagers to involve women in each and every aspect of village life.

Similarly in rural Bangladesh where, although women are generally restricted to a subordinate role, they are encouraged to participate in most NGO projects and to reaffirm their status as fully-fledged partners in social and economic development.

> The goal of the project was to encourage women to become aware of their rights, to overcome their passiveness and to take initiatives. In our meetings with the women, they observed that thanks to their participation in the group they were no longer afraid of leaving their houses and of being seen in the village. Before, this was unthinkable.

In Bangladesh men do not always look kindly on efforts to promote women's rights. In one instance an NGO which had been organizing women's co-operatives was forced to start a co-operative movement for the male villagers in order to avoid problems.

In countries such as Kenya, women take a very active role in small projects despite the fact that their situation is particularly difficult and precarious, especially in isolated rural areas. In this country, which has the highest birthrate in the world, women have to assume a crushing workload which includes most of the agricultural tasks as well as domestic duties, including gathering firewood and carrying water. Faced with the despair of seeing their children suffer from disease and malnutrition, many of these rural Kenyan women who 'work like beasts of burden' have decided to organize in order to find ways out of the crippling cycle of poverty and underdevelopment.

> The women started forming groups in 1976 to find the means of developing their resources, improving living conditions, and giving their children access to secondary education.
>
> As women we are already accustomed to helping one another. Then, one day we decided we were tired of being put down and not having anything. We started looking for solutions and we decided to try vegetable farming. Someone showed us how. With the money we

earned from our vegetable garden we bought a goat and that's how we got started.

Throughout the developing world women are organizing, setting up agricultural and crafts projects, planting trees and gardens, stocking fish ponds and breeding small livestock. They are learning how to provide better nutrition, health care, and education for their children.

As a participant in an NGO development seminar in Togo observed, 'If the women get involved in development, the future of Africa will be ensured.'

POPULAR CELEBRATIONS

Various approaches were observed of the ways in which community groups and NGOs make use of popular festivals, traditional celebrations, and cultural events to promote awareness of common goals and to further development objectives. In Brazil the use of popular theatre and agricultural festivals proved to be an effective instrument for enlisting villagers in collective efforts:

> the batida, or group husking of maize and bean crops in the evenings after the harvest in the villages of Bahia in the nordeste region;

> the traditional 'bumba meu boi' fertility rite, which is enacted at each spring planting by entire rural villages around the central symbolic figure of the bull in much the same way as it was celebrated by early Portuguese settlers;

> peasant theatre, in which villagers improvise their own socially relevant dramas on themes relating to the struggle to overcome poverty and underdevelopment.

In India, the poor pupils of the Seva Sarva schools receive more than a basic education, they also learn about their environment and to question the circumstances that condition their lives. They learn how to take a stand on local issues and to consider possible solutions, while their parents regularly visit their classes and become involved in their education and awakening to social and economic realities. A special event was organized for them: a three-day excursion to Madurai, where they were given the opportunity of living and learning together in an urban setting. Sharing quarters in a camp, they used their many talents to express their awareness of social and economic issues in theatre, song, and dance. They visited the major sights of the city, the airport, the Meenakshi Temple, the Church of Saint Mary, a daily newspaper, the circus, the wealthy neighbourhoods and the slums, the post office, and so on.

A display of their artwork was organized, at the opening of which a pupil from each school performed or recounted their adventures in Madurai. At the end of the event two of the Seva Sarva pupils summed up their experiences in the city:

> We went to Madurai with some strong preconceptions. We were convinced that life in the city was better and easier than here in the villages. But it is really quite different there. We saw both sides of the city — the rich and the poor — and what a big difference there is between them. Many of the streets are filthy and inhospitable. We have a lot to learn about the social and economic development of the city. But life in the villages is better and more peaceful. We shall never leave our villages to live in the city, we prefer to develop our own villages.

ENCOURAGING VILLAGE ORGANIZATION AND DECISION-MAKING

Mr Chandra Sermaran of ASSEFA described the first step: awakening the village.

> It is a process which is applied in areas targeted for development. The promoter asks villagers about their needs and problems. Then he returns a month later. A group meeting is held in the village. Priority issues are discussed and two or three volunteers, or Sevaks, are recruited. ASSEFA then provides a year of training for the volunteers who are given a monthly stipend of 50 rupees.
>
> Groups of ten volunteers are trained in each region. Each trainee is required to present a two-minute report on a rural problem of his or her choice. Actual case histories are presented by the promoters and discussed in the assemblies. Theoretical and practical training sessions are carried out in the villages. The Sevak volunteer groups learn how to analyse and discuss problems and find solutions together. They must learn how to organize reimbursement of loans and how to carry out programme evaluation. Once they have completed their training they are given a small budget to administer so that they can begin to apply their knowledge to real-life situations.

S. Loganathan added:

> ASSEFA's main concern is to develop human beings and not only villages. People must participate, learn to think for themselves and become self-reliant.

It is in this spirit that the Sevak volunteer worker will continue his work in his own village. The entire village gathers for a preliminary meeting. We attended several of these meetings, held in the evenings in many of the villages. The group progressively forms as the interest of the men of the village is kindled and they realize their collective interests. The children look on from a distance while yet further away the women wait under a tree or in front of their houses.

This village assembly becomes the basic decision-making body. In the course of the proceedings the needs of the community are defined and debated. Sometimes the discussion becomes quite animated and it takes all the authority of the ASSEFA regional co-ordinator, Mr Lingam, to get the villagers to reach a consensus. The women gradually draw closer as their shyness gives way to curiosity.

As the last order of business the village decides to elect a president and an executive board, which according to the ASSEFA rules must include a woman, a young person, and a member of the untouchable caste. No one dares to object to the ASSEFA rule. The women are then invited to join the men in their meeting and they slowly gather round, crouching on the dusty ground. At first there are no candidates for the offices, but names gradually begin to emerge from the whispering groups, until someone finally stands up and proposes a nominee. The assembly goes on to elect the village president and officers.

A community fund of at least 1000 rupees is collected, each villager contributing according to his means. The money is deposited in the local bank to be used to help families in case of sickness or accident. The village assembly, or Gramsabha, then decides to convene regularly every fortnight in order to oversee the progress of community projects and to deal with any problems which may arise. A representative of the Gramsabha will be appointed to solicit loans from the bank on behalf of the villagers. Half of the earnings from the village's productive investments is deposited in the fund, and one third of the total earnings is divided among the villagers.

Most of the projects visited had originated in a more conventional way, generally starting with a group effort towards acquiring new skills or to provide needed services in communities or villages. One frequently encountered collective undertaking was the setting up of co-operatives.

CREATING THE FACTORS OF DEVELOPMENT?   157

The co-operative is important as a tool for bringing villagers together and to combat divisiveness. The co-operative is also a training centre; a professor of agronomy has been spending two hours each week for three months in order to train us.

In some instances group consciousness is aroused by the struggle for the recognition of rights that have been denied and that individuals are powerless to carry on by themselves. A common example of the abuse of the rights of the rural poor is the seizure of their land. At times progress achieved by a neighbouring peasant group is enough to move villagers to collective action.

Another means of stimulating group awareness and action is to encourage villagers to re-establish traditional mutual aid societies or to breath new life into dormant community structures such as those found in the mountain villages of Peru.

Many of the groups we work with are beginning to practise traditional forms of farming and exchange which had been neglected for years. One such custom is the verbal agreement between Indian peasants by which one party provides the seed while the other promises to work the land. The produce is then equally divided between the partners.

In Kenya, for example, a development project set up by a women's group ensures through a mutual aid agreement that each member of the group is in turn allotted a small fund for her work and maintenance. In most of these cases the group structure already existed; it was merely a matter of organizing activities around it.

In Burkina Faso the Naams, traditional leaders of village groups, have been successfully enlisted as agents for modernizing and developing their communities. Traditional community groups are often convenient facilitators or instruments of rural develop-ment efforts and must not be overlooked. They are the natural promoters of village or community development.

Marginal groups should not be overlooked, either, whether they be the untouchables in India, the poorest segments of the population, landless peasants, pariahs, or lepers.

In Nigeria we visited a project set up for and by lepers which was designed not only to provide treatment and medical assistance, but to enable them to manage their own economy and development. The project was initiated in 1976 by an Irish nun who began working in villages where lepers were confined. In 1982 there were 443,000 people afflicted with leprosy in Nigeria, living in colonies and villages throughout the country. The project visited involved

10,000 people and served as the administrative centre for sixteen villages of lepers in one of the Nigerian states.

This colony had been originally set up in 1932 by a Belgian missionary order which had, like many charitable groups, concentrated on providing medical help and aid for these segregated groups. Their principal activity was attending to the immediate needs of the victims of the disease, stabilizing them and administering medical treatment.

> I have been here since 1953. When I arrived, I still had a few fingers and toes. Now I no longer have any fingers on my hands and I have lost my feet and have gone blind. It all happened in a matter of years. I was born in 1920 in a nearby village, and before I got leprosy I was a farmer. Although I had been married since I was nineteen years old I was forced to leave my wife. I don't even know what became of her. I haven't seen her since I came here. I don't even remember what her voice sounded like or what she looked like. Here I've known hunger and thirst.

The objectives of the project are fairly simple and precise:

> All the men and women here, regardless of the extent of their disability, must regain their human dignity: on the one hand, by patiently working to regain the use of their bodies which have been impaired by the disease. On the other, they are provided with the opportunity of pursuing some kind of income-producing activity which enables them to become economically self-sufficient, no matter how handicapped they might be.

Without listing the considerable moral and material obstacles the Irish nun encountered in organizing this project, it was obvious that the remarkable results achieved had been possible thanks to her patient dedication and concern for the beneficiaries of her work.

The first goal of the project was to enable the participants to attain self-sufficiency in food production and supply. This was achieved thanks to the creation of a community farm. Before the project was set up more than 200 people in the colony would die every year of malnutrition.

> We want to organize the production and marketing of our agricultural produce along the lines of a co-operative which can serve as a model for our communities as well as for rural villages not restricted to lepers. This is why we are in the process of extending our training programmes.

Even in the case of lepers, who are normally considered to be a handicapped group in need of complete assistance, development efforts can only produce lasting results if the concerned population groups assume responsibility for the project.

> In these rural communities which have been destabilized by the massive arrival of Western consumer goods in the seventies and eighties, the group spirit must be rekindled by village leaders who have acquired production and management skills through intensive training programmes. What we would like to see is that these people should stop waiting for a miracle to occur. Whether they are lepers or not, they have to learn how to become their own miracle-workers.

Once lepers in the surrounding villages have been trained at the project centre, they can return to their communities and apply the agricultural techniques they have learned in their own family plots and gardens.

> In a year or two, they will not only be able to produce enough food to satisfy their own needs, but will have enough extra produce and seed to sell to others.

Thanks to the training they receive, they learn how to store and manage surpluses and resolve any production problems which might arise.

The second fundamental objective of the project is a social and moral one.

> Rejected by society which is afraid of them, lepers need to regain their human dignity and self-respect. If they are capable through their own efforts of becoming self-reliant and learning to fend for themselves, then, despite their disabilities, their pride and sense of being normal people can be restored.

But in order to work they need to be able to regain mobility and the use of their limbs, even though they are often almost totally handicapped. Artificial limbs had to be developed to help them overcome physical disability. However, such devices are not manufactured in Nigeria and the cost of importing them would have been prohibitive. Therefore, while the more able-bodied villagers began to farm, the Irish sister set up the first rehabilitation centre to produce artificial limbs and provide physical therapy for the more handicapped individuals. In eight years the centre has helped over 400 severely handicapped lepers in the colony and in the sixteen surrounding villages to regain mobility.

Although I have lost my fingers, I have learned how to use my hands as they are. I already could no longer walk and I lost my foot completely. At the rehabilitation centre they made a wooden leg for me and I was able to learn how to walk again. Now I can work in the fields just like anyone else.

Besides the additional income provided by the sale of surpluses from the gardens and farms, the participating groups can supplement their earnings by working in small crafts industries for which the project provides training.

Some of the women lepers have begun to sell produce on the roadside outside the project. These women have not as yet developed many of the outward signs of the disease, since their condition has been stabilized through early medical attention. Thanks to their efforts the members of the communities and villages have rendered the project almost self-sufficient. The sale of its produce is almost equal to expenditure.

The concluding observation on the project was made by one of the lepers: 'Now we have enough to eat, I receive proper medical attention and I have learned how to walk again.'

The major achievement of the project is that it can be reproduced elsewhere, wherever the same problems are found, without the need for large financial outlay, for its success is above all dependent on the capacity of people to struggle against despair and misfortune.

I know my future is here within the leper colony and that I shall never leave. But it doesn't matter if you only have a little space to live in. A lot can be done with a little. As you can see, I have lost my fingers and toes, but I can still work. I've requested to be trained as a nurse. Once I've been trained, I will assist the doctors and health workers, while at the same time I can earn some money and make my life meaningful.

STRENGTHENING THE GROUP

Sometimes outside project workers must commit themselves to living within communities and sharing the life of rural villagers while they try to help them find ways of improving their lives. In several instances we observed this approach, which obliged NGO workers to become directly and deeply involved in their work with the community. In the Maisons Familiales et Rurales project in Togo, project leaders often spend years living in communities before they are actually 'adopted' by the group and can at last begin openly to propose development alternatives.

The same was true in Bolivia where in one Andean project the NGO promoter had been totally accepted and integrated into the community after spending years with them.

> He lived with us day in, day out, and like us he slept in an adobe hut. He never did anything without first consulting us. He understood our problems and when he went to La Paz, it was to defend us when our rights or interests were threatened.

But this promoter was called back home. His successor and the new team keep their distance from the peasants and are no longer in a position to get things moving. They are not aware that first one must respect the integrity and specific character of the Andean peasants.

In Mali we visited a project in which the arrival of NGO workers in charge of digging wells deeply disrupted the lives of villagers.

> These NGO teams dislike our food, they hate our soups and sauces, our traditional dishes made with millet or maize, and our pastries. They think they are great benefactors because they've helped us get water, so they think they should be entitled to have 'proper' food to eat. We have to import white rice, chicken, and meat for them ... they really look down on us.

In other instances, group effectiveness has become greater because the NGO has remained on the sidelines and left villagers a free rein in running their project. In Mexico, for example, one NGO project leader purposely avoided learning the local Mayan dialects used by the *campesinos* with whom he was working. He wanted them to 'feel they could talk freely', even when he was present.

Lastly, exceptional circumstances or unforeseen events, such as a natural disaster, can help bring a group together and cement group solidarity.

> Last year's drought turned out to be a godsend for the Bolivian Altiplano, since we all had to pull together in order to confront the emergency with strength and determination. We succeeded beyond expectation, for in only a year we were able to achieve what would have taken a decade to accomplish under normal circumstances.

Once a group has organized, it grows stronger and more confident as each of its members discovers his specific function and natural leaders begin to emerge. These group leaders are often not necessarily traditional figures of authority such as village chiefs, or even the most respected, affluent, or educated members of a community.

NGO workers are constantly seeking to motivate groups to take on responsibility for managing their programmes. All members of the community — men, women, and children — are urged to participate. This is the cornerstone of their action.

... in our communities each person trained in agriculture in turn teachers a fellow farmer. But this does not mean that it gives him a right to tell others what to do.

Each community must select its own leaders instead of allowing 'little bosses' to be imposed upon them. It is all part of a truly democratic process which begins once the community decides to start organizing and working together.

Once the community has decided to start working together, they begin by setting up democratic decision-making. Our task is to help them establish the appropriate structures in order to do so effectively, a village council or assembly, which will be recognized by Government. We also urge them to elect officers and committes to deal with each aspect of their development process. After five centuries of colonial and class domination and alienation, not to say serfdom, this is not always an easy task.

Once villagers have organized their communities they should then be encouraged to seek legal recognition by local and national authorities in accordance with legislation prevailing in each country. With the exception of Zaire, where NGOs tend to prefer to remain 'underground' for the reasons discussed earlier, most of the projects visted had received appropriate legal recognition. But the need for legal status is not always obvious to rural villagers, and it is incumbent upon NGOs to ecourage these communities to overcome their natural mistrust of the government and work within the letter of the law. Villagers soon recognize the advantages of organizing and obtaining legal recognition in terms of the increased support and access to funding which it often provides.

Once the group is organized and has a legally recognized status, the next logical step is for it to set up lines of communication with the various partners it will need to work with to further development goals — the administration, local authorities, banks and other funding agencies, and so on. At this stage villagers must have a fairly clear idea of their needs so that these can be articulated at the local, regional, and national levels.

Villagers must be in a position to defend their rights and interests knowledgeably in any gathering where development problems that affect them are discussed.

Training villagers is not a goal in itself, but is rather aimed at encouraging them to become self-sufficient so that they can manage their own development and that of their community.

One of the most positive developments is that now, after only three years of organizing and training, these village awareness groups can stand up for their rights and interests even before a group of university professors and development experts.

Villagers not only learn to work together democratically, but also are prompted to act in concert to defend their collective interests.

Many of these groups have already gained legal recognition and with our technical advice they are now in a position to go before the courts to defend their interests.

In rural areas, economic survival can only be ensured with certainty if community groups organize. These groups are then in a position to manage the local economy and defend themselves against exploitation, the threat of expropriation, and the takeover of their land by their oppressors.

Six neighbouring communities which had not been given access to electricity decided to join together and send a petition to the prefect.

Now that the association has obtained legal recognition as a small farmers' association, it can wield greater influence and is even in a position to lobby government to make it aware of the rights and needs of peasants — land, health care, education, and support in marketing agricultural products.

In many parts of the rural Third World, the defence of the rights and interests of the rural poor has not been considered as important an issue as in Latin America. There, the rights of landless peasants in particular are threatened on all sides. Indian groups are acutely aware of the fact that they have to struggle to protect their basic human rights — the right to exist, the right to survive, and the right to respect for their cultural integrity. In all the Latin

American countries visited, the defence of the rights of the rural poor, mostly Indian groups, is one of the fundamental priorities of NGO action. In Bolivia, where land reform supposedly enabled the impoverished peasants to gain access to the land, many peasants are still subjected to the arbitrary rule of the *patrones*. It is only through mutual aid and collective action that peasant groups are able to defend their rights.

The same holds true in Brazil, where NGO leaders in one area observed that 'our most significant accomplishment in the past ten years has been that, on the one hand, peasants have begun to organize in defence of their right to the land they have been farming for generations, and, on the other, that share-croppers and small farmers have organized associations and peasant unions so that they can afford legal advice and protection in their struggle against *fazenderos* and the government and para-governmental agencies which oppress them.

In most African countries, the rights of the rural poor to ownership and use of the land do not yet appear to be major concerns. In countries such as Kenya, where arable land is growing extremely scarce while the population continues to increase at an alarming rate, this problem may well become apparent within a few years.

In Asia, however, the defence of the rights of peasants, and of human rights in general, are considered fundamental issues, and NGOs work to provide legal assistance to a number of communities which face difficulties in protecting their rights. In Bangladesh, for example, two NGOs work closely with rural groups to promote awareness of their legal rights and to help them defend these. One NGO is a legal aid co-operative, while the other is a voluntary association of lawyers who provide free legal assistance to rural groups and associations.

Understanding the need for education
Of the 93 projects visited in the course of this study, 17 were training or demonstration centres, model farms, or schools, while another 15 were integrated within village or community development programmes. The remaining projects were nominally rural development projects without a formal education or training component. Nevertheless, each and every one of the 93 projects was either directly or indirectly concerned with training or educating the rural population.

At times training was part of a 'hands-on' approach, at others skills acquisition was ensured in the context of a training facility or by demonstration techniques. Other more pedagogical methods involved literacy and adult education programmes, traditional schooling, and at times the use of more sophisticated technologies, such as audiovisual aids and radio.

> We have more than 350,000 listeners every day. We reach hundreds of communities through our broadcasts and we know that people listen to our programmes because they are in the languages they use, rather than Spanish which is the language of the ruling class.
>
> Our two radio stations — one broadcasting in Tarija province and the other in Chuquisaca — are very effective consciousness-raising tools. We can provide an impressive flow of information useful to the Indian rural population, ranging from agricultural and weather bulletins to discussion of socially relevant issues, popular education, traditional music, all of which help strengthen grassroots groups such as peasant organizations, women's clubs, farmers' unions, etc. It would take dozens of our workers months of travel throughout an extremely vast area to reach as many people as radio does in a matter of minutes.

These passive educational techniques eventually move rural villagers to becoming directly involved in training for development. This was precisely what a Bolivian *campesino* working on a collective development project in the highland village of Corta confirmed.

> When we brought a transistor radio back from La Paz we spent hours listening to it. And then the batteries gave out and a new set was too expensive for us to buy. We had become accustomed to listening to local and international news in our own Aymara language. When the radio stopped working it was as if a door had closed on us. We asked the padre for new batteries, but he told us that he didn't have any and that if we wanted to get the news we should read the local community bulletin. But neither my wife nor I knew how to read. We asked our daughter who had been through primary school to read us the news, but she would just make it up or claim she had to go to her pottery class at the village community centre. So we decided that we would learn how to read together. And when the next literacy programme started we joined the beginners' class. Now we both can read, my wife better than I because she is younger and knowledge stays in a young mind better than an old one like mine.

The need for education is not always so obvious in rural Third World communities, whether it concerns children or adults.

Only recently have young Indian girls decided to stay in school until the end of their primary education. Most of them only attend school for the first three years, then they drop out. One of our major struggles is to persuade girls to complete their primary education and then, if possible, to attend follow-up technical and practical education programmes.

The education of children in some areas is still considered a waste of time, but this attitude is changing rapidly. Parents now seem intent on seeing that their children get at least a primary education, even if they cannot afford to send them to secondary school which is often expensive and located at a great distance. For example, in Nigeria, even primary education is subject to tuition fees which can average 10 naira a term and 50 naira a term at the secondary level. To give some idea of the sacrifice payment for tuition represents, a schoolteacher in Nigeria earns an average of 145 naira a month.

In Cameroun, the Volontaires du Progrès provide informal community education programmes, 'Classes under the Trees', to youngsters who drop out of school after the primary level.

The Kalahan Educational Foundation in the Philippines has a programme especially tailored to provide education for children from highland areas who are traditionally stigmatized by the inhabitants of the valley areas, where most schools are located. This programme provides in their own village environment a basic secondary education which is designed with their future occupations (farming or crafts) in mind or to enable them, if they choose, to continue higher studies at university in Manila. The 250 students attending this secondary school located high in the mountains, live 'on campus' in houses that they either build for themselves or rent, and they farm their own small vegetable gardens for food. Their tuition fee is very small and does not even cover the cost of the programme. In order to meet the remaining costs a small industry has been set up which enables the students to produce marmalades for sale and export.

Once, thanks to the initial consciousness-raising stage, rural villagers have recognized the need for education, NGOs generally provide either formal education or training programmes geared to meet their needs within the context of the development project.

We visited a number of training centres which offer both theoretical and practical training in agriculture, animal husbandry, and public health. Adult literacy programmes are also provided in many instances, generally accompanied by or given in connection with technical or practical education. Technical education is aimed at enabling villagers to acquire essential skills and equipping them to deal with the problems they encounter in their daily lives.

In Mali, the Friends Service Committee has set up a literacy programme around basic skills acquisition courses in such areas as community improvement, basic skills, primary health care, marketing agricultural produce, organizing and running co-operatives, and so on. The Committee provides educational materials, lamps, paper and pencils, blackboards, as well as technical manuals in Tamashek, the local language.

In Bolivia, Javier Albo, a local NGO leader, explained how his organization, CIPCA, conceived the education and training of the adult rural population.

> Indoctrination in whatever form, whether it be Christian, Marxist, or other ideologies, is useless, counterproductive, and represents a dangerous 'bludgeoning' of the minds of rural villagers. Education, on the contrary, should instil the desire to learn more, as well as practical skills for the entire community. A complete education programme can be set up around learning how to use and manage new technologies, for instance in mechanizing agricultural production. This can be accomplished working with the local food crop, in the case of the Indian population of the Altiplano, the potato.

The same practical approach was in evidence in Togo and other African countries where rural workers of the French NGO Maisons Familiales et Rurales are involved.

> We go from village to village and try to identify the precise problems and needs of the men and women in rural areas. Many problems are brought up — lack of water, disease, crop failures, etc. This year we have chosen the following themes for our rural education programme:
>   water: its cycles and management
>   beans: why this traditional crop is failing
>   insects and insecticides
>   women and sewing: mending to get more use out of clothing
>   maize: a new two-month variety.
> These themes will then be developed in three-day village training sessions attended by interested individuals. The trainees will then receive post-training support and advice from the local team to see that they have properly applied what they have learned.

The methods and approaches observed were too numerous to be

described here, but suffice it to say that 53 out of the 93 projects consider education and training as a priority target.

Each NGO intuitively or systematically tailors its programme to the needs of the community where it is involved, as well as to the level of receptivity and acceptance of the group. Various groups are targeted — men, women, the elderly, etc. — and the entire community is encouraged to become involved in some form of education or training.

Some programmes have a remarkable success rate, with results which can be measured in economic terms or in terms of improved health and living conditions in villages. Another indicator of success is the regular increase of people requesting training or attending programmes. Others do not do so well for a variety of reasons which can stem from the quality and appropriateness of the courses or be a result of difficult local material conditions. For example, if the training centre is located too far from potential participants or the site of the training is not equipped to house or feed attending rural villagers, attendance and interest will decline. If programmes do not take into account villagers' work schedules and the fact that some potential participants might be forced to stay at home to take care of farming, stock, or domestic duties, the programme will also suffer.

TRAINING RURAL WORKERS AND EDUCATORS

Besides educating children and training adults NGOs also provide for the training of rural educators and workers among villagers who will in turn be responsible for managing development projects and imparting knowledge and skills to their communities.

This is one of the primary tasks of Maisons Familiales et Rurales, which trains local villagers to assume responsibility for rural development training programmes in villages throughout Africa. The same holds true for the International Institute of Rural Reconstruction (IIRR), which is involved in the Philippines, India, Colombia, and Kenya. Comparable training programmes are available through the Centre for Rural Technology Development (CRTD) which is sponsored by Philippine Business for Social Progress (PBSP) and which has trained workers from the Philippines, Japan, Thailand, and India.

IIRR and CRTD are both involved in what might be called 'applied research', since the theoretical approaches which form the basis of training programmes are put into practice by volunteer workers on farms. Unlike must rural training programmes, which are relatively short in duration, training development educators and workers requires more time and effort: in the case of IIRR, training programmes last from four to six weeks, while most training programmes offered at the grassroots level last only a few days. Many of these training programmes for rural educators are attended by professionals who are not themselves directly involved in development work, but who are eager to improve their knowledge of the rural milieu. This is the case with doctors who work in rural areas.

INTEGRATED PROJECTS

It goes without saying that not all the projects visited followed the approach to rural development which we encountered most frequently — beginning with addressing basic needs and then training villagers to identify and resolve longer-term development goals. However, this is the general pattern, going beyond the scope of a single action in one particular area. Once a project has begun it becomes apparent that most of the problems are related, and that only an integrated approach can ultimately succeed in addressing interrelated factors.

However, lack of resources prevents most NGOs from launching programmes on several fronts at once. Priorities must be set within the general framework of the development programme. Most recent projects are set up in this manner, while the older projects have progressively evolved toward a selective targeting of development goals within an overall strategy, dealing with one problem at a time as it arises.

A project can be integrated in two different ways:
1. In terms of agricultural production. For example, the activities of a farm can be integrated in order to ensure food self-sufficiency and, if possible, the production of surpluses for sale. An example of this type of project integration was cited in Chapter 9.
2. The project integrates a variety of actions within a specific field, such as health or agriculture. In health, for example, the project focuses on all aspects of health care and sanitation, while in agriculture, the project is designed to promote better use of land, improve farming, and satisfy local food needs and provide surpluses for sale.

In our opinion a project can be considered to be integrated when it addresses the following areas simultaneously:

agriculture
health
education and training
economic problems.

The three areas that are generally covered are agriculture, health and training. Next in importance was the combination of agriculture and economics. Lastly, agriculture and training were often coupled, or agriculture and health.

Nineteen of the projects visited could be classified as integrated according to our definition; eleven of them in Latin America.

In Asia, two out of three projects are concerned with at least two different areas, generally agriculture combined with either health or training. In Africa, the majority of projects still tend to be centred on one area or development effort: agriculture is the priority area of concern. Less than half of the projects visited there covered more than one area. In total, of the 93 projects visited, 60 had at least two major fields of activity, and at times several others.

These figures have been given to show that NGOs tend to recognize the need to diversify development efforts in order to address all areas of social and economic importance.

Learning about primary health care and hygiene
The first step in training villagers in primary health care and hygiene is to teach them how to find clean sources of water, the priority concern in most rural development projects. Besides knowing how to purify water supplies from springs and wells, villagers must also learn how to identify water-borne diseases and prevent them through proper hygiene and sanitation.

> At all water sources we post a sign which recommends that drinking water be boiled first, that all utensils be washed, that the surrounding area be kept clean and that water be disposed of outside the house once it has been used.

Once villagers have begun to use clean water they understand how beneficial it can be.

> When we use well water for watering plants the vegetables are no longer polluted and our children no longer become sick.

Next comes learning about proper sanitation and the use of latrines. Not all villagers recognize the need for proper hygiene and sanitation, but once the problem has been properly explained and villagers understand that latrines can also be a good source of organic fertilizer, their interest grows.

Latrines are discussed in classes at school and in informal community gatherings.

We have built 80 individual latrines and we keep getting more requests every day.

Villagers in Peru built 200 latrines thoughout their communities, on the roadsides, in the fields, each one having a distinctive decoration.

Hygiene and sanitation can be promoted along with primary health care through formal training or in small informal teaching sessions which are held in schools and rural clinics, or simply in one-to-one discussions between health workers and villagers.

Women have an important part to play in propagating good health and hygiene practices in rural areas. They learn how to care for their children, how to diagnose and prevent common diseases. They also learn the importance of immunization and see to it that their children and families are properly inoculated.

Thanks to our inoculation campaigns against polio and measles, child mortality in this part of the Bolivian Altiplano has dropped to the levels found in industrialized countries.

Health and hygiene are a primary concern of most NGOs working in rural areas, since many Third World nations do not have the means to provide adequate health care in these regions.

If we are involved in health care it is because there is practically no public health care available here. In Peru there is no rural health policy, nor is there preventive medical care or health education in rural areas.

Not far from here there is a large hospital, but the doctors do not remain on duty; they only appear once a week to take medicines away for their private practices. The three nurses spend the day sleeping and the patients are left to their own devices. (India)

Here medical care is not free; you have to pay for everything — syringes for injections, etc. . . . The emergency room is a disaster; they just let people die. They don't even have medicines or antibiotics here. (Philippines)

Besides health and hygiene education programmes, many projects train rural health workers to provide care and prescribe some types of medicine.

The NGO helped train 50 workers in first-aid care with the co-operation of the Red Cross.

The medical team, a doctor and two nurses, also carries out research into traditional medicine. The purpose of their research is to train rural health workers from rural communities to provide health care and training to their fellow villagers.

NGO projects are instrumental in setting up rural clinics or health centres in areas where the government is unable to ensure health care.

The clinic was over ten miles away, too great a distance to travel for most of the villagers.

Most of these rural clinics are conceived along similar lines. They charge a small fee for treatment, except in cases where the patient is destitute: charging for services makes the beneficiaries of these services aware of the value of the care they are receiving. The cost of a consultation often includes the medicines prescribed. Many of the facilities are rather primitive, such as one we visited in Kenya which was located in two tiny rooms and where the medicines distributed were wrapped in newspapers. Others are better equipped and offer full hospital services.

The Centre is located in a beautiful old mansion where women and children receive care during the period of treatment and convalescence. We saw two infants who had severe burns and had been improperly treated by local physicians: the Centre had taken them in and they were receiving qualified care. The women are responsible for looking after the quarters where they live with their children; they clean and cook for themselves. Groups of six or seven women live in each room; there are fifteen rooms in all. They learn nutrition — how to prepare food to retain its nutritional value. Medicines are kept in a butane-powered refrigerator in a separate room. Children are given inoculations there.

On the days the Centre is open for consultations, once everyone has seen the doctor, a nurse gives a primary health education class to the patients. She shows mothers how to determine whether a child is unwell or undernourished. She recommends proper eating habits and basic ideas of nutrition so that the women can improve their cooking habits. While mothers stay at the Centre during convalescence, they work in the Centre's vegetable gardens and thus learn how to apply these techniques when they return to their home villages. (Our team in Bangladesh.)

In Egypt, a clinic set up by one project provides medical care and treatment three days a week. Two doctors, a nurse, an assistant, and two health workers from the village are on duty at the clinic. A preliminary examination costs the equivalent of $0.50, which includes two follow-up visits if necessary. The catchment area of the clinic covers fourteen villages with a total population of several thousand people. Each patient's file is kept on record for future consultation.

> The waiting room is in effect a primary health care training centre where the symptoms of disease and preventive care are explained using pictures and question-and-answer techniques.

Although, according to estimates made in the course of our visits, only one out of four rural development projects has provided some form of health care facility such as a clinic, this represents a great stride forward in comparison with the situation prevailing before most projects were launched. Some projects even tend to be somewhat over-ambitious in terms of health care: in Togo, for example, we visited a clinic under construction which appeared to be much too large in relation to the locally available health care personnel. Although the local health needs are immense, government funding remains very limited.

Training in nutrition is provided in a variety of different formats, either through formal education techniques or in demonstration classes in village training programmes.

Training sessions in nutrition are provided by NGO workers to future educators as well as villagers in programmes similar to those set up in health and hygiene, agriculture, and animal husbandry. Locally trained educators eventually take on the task of providing their fellow villagers with courses in nutrition. Women's groups are especially important in carrying out this work. They receive training in nutrition along with courses in maternal and child health care, or when they visit rural clinics.

In Togo, for example, the women of one village requested special training from the local NGO worker in how to prepare rice so that it would be 'more nourishing for our foreign guests'. This request was occasioned by our arrival in the village.

In Bangladesh, two young Mennonite missionaries spend three days each week travelling from village to village to instruct mothers in the science of nutritional cooking. An average of twenty women from a village meet under a straw-covered shelter where a primitive oven has been prepared in the ground. This type of oven is traditional throughout Bangladesh. They listen attentively then together experiment with new recipes. The poorer segments of the population eat rice with some spices added (once or twice a day, depending on their resources). No meat or fish is added; fish is sold immediately it is caught in order to buy rice. The two Mennonite women teach the villagers to add soya noodles to their rice dishes in order to increase protein intake and nutritional value. They also show them how to combine wheat and soya flour in the preparation of chapatis, as well as how to prepare vegetables so that they retain more vitamins.

Another effective means of improving nutrition is through the introduction of new and more nourishing varieties of grains and vegetables, improved stock raising, and the breeding of small livestock such as rabbits, guinea-pigs, and poultry. Community, school or individual vegetable gardens can also have a positive impact on nutrition, as we have already seen.

School programmes provide another excellent opportunity for improving knowledge of good nutritional habits. In Colombia many communities have organized 'nuevas escuelas' where children are given their own school gardens which they learn to care for. The produce from the gardens is distributed among the children to be consumed by their families. Parents may also attend these school nutrition programmes and learn to start their own family gardens. These new schools are true community learning centres.

In some projects teaching and giving children advice is often not enough. Immediate urgent solutions must be found and applied. In Bolivia since 1984 undernourished rural children receive supplementary meals at school. Children attend school from 7.30 a.m. to 2.30 p.m., with a lunch break at 11.30 during which they normally eat the lunches their mothers have prepared for them before they left home. However, most of the children have not been provided with a nourishing meal and they are given various supplements to their lunches which are prepared by the teachers during their break.

The same is true in India in one project where a workshop of 36 women rural workers recruited among the poorest groups of widows or mothers prepare special meals destined to supplement the nutrition of infants and young children who are undernourished. These rations of about a pound each are wrapped in cellophane and distributed to mothers on a regular basis. They are made up of 300g. of wheat flour, 100g. of lentils, 25g. of peanuts, and 25g. of powered milk — all designed to provide a balanced nutritional supplement to children's diets.

In the Philippines one NGO we visited is concerned principally with general development education and the health problems associated with poor nutrition.

> We have a lot of information on the problems of diet and nutrition. The major problem is that the farmers who produce eggs and vegetables do not eat them at home but only sell them. Our job is to help them increase their production so that they will have enough to sell and some surplus to feed their families. We are working to help improve the use and preparation of rice, although this often implies changing deeply rooted food traditions. We also came up against a lot of resistance and opposition when we tried to introduce breeding and consumption of rabbits. It was a complete failure. We have a special team which works with women. They play a major role in matters concerning food and nutrition.

In another region of the Philippines the inhabitants of one valley had only sweet potatoes to eat. The educators in a project there gradually helped the people learn how to cultivate other food crops and improve their nutrition.

> Before, we only ate sweet potatoes and a little rice. Now we have vegetables and pigs. But we only eat pork on special occasions. We eat chickens and ducks more often.

In some areas, besides vitamin deficiency, there are health problems such as goitres caused by lack of iodized salt in mountainous regions.

Nutrition problems are not always caused by poverty alone: sometimes they result from certain customs and beliefs which must be dealt with slowly and with great patience.

HOUSING IMPROVEMENT

In most developing countries housing is adapted to local climate and has evolved over time to meet local needs in a specific cultural environment. To many Westerners this housing can appear somewhat primitive.

Progress in this area has not always been introduced with the natural and cultural environment in mind. In most tropical areas of Africa, Asia, and Latin America, corrugated iron roofs have replaced traditional materials, although they do not always provide the best insulation in warm climates.

In one project in Indonesia the technicians have tried to replace the use of corrugated iron for roofs by a novel form of fibrocement made of cement and the locally abundant palm fibre. The moulds for this new type of roofing were bought in Surabaya and brought to the island where the project is located. The mould is made of two plates which press the coconut fibres into a thin layer of cement. The lower plate is surfaced by a sheet of plastic to make the surface smooth and waterproof. The price of producing this type of roofing is four to five times cheaper than buying corrugated iron sheets.

This is not always the case. Thus in Cameroun, in order to improve or 'modernize' his home a villager must spend more than twice the cost of the materials he would need if he had built according to traditional methods and using local materials. But it can be a good investment, for his traditional dwelling normally only lasts five to six years whereas a house built with modern materials will last him from 30 to 40 years.

Traditional dwellings in the Camerounian region of Upper Sanaga are very precarious. Their wooden piles and beams are rapidly eaten away by termites.

> This forces peasants to spend a great deal of time reinforcing and repairing their dwellings. Then it takes quite a few days for the entire family to rebuild the home every five to six years. A traditional house will require twenty cubic metres of 'poto-poto', a mixture of fifteen cubic metres of clay, which must be carried from the river bank, and five cubic metres of straw, which are mixed with around 5,000 litres of water, necessitating, given the size of the buckets, at least five hundred trips from the source of water to the construction site.
>
> Given the amount of labour involved in cutting trees, collecting wood, and building the main structure, constructing this house can take three men and two women at least 800 hours each, or a total of 4,000 hours of work. (Our team in Cameroun.)

In this village the project helped introduce clay bricks which are baked in an open community oven operated by bricklayers who have been trained by NGO workers. Villagers have now become expert in building houses with these sturdier and more durable materials. Villagers are also given loans to rebuild or improve their housing using the bricks, and they can invest the time they had been spending improving their traditional houses on farming and other income-producing activities.

In other areas NGO projects strive to improve the comfort and sanitation of housing, as in one project visited in Brazil. But at the present time improving housing does not appear to be a universal concern of NGOs, to judge by the number of projects we found in the course of our study. Of the 93 visited, only sixteen were concerned with improving village housing.

Learning to control population growth
In the course of this study we have seen the problems which result from population growth throughout the Third World and the ways in which it limits development in these areas. This is a very sensitive problem, and one which rural populations are often unwilling to recognize. In many countries the subject is taboo or at least difficult to discuss, and the majority of NGOs seem to fail to address this problem: we encountered only twelve projects that promoted family planning successfully. The reasons for this may be religious, personal, or multiple.

> Parents think: my child has one mouth, but it also has two arms!

> Polygamy is practised in our communities. There is competition between a man's various wives to see who can bear him the most children, since it is considered that she thus deserves to be his most beloved wife.

> Our women here are very fruitful, many have twelve children, and that is considered a great blessing.

> The people here are mostly Catholic, and contraception is not accepted by the Church.

The reasons are sometimes merely pretexts that hide deeper and unavowable motives.

> I stopped taking the pill because it made my ears itch.

But in most cases women seemed to want to have access to means of contraception: 'What's the point of having so many children if you can't take care of them properly?' Husbands do not always agree. 'My wife only wants two children, but I would like to have four; we shall see ...'

In Kenya, which has the highest birth-rate in the world, one NGO project is attempting to promote family planning with what is considered a great deal of success.

> To introduce contraception in the villages we have trained 26 health workers since 1980. They distribute contraceptives and spermicides

free. In the beginning the villagers were very reluctant, believing that contraception would cause birth defects or that women would become ill. Now they understand better. Couples who have adopted family planning in the past two or three years have begun to persuade others to try it. Now even the village men are coming to request contraceptives on their own initiative. This represents a true change of attitudes in the Luo tribe, which is very attached to the traditional polygamy and large families with many offspring.

But when we asked if these practises had brought about a significant decrease in the Luo birthrate, it appeared not.

When one considers the number of people involved, it is very difficult for 26 workers to keep accurate statistics. Nevertheless, it is my belief that the number of births is rising. When I visit the villages I see more pregnant women every day than I used to see when I first came here. And what is even more distressing is the number of pregnant adolescents and unmarried women.

In India in one region covered by a project. 'Women almost always ask how they can avoid having children. Some even ask to be sterilized. But most of them do not know what to do, and the men never bring this subject up.'

Besides these failures we find one project which seems to have succeeded in controlling population growth. It was in Thailand, where family planning is considered to be a cornerstone of integrated rural development programmes. The project founders considered 'family planning to be the first development priority. If not, all economic progress is defeated by the new mouths that have to be fed. Development without family planning does not help improve the standard of living, rather it causes it to regress.'

The project was inaugurated in 1974. It is carried out by a very large Thai NGO which was formed to implement a programme which today is administered by 600 regular workers, with 16,000 volunteers who work through 17 centres in 16,200 villages in 48 of Thailand's 73 provinces. The results achieved after ten years are spectacular — the average demographic growth rate in areas covered by the programme has fallen from 3.3% to 1.6%.

The methods used are akin to those to promote a new product.

No stone is left unturned in this American-style publicity campaign: key rings containing the new brands of contraceptives are distributed during official dinner parties. Taxi-drivers, hairdressers, and shop-keepers become the smiling publicists in this uncommon advertising campaign. One day the attractive female workers on the family planning team distributed free contraceptives to the policemen of Bangkok. Contraceptives are distributed free of charge throughout the country in village markets, in fairs, or around Buddhist temples during religious celebrations or weddings.

One clever approach to this campaign on the part of the person who thought it up was to strip away the emotional charge around what was considered a taboo subject and bring it out into the open. In this effort Buddhist religious leaders were helpful. People even began to talk about contraception with humour, and therefore made it an easy subject to bring up without embarrassment.

The King's birthday is celebrated each year with the gift of 1,190 free vasectomies which are offered to the public. Specially equipped buses which give out information and are equipped for sterilization criss-cross the entire country. Everyone knows the NGO's slogans by heart, such as 'a condom a day keeps the doctor away', or the tiny inscription on each key ring containing a contraceptive: 'In case of an emergency, break the glass'.

There is more to it than mere gadgetry and slogans, for these are always accompanied by solid measures to promote development — distribution of free oxen and pigs, financial help to build up emergency food stocks. The NGO also works to secure low interest loans for farmers who practise family planning and who need money for farming. (Our team in Thailand.)

One of the main reasons for the success of this programme is that, in contrast to the situation in most other countries, it is integrated in the national health policy and the Government solicits and accepts the support of the private sector in this area. It should also be noted that Theravedin Buddhism which is practised by 95% of all Thais does not oppose family planning, since it helps improve the quality of people's lives. Moreover, Thai women tend to be independent-minded and take decisions regarding their family life very much on their own without asking their husband's advice. The fact that 86% of the population can read and write is certainly not a negligible factor.

However, this project is not representative of major trends in the Third World in terms of population policy. This is all the more disquieting since it is a matter of no little urgency.

Learning to use local resources and protect the environment
While most NGOs begin a project by urging villagers to achieve self-reliance in terms of food production and primary health care

and hygiene, development education and practical training rapidly become the central focus of programmes. Education and training are in fact the foundation of all future economic progress. An important step in this process is learning how to make good use of local resources, whether material or cultural. This is why project leaders and workers must have a thorough knowledge of the milieu in which they are working.

> If from the very beginning the project workers fail to recognize the importance of local social and economic factors, attempts to mobilize the population and encourage it to assume control of these factors are doomed to failure. It is not enough to introduce improvements in farming, soil conservation, and other areas; all technical and economic progress must stem from the actual needs and fit the abilities of the concerned group.
>
> We do not believe that the 'peasant revolution' theorized by the social thinkers of 19th-century Europe really applies to the Andean milieu. Our task now is to help these Indian societies learn how to apply age-old traditions and techniques in order to foster development. Then we must know how to withdraw quietly and let them resolve their own problems.
>
> There is no need to impose Western economic models on secular Indian cultures. We have to adapt the traditional Indian culture to modern circumstances and make use of ancient technologies so that each member of the community can take part in the collective reawakening of these communities.

In some cases NGOs fail to understand the importance of integrating local traditions and technologies in the development process and the project never really gets off the ground.

> The people in these communities had not been well prepared for the project. The preliminary studies by the specialists had not taken into account the cultural and historical factors.
>
> The NGO team was not familiar with our traditions and way of life. We tried to tell them, but they would not listen and said they knew better.

Although at times NGOs fail to recognize the value of cultural resources, most of them readily make use of available material resources. We noted that many project workers had succeeded in making good use of local conditions and technologies to achieve economic goals, whether they concerned the entire community or its individual members. We saw hundreds of examples of innovative technical approaches to farming and irrigation, construction and small industry, which owed nothing to modern industrial techniques but were conceived by adapting traditional technologies to meet social and economic challenges.

In many areas women were the principal agents in this process of making use of the old in order to forge the new. The ubiquitous adobe brick used in the construction of homes and community buildings is generally the product of women's skills. Wells are often dug using simple, age-old technologies; small dams are built using locally available materials, as we have seen earlier in this study.

Of course, some projects can afford to introduce more elaborate modern technologies, but the beneficiaries of these projects do not seem to participate as readily.

> Until now, peasants tended to reject modernization. On a modern highly mechanized farm there is no place for the manual skills which abound throughout the rural Third World. Therefore we are reluctant to introduce modern technology, not only because it is alien to the cultures here but also because it often precludes people's active participation and prevents them from using familiar technologies.

In many other small projects simple imported technologies are introduced where project leaders might have been better advised to try to adapt more familiar local technologies to the development tasks at hand. But the opposite is often true — the introduction of small labour-saving devices or techniques can at times play a decisive part in encouraging villagers to become involved in a project.

There is therefore no hard and fast rule concerning the use of local traditional approaches versus the introduction of new technologies — it is up to the good judgement of project personnel and the villagers themselves.

The Nigerian leper colony described earlier in this chapter, perhaps because of its necessary isolation, has been forced to make optimum use of local resources and talent in order to find local answers to difficult and unusual circumstances.

As mentioned earlier, the lepers make artificial limbs in their workshop; they also manufacture furniture for the local hospital, the school, and their homes and for sale outside the community. They make their own shoes and sandals, which are adapted to the physical disabilities of each member of the community. There is also a small metal workshop and foundry which produces small agricultural implements (including feeders for the chicken houses), as well as pots and pans and the metal components for the artificial limbs. Another workshop makes clothing for the community as well as the children's school uniforms, and the women work at home, weaving and knitting clothing for sale outside the colony.

Remembering that this community also produces most of its own food, it is evident that no effort has been spared to make full use of local talent and resources in order to ensure self-determination and self-reliance.

In the field of health care, too, we found a number of NGO projects in which novel ways of making use of local resources had been discovered.

For example, in one project in Bangladesh, rural villagers manufacture medicines in what must be a unique undertaking in the Third World. This internationally known industry is even in a position to compete successfully with the large foreign pharmaceutical companies which, in order to develop and produce new drugs, are forced to make large investments.

This is no small project since over five million dollars have been invested so far — in part by a group of Northern NGOs (NOVIB, Christian Aid, and Oxfam) with the remaining two-thirds of the financing covered by loans. Even though priority is given to production, social goals are not neglected. The workers are recruited among the poorest classes — one of the goals of the project — and each worker receives an hour of training each day. The personnel of this industry are aware of the fact that thanks to their efforts they have contributed to increasing the supply of low-cost medicines in Bangladesh. In fact, in a matter of a few years competing pharmaceutical companies have been forced to reduce their prices to the levels set by the local drug industry.

In Bolivia, thanks to the efforts of NGOs, traditional medicine is being practised more widely. Traditional Kallawaya medicine men have organized popular medicine training courses in rural areas and have encouraged villagers to use medicinal plants grown in community gardens. To date 54 of these community gardens have been created and numerous health workers have been trained in traditional medicine.

The Kallawaya healers themselves undergo a severe training programme which lasts eleven years. The ancestral tradition is transmitted within each Kallawaya family, but a father cannot train his son, he must rather reveal the science of healing to his nephew. This science goes back to pre-Inca times and it is practised by a lineage of the Aymara Indians. The Aymara culture is still very strong in Bolivia, in particular, and plays a dominant role in these societies thanks to strong family and community ties. The strength of this culture is attested to by the fact that it survived even the long period of Spanish colonization.

This revival of traditional medicine is not really a rebirth of an ancient science, since it has continued to exist thanks to its unique form of transmission within families from generation to generation. What has happened is that its influence is spreading to broader segments of the population, and in rural areas in particular, since this type of therapy is in perfect harmony with secular traditions. Another reason for the success of traditional medicine is that most rural communities cannot afford modern Western medicines. At the present time 70% of the Bolivian population uses traditional Kallawaya medicines and healing techniques.

The philosophy of the Kellawaya healers is best expressed by one of its practitioners:

> Disease in a man, woman, or child is generally brought about when a natural system breaks down and begins to dysfunction. But one must understand how and why this dysfunction comes about. And the afflicted person no longer has the strength to try to discover alone the reasons for his or her sickness. Sometimes the sick person does not possess the strength to heal himself alone. One person's sickness is everyone's concern. Of the living as well as the dead, of those present and those who are away. This is true also because sickness and healing are matters which are affected by language.

Protecting the environment is not an easy problem, and rural communities have taken a long time to understand the impact the environment can have on their well-being and development. But it would appear that they have not taken quite as long as governments to understand the necessity of protecting and enhancing the environment.

One significant example of this is the international programme to fight desertification which was approved several years ago, yet which most concerned governments have as yet to act upon. In contrast, NGOs and project leaders have taken numerous initiatives to protect the environment and to include environmental criteria in their development projects.

In Ecuador: 'An important aspect of NGO work to further development concerns environmental action. NGO reforestation programmes have been instrumental in planting over 700,000 eucalyptus trees every year.'

However, this is not yet an overwhelming trend among NGOs. Out of the projects visited only 23 had carried out reforestation or agro-forestry programmes and only eight promoted the use of alternative energy sources for fuel and cooking.

Energy resources. We found only two projects which advocated using fuel-efficient ovens in order to save wood.

> ... making eathern ovens to replace traditional three-stone outdoor hearths. These fuel-efficient ovens help save wood by improving combustion. We have also developed compressed fuel brickettes made of cow dung and straw from millet stalks to replace wood.

Many organizations have tried to introduce this type of improved oven in African rural areas. However, after a while villagers abandoned the new ovens and the women returned to their traditional hearths — introduction of the new technology had not been accompanied by an appropriate education programme to explain to villagers the advantages of using fuel-saving ovens.

Biogas does not appear to have a very broad impact either. In each case where biogas was introduced, whether in Togo, Egypt, or India where we saw the results of these efforts, it did not succeed for a variety of reasons. In Egypt, the biogas production facility we visited was part of a project which was almost fraudulent. In India, 'A few biogas systems are used for cooking, but on the whole biogas technology has been a failure. People do not like to cook with gas which is produced from human wastes: they prefer using animal dung.' An ambitious biogas programme was set up in Togo, but owing to limited resources it has not been very successful. Its principal achievement until now has been to have encouraged villagers to instal latrines in their village.

Reforestation. Reforestation has been much more widely practised.

> The women folk asked the Naam affiliates to assist them in reforestation efforts, since they are burdened with the task of finding firewood for cooking. The choice of areas for planting trees was made in accordance with the degree of erosion of the terrain and the needs of the chosen trees. (Burkina Faso)

> The NGO has set up its own greenhouse and sells saplings at the subsidized price of five sucres each, including transportation to the

planting sites in the rural communities as well as a follow-up training programme to explain how to plant and care for the trees. Initially the peasants were not too keen on joining the reforestation *mingas* because they were afraid the government would take over the new forests. However, they finally decided to pitch in and 4,000,000 trees have been planted in the past ten years.

We have set up greenhouses for trees and flowers, planted lemon, mango, and eucalyptus trees. Thus we can show visitors that it is possible to encourage people to take a positive initiative. (Bolivia)

In Kenya we visited another greenhouse which had been created by women's groups. One of the local villagers who attended agro-forestry classes and who knows the Latin names of all of the species has returned to her village to show the other women how to plant and care for the trees.

Some varieties are used for fence posts or building granaries, while others help enrich the soil and are planted in conjunction with other varieties such as coffee trees. Fast-growing varieties can be used as a source of firewood and charcoal. We can supply hardwoods for construction, etc. The women say that trees are more important than men, since they use them for cooking, building, and maintaining their homes.

The initial resistance and mistakes have now been overcome and the days when NGOs 'had villagers planting trees without rhyme or reason' are over. Now most NGOs know what varieties to plant in accordance with local conditions whether it be in Asia, Africa, or Latin America.

It will probably take decades before the damage caused by the indiscriminate cutting of trees is repaired, but a step in the right direction has been taken thanks to the efforts of NGOs.

Learning how to produce more and of better quality
This is a basic concern in 54 of the projects we visited. It is also the primary goal of communities which are determined to achieve food self-sufficiency and if possible the production of surpluses which can be sold to produce income for local populations.

With a reasonable amount of effort and capital these valleys — if they were more accessible — could become centres for intensive food production. But for the time being malnutrition remains a chronic problem and the soil has become almost infertile since the peasants do not have the means to buy fertilizers.

To achieve food self-sufficiency a major effort is generally made to improve the quality of the soil and to promote a more rational use of the land. In most areas the soil has been depleted of its nutrients through overcultivation and inappropriate use. It needs to be regenerated. The problem is all the more acute in areas where arable land is scarce either because of the type of terrain (mountainous or infertile areas) or because the land can no longer feed a rapidly growing population.

> We can longer survive by farming these lands which are becoming infertile and which produce less each year.
> The four communities have a total area of arable land of 716 hectares for 711 families — in other words barely more than one hectare per family. The poorest of these communities has only an average of 0.6 hectare per family to farm.

In some cases the depletion of the soil has been caused by drought, a world-wide phenomenon in recent years.

> The Andean valleys and the Altiplano have been suffering from severe drought for the past sixty years. This is the worst drought that has ever been experienced here.

In other areas, floods have rendered the land infertile.

> Available arable land has decreased by 208,900 hectares while food production has gone down 29%. Over 1,600,000 rural villagers have been affected by this disaster.

In 42 of the projects visited we found programmes for improving the quality and use of soils. This improvement of soils entails finding appropriate ways to help prevent continued deterioration of farming land.

CONTROLLING EROSION

In most of the projects which address the problem of erosion, the most frequently applied remedy was reforestation in order to stop loss of topsoil which is carried away by rain or wind.

IMPROVING IRRIGATION

We have already mentioned this problem, but it also belongs in this chapter since irrigation is an important means of improving land use and increasing cultivated areas. Water problems are, of course, part of 'basic needs' — without water no development is possible — and require the mastering and use of appropriate technologies.

In one project seen in Western Bengal, an irrigation scheme was set up which has enabled farmers to obtain an extra crop of rice, wheat, and some vegetables each year, and in some cases two extra harvests. Water can work miracles: a cabbage weighing six to eight kilos can be grown in 40 days.

Located in the valley of the Ganges about 25 miles from Calcutta, the area where the irrigation project was set up endures eight dry months each year after four months of torrential rains. The project, which began in 1981, initially covered an area equivalent to 8,000 hectares and another 2,000 hectares have been irrigated thanks to a small additional investment amounting to around 100 dollars per hectare. There is potentially a further 4–5,000 hectares available for irrigation. The total increase in local food crops obtained thanks to this project is estimated at 60–70%, a noteworthy achievement: the irrigated farms provide food for over 100,000 people in the surrounding areas.

The entire project was set up to restore and extend a former irrigation system which had not been used and had gradually deteriorated. Over 50 miles of canals and ditches were cleared and extended by the collective work of village teams, working with the simplest of tools. In this case, as in others we shall cite, the project promoters were wise enough to rehabilitate an existing system and to use local manpower instead of introducing sophisticated technologies or costly equipment.

SOIL MANAGEMENT

In most cases soil management schemes are applied using simple technologies and available resources which are adapted to local conditions and customs.

> Our first need was to avoid the brutal introduction in these communities of ultra-modern technologies, even if we had the wherewithal to do so.
>
> The Andean peasants have an extremely rich store of agricultural and pastoral traditions which are still of value today. This 'capital' lies dormant waiting to be used for the benefit of the very populations for which it represents their birthright. It is up to us to put it to use.
>
> The members of these communities have begun to practise crop rotation once again. They now also use natural fertilizers and compost made from algae which abound in the swamps around the lake. They add chemical fertilizers which they can now buy using the income from the sale of their potatoes.

But NGO project leaders also know when it is wise to introduce new methods and technologies.

We introduced a new variety of legume which helped retain top soil on hillside terraces while at the same time it enhanced the nitrogen level of the soil.

We planted climbing lucerne clover (*Vicia villosa*) on land that was destined to lie fallow for seven years in order to restore essential nutrients to soils which had lost their fertility because they had been overfarmed and crops had not been rotated. Besides replenishing soils with essential organic material lucerne also provides fodder for livestock.

We have learned how to use straw on the rows of the fields in order to retain humidity and provide natural fertilizer once it has been burned before the land is ploughed. Now we systematically use organic material to mulch the soil. This material gradually becomes compost and helps micro-organisms to develop, thereby restoring vital nutrients to depleted soils. This technique also prevents erosion, ensures an even soil temperature, and stops weed growth.

We always use the dead stalks and all the organic material left over from the harvest — whether from beans, maize, or sweet potato — to cover the soil before replanting so that it will be protected and organically fertilized.

IMPROVING LAND USE

There was no way of increasing the acreage each family had to farm, so we decided to try to improve yields through crop rotation and a more rational use of the land. Before, the people here only farmed from March to September. After we had worked with them and trained them, encouraging them to start family rice paddies, they realized that they could rotate crops and farm their plots all the year round. From February to May they could grow sweet potatoes and maize. Then in May rice could be planted in the paddies. After the rice harvest in November the land could be used for growing beans, tomatoes, squash, and other vegetables ... They learned how to plant in rows instead of merely sowing haphazardly. This enabled them to interplant millet and fruit trees.

I used to plant peanuts ten centimetres apart, but now I've learned to leave at least twenty centimetres between plants, and my yields have tripled since the plants have more room to grow. My manioc harvests have also tripled.

These spectacular results are not always to the liking of the farmers who remain attached to their traditional methods.

People thought that I had gone to see the witch doctor since my peanut crop did so well.

Lazy villagers come and steal from my fields.

A second major area for concern for NGOs in their efforts to improve agricultural productivity is seed selection. This was the case in 38 of the projects visited.

Most peasants do not immediately recognize the need for proper seed selection. They often rely on nature to do this for them and are content to plant and reap whatever they can from their land.

We tried to help the Andean peasants understand the importance of promoting proper seed selection, just as their ancient Incan and pre-Incan predecessors did. What this meant was that they would have to plant in order to produce better varieties of potatoes for seeding instead of eating the entire crop.

The greatest achievement of the project is that it helped us improve our varieties of potato. Now with 100 kilos of seeding potatoes we can obtain harvests of 700 kilos. Before, the most we could harvest was 400 kilos.

We now use red maize varieties that give better yields.

In one demonstration farm we visited in the Philippines new seed varieties are carefully tested and tried out so that their advantages and weaknesses are well known before they are introduced.

The family farmer cannot plant the varieties we recommend unless we have already tested them over more than one harvest. We must ensure that we have allowed ample time to experiment with new varieties and farming methods before we encourage farmers to use them. In our experimental farm we have a variety of different plots where we compare different varieties of a crop in varying conditions. For example, on one plot we have three different varieties of rice growing, using different methods with each one and which will no doubt produce very different results. In this way we can select the best variety for each type of land and farming situation.

We also have two hectares divided into eighteen different plots where we are experimenting with Japanese farming methods. These eighteen sections correspond to the complete eighteen-week growth cycle of rice. Then we also have a half-hectare plot where we are working with vegetable crops which can be easily farmed by villagers.

This experimental farm also produces enough food for volunteer workers or trainees who attend our extension programme. Our ultimate goal is to get the people here to learn how to develop their own improved seed varieties which will enable them to increase their yields.

NGO workers are also concerned with crop diversification and rotation. Crop rotation and the wise use of land help maintain healthy soils, improve yields and ultimately benefit rural populations by ensuring greater food self-sufficiency. Another notable advantage of scientific farming techniques is that they can help develop more nutritional grain and vegetable crops and thereby not only increase the quantity of food available in the rural Third World but also improve the quality of food crops.

We have reintroduced the traditional high-altitude crops of the Andes — quinoa and rye — in the community plots. And then, progressively, we have encouraged *campesinos* to try new food crops such as turnips, beets, and cabbages. Thanks to these new crops we have been able to reduce malnutrition caused by the drought and also to improve the nutrition of livestock by feeding animals on the parts of these plants not consumed by humans.

We teach them how to farm new crops that are suited to the local environment, while at the same time we encourage them to diversify their diet and try new foods such as certain types of beans and peas.

Each of the members of the community has his own family garden where he can plant the crops he has already tested on our experimental farm. He can do this without fear of failure or of wasting the precious little acreage he has to feed himself and his family.

I know how difficult it is to get people to change their eating habits, but nevertheless I have been successful in introducing new high-yield food crops which have a much higher protein content than the traditional food sources. First of all I prepare dishes with the new foods and let the villagers try them when I make my tour of the communities.

One of the major tasks of the project promoters is to persuade the peasants to try farming short-cycle millet which enables them to have two harvests a year instead of one. This in itself helps increase food production and encourages the peasants to farm for their own consumption despite the spread of cotton farming.

Learning to produce more and better also involves mastering new and appropriate technologies which help make work easier and more productive.

Thanks to the introduction of a new type of plough we can now increase the acreage of land used for farming local food crops.

People are learning how to water plants properly and also how to graft trees.

> Here people say that bullocks can't be used for work; I didn't think it was possible.

Men and women from this village in Togo were taken to another area to see exactly what could be done to improve farming when animals were used to pull ploughs.

> If I had been younger, I would have packed and moved over here, but since I am married I must stay here.

> Now that I have seen it I am going to try it out, even if the others say it's impossible. I am certain that if I succeed others will want to imitate me.

> Now I am thinking how I can start farming using bullocks to pull my plough. I am going to try to buy the animals with someone else so that we can share them.

PROPER USE OF FERTILIZERS

Even if there were a temptation to improve yields by using commercial fertilizers, most of the communities we visited could not afford to do so; therefore from necessity, they try natural fertilizers or go back to using them.

In Bangladesh, 'Chemical fertilizers are very expensive, and when you use them you need to have insecticides also. Composting involves more work, but the organic nutrients tend to stay in the ground and do not pollute it.'

It is not always easy to persuade rural villagers to use this type of fertilizer, but here are two examples of the many innovative ways rural communities find for obtaining and using fertilizers.

> At the centre we try to teach peasants how to use a new latrine system: in a small hut they dig two holes and when one is almost full they fill it with leaves and wait six months before they extract a high quality organic fertilizer which can be used on all crops.

In the Philippines, villagers grow aquatic plants in rice paddies which are fallow during crop rotation; these are harvested and used as compost.

IMPROVING LIVESTOCK

In most of the projects we visited villagers lacked minimum protein in their diet. Although grains can be nourishing in terms of protein content, in many instances even this source is limited by a variety of factors including drought or lack of land for farming.

Many children are undernourished, some with symptoms of kwashiorkor, since they do not receive adequate protein from the time they are weaned. Many adults also suffer from protein deficiency. Most projects endeavour to find sources for supplementing protein intake among the local populations, commonly by trying to introduce some form of livestock.

Among the projects we visited 25 were in some way concerned with improving existing livestock, while 15 had introduced species new to the community. Small livestock has already been discussed in connection with 'basic needs'. It goes without saying that the climate, the environment, and local customs are determining factors with regard to the introduction or improvement of stock-raising.

Among the projects visited the types of livestock most frequently encountered, other than smaller farm animals such as pigs and poultry, were cattle and goats. In the case of cattle, most of the projects were concerned with improving existing breeds or increasing herds.

> For the past three years we have been practising artificial insemination in order to improve our breeds so that they produce more meat and milk.

Goat-keeping is also expanding throughout the Third World, especially in women's projects. The principal advantage of goats is that they require only a small investment, and they multiply very quickly. In the Kenyan project described in Chapter 10:

> The women thought goats would be an ideal source of income since as the animals proliferate they produce enough income so that the women can start savings accounts. They were convinced that the goats would multiply even faster than their bank accounts.

In Bangladesh, one project had found an innovative approach to goat-raising:

> Here we tried the 'poor women's goat' programme which has been implemented in a number of Bengali villages. This programme gives each village co-operative kids to distribute among the poorest women. Each woman must care for the goat until it in turn gives birth to a kid. The nanny is then sold by the programme and the woman receives half of the money. A qualified inspector regularly visits the women to see that the goats are being properly fed and cared for.

The livestock most frequently encountered were, of course, the traditional farm animals, pigs, chickens, turkeys, ducks, and in some parts of the world rabbits and guinea-pigs. In some villages even these animals were new to the community.

Project workers teach villagers how to feed and care for livestock, as in one of the projects visited in the Philippines where chickens and pigs are fed with a mixture of rice chaff and the aquatic plants grown in fallow rice fields. Villagers also learn how to protect animals from disease through inoculations and proper hygiene. These animals provide supplemental sources of protein and are used to increase income.

As was mentioned in connection with 'basic needs', some projects use bee-keeping as an auxiliary activity for rural families. A family may have one or two hives and produce just enough honey for its own needs or that of a small village. On the other hand, there are projects which have made bee-keeping a large-scale activity which becomes the main source of income for the community. This was the case in one project in northern Peru.

> Within two years, when the community has mastered the techniques of producing honey, they will join the Departmental Committee of Honey Producers. They can then map out a strategy for increasing local production and diversifying the products from the hives — royal jelly, hydromel, and beeswax. This will be a great stride forward for several communities in the Lambayeque Department.

In Kenya, in the Kibwezi area, bee-keeping provides one community with a solid source of revenue and the means of setting up a local industry. Women collect the honey from their family hives and process it in a small factory which the women themselves built. In order to do so they had to learn how to make adobe bricks, until then considered men's work. The honey processing factory was built thanks to the blueprints and supervision of a volunteer NGO worker. Sixty women from the village were given specialized training in apiculture and were awarded diplomas of excellence in bee-keeping.

The honey (which they buy in for processing, since the hives do not yet produce enough) is being marketed with the village label and the women are planning to open their own shop, which again they will build with their own hands. There they hope to sell other products from the village hives.

This project, which also includes goat-keeeping, crafts, and a large-scale reforestation scheme to provide flora for the bees, should eventually provide enough income to support over 2,500 families.

SMALL AGROFOOD AND CRAFTS INDUSTRIES

As we have seen in the case of bee-keeping, many small-scale agricultural projects eventually lead to the processing and marketing of agricultural products. For example, in a number of African rural areas thanks to NGO projects villagers have set up community grain mills for processing millet and other grain crops into flour for local consumption.

This type of mill is almost an economic necessity for most projects, for otherwise villagers have to rely on commercial mills and other intermediaries who take a large cut of their meagre earnings to mill the peasants' grain. The other alternative, of course, is to have the women folk painfully grind the millet by hand, using the traditional household millstone. This task takes a great deal of time and effort.

In one project in Burkina Faso, village mills are set up with the help of long-term, low-interest loans (six years at 7%) made to the women's village organizations. As the loans are repaid into a revolving fund, new mills are financed in neighbouring villages — the so-called 'daughters' mills' — or more mills — the 'sons' mills' — are underwritten in the original village. In the vernacular, the 'daughters' leave the village while the 'sons' stay at home to help their fathers.

In a similar project in Zaire, 'The community mill helps reduce the women's workload. It also provides extra income for the village, since the mill not only grinds grain from neighbouring villages but also markets its own flour. This small project is a fairly lucrative undertaking.' The villagers make good use of the mill, since its rates are lower than those of the competing private enterprises, and it has yet another advantage for the villagers.

> The presence here of the mill has helped raise the price of soya, which is a good thing for the local farmers. In fact, by purchasing soya from neighbouring producers the mill has helped keep prices up.

In Nigeria, in an area where palm oil has traditionally been produced, villagers organized a plantation and oil processing plant which services three villages. The farming and processing of palm fruit enables villagers to earn extra income and it ensures employment for a number of the villagers.

I have four children, and before the project was started here I was forced to ask my father-in-law for food when half of our cassava crop was eaten by insects. I had to replace the cassava they gave me the following year, and if it had been a poor crop we would not have had anything to eat. The palm fruit crop was of some help, but then the middlemen from Umahia would band together and keep the purchase price of palm fruit as low as possible. We often didn't even have enough money left over to buy maize to eat.

I began working on the palm plantation and afterwards I asked if I could have a job with the palm oil factory. I learned how to repair and maintain the machines as well as the electric motors. And now I can make a decent living while my wife and daughters grow vegetables. Now we can survive.

In Ecuador, in Bolivar province, one NGO project trains villagers and finances the production of cheese and sausages by the local co-operative. The technology used in this small food-processing industry is modelled on Swiss cheese-making and the products are sold mainly in a shop the co-operative runs in Quito. It makes excellent Gruyère, Gorgonzola, and Parmesan cheeses from the milk of cows belonging to the members of the co-operative, as well as goat's-milk cheese. The production has first and foremost enabled the local farmers to improve their own diet and then to sell their surplus in the capital. In Ecuador cheese and sausages are considered luxury items.

In Zaire, an association of young peasants has set up a community shop so that villagers are no longer victims of hoarding and speculation on basic items.

> This small project, which was set up to provide the local population with sorely needed basic commodities, will no doubt grow in coming years as a whole network of village shops is set up around the country. Thanks to these shops the prices of basic goods can be kept in line with the demand of rural villagers for low-priced items. And by their very existence they force itinerant merchants to lower their prices.

In Burkina Faso, pig-raising has been introduced in one project. Interested villagers are given low-interest loans to get started. One of the pork producers 'is a cook who sells his pork already prepared. His hams are famous throughout the area and many local expatriates buy them. The income from this business has enabled this man to finance his children's education. Moreover, he is now even able to buy enough millet to feed his family properly and to have electricity in his home.'

In the Philippines a marmalade factory was set up to finance local schooling for the children of a minority tribe which lives in an isolated area and is discriminated against by the inhabitants of the valleys below.

Here in the mountains we have found enough wild berries to use in making jellies and marmalades in our factory

The preserves, bottled and labelled with the name of the project, are sold in shops in Manila. This project also helped local villagers start vegetable gardening in order to diversify the local diet, which up until then consisted mainly of sweet potatoes.

The other main branch of small-scale industry we encountered among the projects was crafts. Local crafts industries are generally aimed at supplying local needs in terms of clothing and small utensils, providing a source of income to villagers through local sale or even export. Among local crafts industries we might mention one that produces hoes and other small farming implements which are manufactured in a small village foundry.

In Burkina Faso, a small local industry produces pots.

It employs four people. The raw material comes from France as aluminium ingots, or is recycled metal parts from old car bodies.

We encountered several small foundries which produced agricultural tools used by local farmers, as well as primitive brickyards or kilns which made bricks used in building projects promoted by NGOs and the undertaking already mentioned, which makes fibrocement sheets for roofing. There is no dearth of projects and successful achievements in an area where most NGOs and local participants have shown great innovativeness and imagination. In many instances secondary productive activities branch out from the initial scheme.

Most of the small crafts industries which produce items for export are located in Asian countries, although we did see some in Africa and Latin America. The products are varied — pottery, baskets, batiks, clothing, toys, and various small novelty items. Although most of these items are produced for export or for sale to tourists, rarely did we find projects which had made efforts to study potential markets before production was begun. This was the case in a number of projects we visited in Bangladesh. In one of them several workshops had been set up: burlap bags, carpentry, shoes, fibreglass. But the people working in the project receive a salary from the project, amounting to a circuitous way of providing assistance rather than helping them become self-reliant. Furthermore, a part of this project which was to have produced silk screens has been closed down: because of drought, silkworms are no longer available. In another project a crafts industry based on burlap was closed since there did not appear to be a good market for burlap artefacts.

We did see one very successful wicker furniture industry which produces custom-made pieces to order from wholesalers in Europe (mainly in West Germany), but for every project that succeeds several are dropped because project promoters fail to address properly the problems involved in exporting goods — the paperwork, export licences, and so on.

Our aim is not to criticize what has been accomplished, but simply to show that for a crafts industry geared to export to succeed it must be able to compete successfully on the world market. Goodwill is not enough.

Learning how to participate actively in the development process
This is perhaps the one area in which NGOs can be decisive in helping rural villagers address development goals. In most instances before the NGO was set up locally, or before it commited itself to a project, the local population was at mere subsistence level.

Most Third World rural populations are at the mercy of supply and demand; it is therefore imperative that they learn how to gauge the market and how to use its mechanisms to their benefit. One of the major obstacles to this is the isolation which frequently inhibits communication between rural areas and the economic and administrative centres of a country. Even when villagers have products to market, they are often not materially in a position to do so.

> The most serious problem confronted by rural villages is their complete isolation. Access is generally only possible on foot, or during dry periods with four-wheel drive vehicles. For the moment there are no lorries coming through here, and during the winter even with a car it is hard to reach the village.

> What holds back development everywhere in Africa is the fact that for weeks upon end communications are shut down between rural villages and urban areas. If people and goods do not have a minimum amount of mobility and there is no way of marketing goods, then rural villages start to decline and inevitably die.

The only way of reaching the village was across a wide river which was full of rapids. One enterprising man decided to make the most of this situation and build a private bridge across the river. He charges a toll to cross the bridge, and the proceeds of the sale of most of the peasants' crops goes to pay the right of passage over the bridge.

We don't have the means of taking our crops to market in La Paz. Therefore the lorry drivers are in a position to set the price they want. It takes my wife and myself two days on foot to take our crop down to the lorry in the valley. I thought the lorry driver would give us 7,000 pesos a bag for my maize like he did the others, but he would only pay me 4,000. What could I do? I had to accept.

Until recently our agricultural surplus simply sat at the entrance to the village where it slowly rotted, while the villagers waited for a hypothetical buyer.

In circumstances like these, when villagers begin to understand that united they are stronger, they begin to act.

They carve a road, by hand if necessary, out of the side of a mountain as we have seen in Peru; they build a track to save four hours of travel, as was the case in one area of Mali; they build a bridge in Indonesia 'which enables them to save the money they had been paying in tolls to cross a private bridge'; they put aside their savings until they have enough to buy a lorry to take their crops to market ... Then, and only then, are they in a position to take on the more serious problem of dealing with the middlemen who often exploit their ignorance or take advantage of their vulnerability.

If the peasants continue to be ruthlessly exploited by middlemen, they will never be able to achieve economic progress.

The lorries haul in fertilizers to sell, and the farmers are forced to pay whatever price the drivers ask if they want fertilizers for their crops.

This, of course, is part of a problem we have already described, that of 'profiteers and pirates', but it is clear that if these obstacles cannot all be overcome at once, at least NGOs are gradually beginning to address them.

In order to combat speculation in basic commodities, NGOs can, for example, help set up consumers' co-operatives which will enable villagers to obtain vital supplies at more reasonable prices. Community shops can also help rural villagers to obtain basic products locally at low cost; these shops can also help bring down market prices for these products, as we have seen in Zaire. Community granaries are yet another way of reducing the power of middlemen, since they can purchase farmers' crops for marketing when prices are high and at the same time they provide rural villagers with the seed and flour they need, bridging, as it were, the gap between harvests. One such granary was visited in Burkina Faso.

Rural co-operatives are another fundamental instrument enabling Third World farmers to improve production and marketing of agricultural produce. We saw a number of successful co-operatives in the course of the study.

Credit unions and savings co-operatives are being developed in many rural areas. We visited several of these which functioned admirably, enabling farmers to finance their activities without having to assume great financial burdens or resort to the handouts of aid institutions or government subsidies. In some areas project workers teach villagers how to start savings schemes, or assist them in finding low-interest loans from local banks wherever possible.

The results achieved up to now have been remarkable, even where savings co-operatives are a relatively new phenomenon. In Togo, the leaders of one co-operative are planning a development project which should be very beneficial to its members. They hope to acquire a small bus for transporting the tourists who will be arriving at the recently inaugurated international airport nearby; there are also plans to purchase land for starting a community vegetable garden and rice farm.

One extremely positive characteristic of rural co-operatives, whether they are set up to encourage savings, to provide sources of credit, or geared to agricultural production and marketing, is that they allow local groups to tackle their problems themselves without being reduced to soliciting hand-outs from aid organizations. Instead of grants they request loans in money or in kind — seed, agricultural equipment — which in the great majority of cases they scrupulously reimburse.

In Bangladesh, GK makes loans to small farmers — money, seed, or fertilizers — while at the same time providing advice and training to villagers on how to make wise use of their capital, avoiding falling prey to moneylenders. To qualify to receive a loan of 100 TK (about $3.50), the farmer undertakes to plant crops of his own choice — sugar cane, jute, mustard, vegetables, etc. — and to reimburse the loan within five years along with ten kilos of rice.

Half the rice will be retained by the farmer for use between harvests — a sort of forced 'saving for a rainy day' plan. The remaining five kilos of rice is stocked by the community and sold on the open market when the price of rice is sufficiently high. This income goes back into the co-operative's fund.

We are told that in this region the interest charged by money-lenders can be as high as 300% per year. Government loans, underwritten by the World Bank, are available at 13% interest, but the red tape and extensive paperwork discourage local farmers from applying: only the more educated and affluent farmers take advantage of government loans. The poorer farmers, and rural villagers who do not have land for farming, have only the NGO to turn to in order to finance their activities.

In Bolivia, CIPCA makes loans to peasants for the purchase of seed and agricultural inputs such as fertilizers and insecticides, as well as for acquisition or improvement of livestock. The NGO charges an annual 5% rate to insure the loans plus an interest rate of 2.4%, which is extraordinary considering the annual inflation rate in Bolivia surpasses 2000%. When a villager borrows he undertakes to repay the loan by the following year. He must therefore pay back part of it with produce.

In Colombia, loans provided by a local NGO to individual farmers must be guaranteed and approved by the community. The loans must be reimbursed on the day they fall due. If necessary a new loan is negotiated for the peasant, but not before he has shown that he is willing and able to pay back the initial one, thereby proving that he is a responsible economic agent.

In Zaire, one NGO encourages peasants to start savings schemes. Interest on their savings is rather low by Western standards — 4% yearly — but the local villagers are not attracted by the rates, rather by the fact that they are putting their money in a safe place where it will not be stolen or spent. They also gain future access to credit.

Savings, loans, and investment plans are readily adopted by rural communities, and they are quick to learn how to take advantage of the expanded opportunities provided by these means. What is new to them is that they can control these mechanisms rather than be victimized by unscrupulous moneylenders, or risk losing their land and their livelihood. These locally administered credit institutions have given many rural communities a whole new lease of life.

The important part women play in ensuring that proper use is made of savings should be emphasized. In most agrarian Third World societies women hold the purse strings, and any action to promote savings and proper management of resources ultimately depends on them. The action of most NGOs in this area depends on women's groups.

CHAPTER 13
Obstacles and Limits to NGO Action

We have seen how NGOs work with and support rural communities which, without them, would be left outside the development process. Most of the projects we visited are still too recent (two out of three are barely ten years old) to determine whether or not they have been successful, in other words, whether they have been able to achieve the goals which they have set for themselves and, in particular, whether they have had a measurable impact on the living conditions of the communities involved. In some cases the reasons for their inability to fulfil objectives were apparent, and it would not always be fair to consider them as failures.

The purpose of this analysis is not to criticize particular organizations, but rather to understand the circumstances which cause a project to advance or to stagnate, so that errors and pitfalls can be avoided by others in future.

In light of the findings of our study, it is obvious that rural development remains essentially a prerogative of government even though NGOs may be able to influence opinion, lobby in favour of the interests of the rural poor, and in some cases force the state to take urgent measures.

NGOs are often not in a position directly to assail all the factors of impoverishment mentioned earlier, but are nevertheless forced to consider urgently the severe impact of these factors on rural populations in the Third World. In the task of fostering the factors of development, on the other hand, NGOs have abundantly demonstrated their imagination and efficiency by helping rural communities to understand and adequately address the problems they face in agriculture, health, education, and training. However, they are not always able to meet the challenge posed by the formidable problems encountered throughout the rural Third World.

The obstacles which lead to the breakdown or failure of projects are of two kinds: those related to the project environment and those which are entirely within the responsibility of NGOs themselves, whether they concern methodology, project personnel, or resources.

OBSTACLES DUE TO OUTSIDE CIRCUMSTANCES

The obstacles to successful project implementation met most frequently in the areas visited fall into six main categories.

Soil and climate

> The lack of rain has become chronic and has slowed down our progress.

> There is no water; the wells are dry and we don't have enough money to dig new ones.

> We hit bedrock when we dig and we can't use dynamite, since you need a special authorization to blast from the Office of the President.

Domestic political circumstances
> The absence of a development policy.

> Unfavourable economic policy (for example, priority given to industrialization versus rural development, cash-cropping instead of domestic food production).

Local economic and administrative environment
> officials
> middlemen
> corruption.

Indifference or resistance of villagers

Demands of lending institutions and sponsors

> Soon we shall be spending all of our time filing forms and loan applications. (Kenya)

> We are forced to use the money we receive strictly for the earmarked projects, even if an emergency arises in the meantime. (Mali)

Lack of financial resources
NGOs are often unable to secure sufficient funding to meet their development goals. They frequently have to deal with financial

shortfalls, and this situation will probably worsen for two reasons:

development projects are growing and new ones are launched every day; each new project has to compete for funding;

funding from private sources has not kept pace with new development initiatives, and the general trend is for private funding to decrease.

This lack of financial resources is a major cause of project failure, mostly when a community has been prepared to start a project which has to be adjourned or abandoned when funding does not become available.

Lack of funds has caused the project to lose its momentum. (Bangladesh)

We know that because we cannot provide food and housing for the villagers who attend our training programme, fewer people are coming now. We simply can't afford to house and feed them, and it is quite difficult for them to travel 20 miles every day to attend courses. (Togo)

This lack of funds is a continual source of complaint, especially among projects which have been set up by grassroots groups. In many cases they have explored every possible local avenue for funding and are left with nowhere to turn. At this point a small financial shot in the arm would probably make all the difference; without it the project is often condemned to stagnation or failure.

NGO-RELATED OBSTACLES

Some of these obstacles are attributable to NGO shortcomings:

although they have the best intentions, they often lack basic preparation, familiarity with the environment, technical knowledge, and teaching experience.

in many instances they lack an overall strategy and methodology in the countries where they are involved. At times they fail to adapt their policies to changing circumstances in the areas where they work.

they are jealous of their independence and often refuse to co-operate with other NGOs or with local officials.

the local follow-up of their actions is generally insufficient, mostly owing to lack of personnel or financial resources.

But in most cases these shortcomings are but the other side of the coin, for NGOs have great qualities which should be stressed:

their dedication and generosity is universally acknowledged.

they stand up for the poorest and most oppressed sectors of the population in the most marginal areas.

they are extremely flexible and able to respond rapidly.

they are attentive to the needs of local populations and their personnel are strongly motivated.

they are able to secure private and public funding and the cost of their operations is relatively low.

they are in a position to take risks, experiment, and innovate.

they promote the use of local resources.

One of the surest signs that a project has failed to fulfil its objectives is when its beneficiaries do not take an active interest and do not become directly involved. In other words, the project has been set up *for* them, but not *by* them.

It would seem that the people are considered as passive beneficiaries of the project and not as dynamic partners from the very beginning of the operation. They are not directly involved in setting the project goals which the NGO workers are responsible for proposing. (Indonesia)

To have been forced to pay a villager from Ambana to do the masonry work on the new wing of the local clinic shows that the NGO has not managed to motivate villagers to participate in the project. (Bolivia)

Since the project was 'completed' two years ago and the local community assumed direct responsibility, it operates like an ordinary farm. A few families continue to work the community plots, but there are no longer any training courses available, nor do people in the surrounding communities seem interested in learning how to improve their farming techniques. This uninterest and passivity are understandable — the local population and communities which were chosen for the project were not given adequate grounding. No preliminary study of the social and cultural factors was made. Moreover, the peasants are not particularly motivated to work together since many families receive cash grants from a US NGO which provides money directly to parents to feed their 'poor' children. (Bolivia)

These examples typify a situation that is frequently encountered among rural projects throughout the Third World. The following observations may throw some light on the causes of this type of obstacle to NGO rural development efforts.

Ill-preparedness
The qualifications of the NGO and its understanding of the local social and cultural environment determine the ultimate success and effectiveness of a project. Unfortunately NGO workers are often ill-prepared for their task. Good intentions cannot replace technical expertise:

> The NGO started a reforestation and water development scheme without technical knowledge in these areas. Now there are specialists in the field, but at the beginning the NGO workers simply recommended that villagers 'plant three hectares of trees' in one area without any regard whatsoever for the species of trees to be planted, the right time to plant, or any real follow-up programme. (Environment Liaison Centre, Nairobi)

> Advocating gardening as a local solution to the food problem in the villages has caused a severe shortage of water. It was then decided to start a water and soil conservation programme, but it was very nearly too late. (Burkina Faso)

> The failure rate of NGO water projects is simply staggering. Throughout the developing world 70–80% of these new wells and pumps are no longer operational. (United Nations Environment Programme)

> Some of the Centre's activities have failed dismally: biogas, brickmaking, weaving, and crafts. These activities were launched without having made the least attempt to study the potential market for the products. Pottery was also a failure since the clay was not of good quality. (India)

> Economic results are low when one considers the level of investment. This is something that does not seem to have particularly preoccupied the NGO; it seemed secondary. (Bangladesh)

> There were some serious mistakes in explaining the purpose of the project — for example, the people thought that loans were grants. (Mali)

> No consideration was given to local expertise and traditional technologies — many good opportunities were lost. (Burkina Faso)

Another serious obstacle to implementing rural development policy is Northern NGOs' frequent ignorance of the local social and cultural environment. Since most of the NGO workers from

Northern organizations — and sometimes even those from the Third World — have an urban background, the rural environment is alien to them. They are often unable properly to perceive and understand the problems of Third World peasants and the peculiarities of the social and economic environment in rural areas.

Some development organizations which have been working in the field for long periods continue to work with rural groups without properly understanding the local cultural factors, the basic motivations and beliefs of the people who are involved in a project.

Thus, as we have already seen, the important role of women in Third World rural societies is often underestimated. Depriving women of their traditional role, albeit with the best of intentions, by following Western development models, generally causes projects to fail or at least to stagnate.

There are numerous codes of behaviour in rural societies which cannot be ignored by those who are responsible for implementing a project. Projects which do not take these specific behaviour patterns into account can hardly be considered as examples of successful development.

In Kenya, for example, if NGO workers fail to understand the importance and significance that the dominant Kikuyu tribe attributes to having a large family, no coherent family planning policy can be successfully advocated or implemented.

Yet another idiosyncrasy encountered in Kenya can account for the failure of NGO development efforts, since they overlooked a fundamental belief system. The Wakamba tribe refuse to use metal farming tools since they believe that they will cause a drought. This belief can be traced back to the period when the British were building the Kampala–Mombasa railroad: Wakamba tribesmen associated the terrible drought experienced at that time with the iron rails which crossed their farmland.

Another interesting example of the importance of cultural factors is given by the Masai tribesmen, who believe that a Masai must have a large herd of cattle in order to ensure respect and social standing. In fact most of their cattle can hardly survive on the disappearing natural pastures — the carcases of dead cattle mark the passage of their continual migrations in search of pastures. Grazing rights are a matter of perpetual conflict with other tribes, often ending in deadly confrontations. The Masai will certainly disappear before they will abandon their almost religious attachment to their large herds of starving cattle.

Questionable motivation

Some NGOs seem intent on acting independently without regard for what is going on in neighbouring villages, often with the result that one group's actions can threaten another's achievements. We have already seen the detrimental effects in Bolivia of some international NGOs' aid and assistance programmes which channel money and food directly into highland communities. This type of aid discourages development efforts and makes charity cases out of rural populations.

Most of these errors and oversights are caused by a lack of knowledge and proper preparation, despite the good intentions and well-meaning efforts of most organizations. Other less ingenuous groups are moved by less pure motives, and not only does their action in some communities produce no good, it handicaps future development.

> The Indian tribes are torn between contradictory development policies and manipulated by 'foreign associations'. The Indian peasant suffers the assaults of proselytizing North American religious groups intent on converting him by offering all sorts of enticements — a tractor for his farm, cattle, an electric generator. This 'generosity' corrupts rural villagers and causes tremendous dissension within communities which these 'missionaries' are quick to exploit in order to gain a foothold in rural areas. (Bolivia)

> This is a rather unusual NGO. It carries out government policy, is run by officials, and forces the local promoters and villagers to work for free — to the benefit of whom? (Indonesia)

> What can one think of a Northern NGO which on the one hand finances a local factory to produce agricultural implements for use in developing rural areas here and then turns around and gives a factory in Europe orders for the same tools? (Indonesia)

In other less extreme cases, some NGOs lack sensitivity and may intervene without proper consideration for the feelings of the population concerned. The result is that they lose their credibility and delay genuine development efforts.

> A German lady came to tell us they were going to supply running water to all the villagers. She came up here twice to tell us about what they were going to do, and we haven't seen her since. We still don't have running water here. (Peru)

We cannot close this chapter on the obstacles to NGO development projects and on failures without mentioning the fairly rare cases in which a development programme is not primarily aimed at helping a rural group but at promoting the interests of the organization which has undertaken to set up a project. These instances cannot be considered as failures, since they generally succeed, but only in furthering their own goals which generally have little or nothing to do with the social and economic development of the areas in which they operate.

We could mention one project in Egypt described in its attractive brochures as concerned with 'community clubs, development co-operatives, technical production unit, carpentry workshop, weaving workshop, chicken farming, experimental biogas production unit, etc.' When we visited the project we found an altogether different story:

The carpentry workshop has fifteen people working there, we were told. Yet there wasn't a single saw-horse or table in the room. On the roof an unfinished windmill had not furnished a single kilowatt of electricity. The only functioning unit appeared to be the weaving workshop where eight women were working. A brick building houses the 'intensive chicken-raising operation'. The door was padlocked, the windows were all boarded up. Through a crack in one window we couldn't see a single chicken, and you couldn't hear a peep coming from inside. The village supposedly has three biogas units, two using an Indian system (reservoir) and the third based on a Chinese model. The two Indian units were functioning. One provided gas to a nearby home belonging to the village chief. None of the other houses were supplied by these units. We were shown a solar power generator which is still sitting in pieces in the carpentry workshop. It had obviously never been used. However, at the head office of the NGO in Cairo we had been shown a photograph of the village with the three solar panels in evidence, three bullocks, an empty sewing workshop, etc. This same workshop is supposedly where the village holds its assemblies. We saw a television set sitting there. But how could it work since there was no power? To us this entire project seemed to be almost an example of 'development fraud'. When one considers the amount of funding that has gone into this project in the past six years in comparison with what we saw oñ the spot, one wonders whether the sole object of the endeavour was to give its donors a clean conscience.

PART FIVE

CHAPTER 14
Economic and Social Achievements

The standard tool for measuring the economic results of any activity is to analyse the relationship of its costs to the benefits derived from it. When it comes to evaluating development projects this approach can be problematic, since the data needed to calculate cost-benefit ratios is often lacking, at best hard to estimate.

NGOs are not always willing to divulge their budgets, or the real costs of their projects: in many cases they actually ignore them, and sometimes they feel it may be better not to reveal the precise investment figures for a project when they are seeking funding from various sources.

To make a precise evaluation of the benefits of a project, statistical data must be collected in the village or community concerned before the project is initiated. Accurate figures must be gathered regarding agricultural production, family income, food production and supply, nutritional levels, infant mortality, in order to measure the potential impact of the project and to chart its progress clearly. These preliminary figures are in many cases very difficult to come by, since in most of these areas the population is more concerned with survival than with vital statistics.

Generally, the only statistics readily available are those published by international organizations or governments; these usually concern countries or large regions and do not enable one to assess accurately the major economic indicators at the local level where a project is to be implemented. Extrapolation from regional or national data is made particularly difficult by the extreme regional disparity we have already observed in many areas of the Third World.

Moreover, this disparity makes it extremely difficult to quantify or interpret data when it is available, since the same economic results can have tremendously varying impacts according to the social and cultural context of the project under consideration. For example, it would be a daunting task to compare the economic costs and benefits of building a school in an African village or setting up a model farm in a Latin American community. Living standards in each case differ fundamentally, and the costs of materials and labour are also difficult to compare.

Although organizing a group can ultimately bring about quantifiable economic results, it is often not measurable in the short or even medium term. In some cases it may never be, although morally or sociologically speaking the action taken is considered beneficial. What economic value can be directly attributed to the defence of the human rights of landless peasants, for instance, or to saving a child from starvation?

Economic results may be readily measurable in some projects, in other cases they are hard to assess, but in situations where the beneficiaries of a project were living in conditions of absolute poverty before action to promote development was begun, charting economic progress becomes relatively easier. Starting from zero, even a modest improvement in living standards becomes immediately evident.

We have already indicated in a number of the projects considered in the course of our study some of the economic benefits observed, as well as changes in living standards as witnessed by those participating in these projects. In this chapter we offer an analysis of some of the economic and social results we have described earlier. We do not pretend, in view of the enormous disparities involved and the dearth of reliable information, to provide rigorous economic indices which can easily be extrapolated in charting trends. At best, we can indicate the general trends and draw some pertinent conclusions from them under the heading of economic and social developments, improvements in health, and population numbers benefiting as a result of projects.

ECONOMIC BENEFITS

In economic terms, results were analysed in each instance where precise data was given by project leaders or workers. The data included local food production; increase of community resources or capital (agricultural equipment or tools, buildings, vehicles, etc.), given in units of these items rather than by attempting to estimate market value which varies widely from country to country; income generated by the sale of agricultural surpluses or other products; and savings.

In charting economic results, we had to establish a basis for

estimating minimum annual income per capita. A base-line figure
of $75 was chosen as the minimum annual income needed to ensure
one person's survival in the rural Third World. This figure
accounts for the daily consumption of 750g. of grain — the food
with the highest calorie to cost ratio — providing the minimum
daily intake of 2,300–2,500 calories to ensure survival, and rice was
the grain chosen as it has the highest calorific value. The price of
rice, a commodity more of which is consumed domestically than
exported, varies from country to country, and only 3% of the
world crop is marketed outide the countries where it is farmed. Its
cost was calculated in relation to prices prevailing on the world
market in 1983, on average $260 a tonne.

Whatever the limitations of this economic approach, it allowed
us to draw certain conclusions regarding the efficiency of small-
scale projects and their impact on local economies. A representative selection of projects visited is shown in Table I.

These projects vary considerably, but they cover the full range
of the types of action observed in terms of project duration (from
one year in the case of the most recently established project to 21
years for the oldest one still under way at the time of our survey),
number of beneficiaries (varying from 300 to 143,000), and in
relation to direct economic results, starting at overcoming absolute
poverty to establishing a significant level of savings on individual
or family income.

We then made a cross-selection of projects in terms of levels of
funding in the three main geographical areas. This was accomplished by indicating the average annual funding available per
project beneficiary, i.e. by dividing total annual project funding
available by the number of beneficiaries.

It can be seen that funding varies considerably from project to
project, ranging from US$0.07 to 100.00, but the majority of
projects have a relatively small average funding allotment per
capita, generally under $6.50 per annum.

The following observations can be drawn from this chart:
1.   No one country or region has a high concentration of either
small or large funding levels. Costs generally depend on local
needs, circumstances, and the judgement of project leaders.
2.   On the other hand, it would appear that the greater the
number of people standing to benefit from a project, the lower
the average funding level per capita. In fact, many of the operations
are similar in nature and cost no matter how many people are

Table I: EXAMPLES OF ECONOMIC RESULTS

Country, age of project	Project population	Annual funding per capita (US$)	Income or situation of each person before project	Income or situation of each person after project	Significant increase in wealth or level of savings
Peru 7 years	20,000	0.50	malnutrition	100.00	12,000.00
Brazil 3 years	16,984	3.60	below poverty line	food self-sufficiency + 20.00	primary school, 16 rural roads, nursery, 6 granaries, community vegetable garden, flour mill and silo, marmalade industry, 3 stockraising units, 5 village shops for basic food items
Philippines 4 years	24,000	0.80	150.00	190.00 to 230.00	45% self-sufficiency
Philippines 1 year	300	25.00	0	food self-sufficiency	village rebuilt
India 3 years	143,000	0.65	food self-sufficiency + 5.00	food self-sufficiency + 24.00	
Nigeria 21 years	63,000	0.07	50.00	220.00	co-operative farm and small industry, roads, bridges, irrigation Overall profit: 2,940.00
Kenya 3 years	400	16.00	malnutrition	food self-sufficiency	school, 50 goats in community stock-raising programme

	Project	Average funding per capita (US$)	Age of project
Latin America			
Bolivia	CIPCA	3.00	6 years
	CICDA	3.00	5 years
	Puerto Perez	0.75	$2\frac{1}{2}$ years
Brazil	MOC	3.50	3 years
Peru	Yucay	0.50	7 years
Africa			
Nigeria	Ossiomo	1.50	9 years
	Uboma	0.07	21 years
Kenya	Kandito	17.00	3 years
	Ogwedhi	6.50	12 years
	Dol Nyalik	1.20	7 years
Cameroun	Gaban	3.00	5 years
	Sanaga	0.10	7 years
Zaire	Nyamilina	16.50	18 months
Mali	Goudam	72.00	10 years
	Ile de Paix	12.00	9 years
Burkina Faso	Niou	0.17	10 years
Asia			
India	SSS	0.65	3 years
Philippines	CRTD	0.80	4 years
	Kalahan	27.50	12 years
	Zambales	100.00	9 years
Bangladesh	Palli Gono	4.00	6 years
	Pullati	1.00	5 years
	GUP	0.50	12 years

destined to benefit (rural clinics, model farms, community centres, etc.).

3. Generally, the younger a project is the higher the level of funding required. This can be explained in part by the fact that many projects receive an initial grant with which they have to finance the entire project or a good segment of it over a period of several years.

4. In the examples chosen, there are three notable exceptions to the rule — Kalahan, Zambales, and Goudam. In the case of Kalahan, the project was designed to build and staff a secondary school in a mountainous area; funding was not intended to provide the basis for 'productive' and income-generating activities and therefore the initial investment was greater. However, in parallel to

Table II: EXAMPLES OF SOCIAL RESULTS scale 1–10

Country and age of project	Group organization	Self-reliance	Persons trained	Local project workers	Training programmes	Legal aid, defence of human rights
Kenya 3 years	8	9	8	8	9	–
Kenya 3 years	8	7	8	5	7	–
Kenya 12 years	6	5	6	5	5	–
Cameroun 5 years	6	6	7	7	8	–
Cameroun 7 years	7	7	8	5	8	–
Zaire 3 years	8	8	6	7	8	–
Mali 5 years	3	4	7	3	8	–
Mali 8 years	1	1	1	1	1	–
Nigeria 9 years	9	9	8	5	9	–
Nigeria 21 years	8	9	8	9	8	–
Egypt 3 years	7	8	6	6	8	–
Philippines 4 years	7	7	5	5	6	7
Philippines 12 years	5	4	8	3	9	8
Philippines 9 years	8	4	7	3	6	6
Bangladesh 6 years	8	8	8	5	8	7
Indonesia 1 year	7	8	7	7	7	–
Thailand 10 years	8	9	8	9	8	–
Brazil 3 years	9	9	8	6	7	8
Peru 7 years	9	8	8	9	9	8

Table III: EXAMPLES OF RESULTS IN THE FIELD OF HEALTH

Country and age of project	drinking water	hygiene introduced	maternal and child care	clinic	pharmacy	health workers trained
Kenya 6 years	6	6	7	7	7	6
Zaire 12 years	–	7	8	8	–	8
Philippines 9 years	5	2	2	8	–	–
Brazil 3 years	8	8	8	–	8	8
Cameroun 5 years	7	5	7	5	–	–

– action not carried out by project

this project a small industry is being set up which should enable the local population to become more or less self-sufficient by 1988. In the case of Zambales and Goudam, complete village infrastructures had to be created, accompanied by a specially designed programme to encourage nomadic groups to become settled. In both cases the population groups are relatively small — 500 and 1000 people respectively. These projects might be more accurately described as research projects which are designed to advance sociological as well as economic understanding of the problems of settling nomadic population groups.

5. The level of funding per capita does not necessarily reflect the real needs of the groups concerned, but only gives an idea of the amounts of funding that project leaders were able to secure to finance projects in relation to the commitments and motivations of sponsoring agencies or funding sources. Some NGOs manage to be very resourceful in soliciting and obtaining funding, while others have greater difficulties in raising money and their projects suffer accordingly.

6. New funding for projects should not be made in terms of previous levels of funding, but in direct response to local needs.

SOCIAL BENEFITS

In social terms, results are generally reflected in an improvement in living conditions of the populations concerned in any or all of the following ways: improved group cohesiveness; ability to ensure self-reliance; number of people trained or educated (literacy and skills acquisition); number of local project workers established; action taken in the field of legal aid and defence of human rights.

These results again, are practically impossible to measure in absolute terms, so a grading system was devised to score social results on a scale of 0 to 10, each social development factor being considered individually in order to establish a numerical score. For example, results in education and training for a particular project were evaluated in connection with the number of persons trained or educated in relation to the potential number of persons within reach of the project, rather than by comparing numbers of people benefiting from these programmes from project to project.

The area in which the most significant results have been achieved appears to be that of social and group organization. NGOs have through their work been able to restructure and reactivate village and community life in many rural areas as the first step in improving living conditions and promoting self-determination and self-reliance.

However, in this area success remains unevenly distributed. The training of local project leaders and workers among the population groups concerned leaves something to be desired. In many instances not enough time and consideration is given to this important task, judging by the fairly poor success rate of projects once management is taken over by local leaders. The phasing out of direct NGO involvement and the progressive takeover of the responsibility for projects by the population itself must be the ultimate goal of any development project. The great majority of the projects visited had not had enough time to mature and to demonstrate in this manner the coming-of-age of the beneficiaries, but in this particular area Latin American projects seemed to have achieved a remarkable degree of progress. Locally trained project workers and leaders proved to have a high level of qualification and efficiency in their work.

Lastly, it is noteworthy that in most areas of Asia and Latin America great strides have been made in the defence of human rights, while in Africa this activity remains largely non-existent.

IMPROVEMENTS IN HEALTH

In the field of health, the elements considered were the progressive decrease in the level of disease in the project area as well as overall improvement of the health and hygiene of the population thanks to the introduction of basic hygiene and maternal and child health care; improved access to drinking water; the setting up of a health care network (clinics, rural pharmacies, etc.).

These results were also scored on a scale of 0 to 10 in relation to the progress which could be achieved in the given circumstances, and not in terms of rigid criteria.

Results in the field of health and hygiene, from our observation and experience in the course of the project visits seem to lag behind achievements in other areas.

A variety of specific actions have been carried out by NGOs from both the North and the South. However, significant improvements in the area of health generally depend on a number of complex factors including programmes to improve hygiene, immunization campaigns, better understanding of nutritional needs, not to speak of the availability of actual health services, provided for by governments through regional planning or thanks to the action of private groups.

Hospitals and clinics are needed, as well as roads and transport to provide access to them. Drugs at affordable prices are also an important factor, and sufficient qualified health care workers and doctors. Most of these factors are outside the control and prerogatives of NGOs. They remain within the responsibility and purview of governments, whether local, provincial, or central. Even when all these criteria have been satisfied, actual results often take years to materialize. Once the health of adults or children has deteriorated because of poor hygiene, lack of suitable drinking water, undernourishment, or malnutrition, it takes long and patient efforts to restore health to a community.

In our analysis of the 93 projects, we encountered a number of efforts to improve seed varieties. This type of action can generate fairly high yields in a short period of time, and the effects are often lasting.

The basic diets of most of the rural villagers tend to be fairly traditional and stable: potatoes, beans and maize in Latin America, rice in Asia, millet in Africa. Any improvement in yields of these crops can have an immediate impact on the nutritional needs of the populations concerned and enable them to produce surpluses for sale to neighbouring communities, representing an additional benefit in terms of food production and supply.

In the Philippines, for example, local NGOs have worked with farmers to help them introduce high-yield varieties of rice which enable them to almost double the amounts harvested. The introduction of new varieties is accompanied by traditional rice-farming methods based on Japanese models. The results obtained in these projects exceed the highest yields observed in Japan.

In Latin America, peasant farmers have developed, grown, and distributed their own seed varieties, in order to avoid having to buy them from middlemen who take a huge profit and charge exorbitant prices. Many of the groups who have worked to become self-sufficient in terms of seed supply have been able to double the income derived from their crops in a matter of only two years. This was the case for some bean and potato crops.

In one project visited in Brazil, the increased income was immediately put to use in financing community endeavours and infrastructure, such as setting up clinics, building schools, and making roads, for which the Brazilian government was not in a position to assume responsibility.

POPULATION GROUPS BENEFITING FROM DEVELOPMENT PROJECTS

The number of people who benefit from a project depends first of all on the density of the population and the size of the project area. The actual number of project beneficiaries often differs from the number initially targeted, since actions involve different segments of a group at different stages of a project's development.

Moreover, the percentage of the local population which benefits from a project varies in relation to the nature of the project. Where water development or health are concerned (well-digging, irrigation, sanitation, health care, rural clinics, etc.), the entire population is often involved and benefits directly. On the other hand, in agricultural improvement projects the percentage of the population benefiting drops considerably, since this type of action directly involves specific groups on a longer-term basis in which training and experiment play an important part before the benefits are felt by an entire project population.

Below we have selected, again from the three main Third World regions, a group of projects to illustrate the number of people involved in each case and what percentage of the population actually benefits directly.

In the light of these findings, together with those in other areas, we can estimate that NGO projects throughout the Third World affect millions of people. The results are fairly uneven, according to the various regions, the methods used, and the populations, but it is possible to make the following observations:
1.   In Africa the beneficiaries of a project can be estimated to be in the thousands, in Latin America in the tens of thousands, and in Asia in the hundreds of thousands. This is of course relevant to the density of population factor mentioned earlier, but the NGOs' development approaches and the openness of the recipient populations do play an important part in the scale of a project and its outreach.
2.   In Latin America whole regions have been pulled out of the zone of absolute poverty thanks to NGO development projects, and their efficiency in these areas approaches the optimum level. An important part of development work in this area is that of

Latin America

	Project	Project Population	Actual Beneficiaries
Bolivia	Altiplano	28,000	100%*
	Camacho	5,000	50%
	Puerto Perez	12,500	20%
Brazil	MOC	16,980	100%*
	CCDH	16,000	100%
	Fortaleza	20,000	30%
Peru	Yucay	20,000	100%*
	PISCAA	2,915	100%*

* Essentially agricultural projects, but because they are integrated community development programmes the percentage of the population which benefits from them is higher.

Africa

Cameroun	Gaban	2,000	80%
	Sanaga	80,000	80%
Burkina Faso	Niou	38,500	25%
Mali	Segou	8,000	100%[1]
	Goudam	1,000	100%[2]
	Bandiagara	40,000	50%
	Tombouctou	20,000	100%[3]
Togo	Bouvolème	5,000	30%
	Manga	5,000	10%[4]
Zaire	Madiata	20,000	50%
	Jomba	5,000	100%[5]
Kenya	Homa Bay	2,000	25%
	Ogwedhi	2,000	80%
	Saradidi	50,000	10%
	Kibwezi	20,000	60%
Egypt	Der El Maymoun	1,000	100%
Nigeria	Ossiomo	6,500	100%
	Uboma	63,000	80%

Asia

Bangladesh	GUP	153,000	80%
	PGUK	8,000	15%
	Pullati Kandi	3,000	90%
Indonesia	Baturaja	36,400	50%
	Bali	110,000	
Philippines	Cavité	80.000	60%
	Laguna	24,000	40%
India	Amta	143,000	100%
	ASSEFA	24,242	80%
Thailand	PDA	11 million	[6]

[1] water projects
[2] nomadic population settlement scheme
[3] percentage covering health component of project
[4] recently established project
[5] community shop benefiting the entire group
[6] percentage hard to estimate, since family planning has caused population growth to drop by half

making local populations aware of their rights and of what can be achieved through group organization. In many instances these population groups — especially in the Andes — have reactivated dormant community structures and collective agricultural practices which had nearly disappeared.

3. In Africa the work of NGOs is somewhat more fragmented and takes place on a much smaller scale. Following in the wake of 'rescue' operations, NGO programmes are often geared to helping people pull out of absolute poverty and malnutrition to begin to learn the rudiments of agriculture in order to satisfy their basic dietary needs.

4. In Asia, many projects focused on the defence of rural populations' rights and on ways to improve technologies to make them more efficient and productive. Generally speaking, land is used optimally in Asia, but the pressure of demographics is the main concern.

If we compare the number of people already benefiting from NGO development projects with the approximate number of NGOs working throughout the world, it is possible to draw the following conclusions.

In Latin America, since the average project involves population groups in the tens of thousands and the number of NGOs is estimated at around 2,500, it could be estimated that about 25 million people benefit by NGO development projects in this region.

In Africa, the same method enables us to estimate the number of people benefiting from NGO development projects there at 12 million people (on the basis of 1,000 persons involved in each of a total of 12,000 projects).

In Asia, one can reasonably assume that the number of projects is not below 30,000, and even choosing an average of 20,000 beneficiaries for each one, the estimated number of beneficiaries in this area comes to 60 million people.

Therefore, using rather low estimates and in a fairly pessimistic perspective, the total number of rural inhabitants around the world benefiting from NGO development effforts must come to around 100 million people.

CHAPTER 15

A New Approach to Development

On the basis of interviews carried out in nineteen countries and covering a total of 93 projects, we have attempted in this study to draw up a 'state of the art' assessment of NGO activities. Thanks to the methodology and criteria used, we were able to produce a representative selection of NGO rural development projects, as close as possible to reality. If this survey is not exhaustive — and how could it be, given the number and extreme diversity of projects? — it does at least give us a perspective on the phenomenon.

At this stage, we now ask ourselves what action could be taken in order to optimize this new development approach. Is it possible to foresee increased efficiency, a wider scope for projects, quicker implementation, and in what conditions? Despite the extreme diversity and intertwining of the problems encountered, a new trend is emerging and this we shall attempt to analyse.

In the course of the study it became apparent that there are three distinct types of problem which are generally grouped under the general heading of development. However, each of these types of problem requires special treatment and they occur in a logical order which must be respected. At the risk of repeating ourselves, we shall briefly restate these problems, remembering that in the field there is a certain amount of overlapping:

villagers' basic needs;

factors of impoverishment afflicting rural populations;

factors of development, of which villagers must become the initiators and managers.

In order to examine these factors we must, on the basis of the information collected, try to develop a global view of rural development which accurately reflects the perceptions and experience of public and private institutions involved in the process. In fact, on the basis of the information gathered from NGOs in both the South and North, it would appear that a decisive re-ordering and rethinking of development is taking place which points to the emergence of a global view.

We shall see that this new approach requires a new understanding of the respective roles of the agents of rural development as well as redefinition of relations between these various agents. By promoting a better understanding of each agent's role and responsibility in the development process, it should be possible to overcome obstacles to action, to extend the present scope of NGO operations so that new rural development strategies can be conceived and put into practice which are better adapted to the needs of the concerned populations, and to ensure that those who are responsible for development have the appropriate means at their disposal.

A GLOBAL VIEW OF RURAL DEVELOPMENT BASED ON NEW PERCEPTIONS AND PRIORITIES

The initiative shifts from North to South
As we have seen, one of the main concerns of NGOs in industrialized countries is that villagers themselves participate actively in development projects. The success of a project depends to a large extent on the degree of participation of the population concerned by the project. The increasing number of Third World NGOs is evidence of the fact that villagers no longer wait to be invited to take the initiative to improve their living conditions. This new development was observed in varying degrees in all the countries visited, and must henceforth be taken into account.

Development policies should recognize the needs of rural populations
To this day, rural populations are frequently excluded from discussion and decision-making concerning development policy. But the fact remains that in most poor countries a majority of the population lives in rural areas. Paradoxically, it is precisely this sector of each country's population that is still unable to feed itself adequately, let alone produce sufficient food for the entire country. They constitute pockets of poverty which completely destabilize a country, both economically and politically.

*Domestic food production should take priority over cash crops for
export and industrial development*
The analysis of the factors of impoverishment in Chapter 5
underscored the reasons for and negative effects of policies to
promote cash crops for export, policies which are implemented by
most Third World countries. Through their full-scale support of
export industries and crops, governments of these countries hope
to earn the foreign exchange needed to finance Western-style
industrialization and grandiose prestige operations, and in particular to help cope with the crushing debt resulting from large-
scale public works projects.

There is no question of suggesting that these countries renounce
cash crops altogether. However, they should be convinced that top
priority should go to satisfying the food needs of the population
through domestic production. In this context, what is to be
avoided are the damaging side-effects of cash-cropping, not to
speak of the pressures this policy places on a country's balance of
payments when it is constrained to import food to feed its own
people. The first of these negative side-effects is the depletion of
soil nutrients through the systematic abuse of extensive cropping
methods. Next comes the pressure brought to bear on small
farmers to leave their land, in order to create large estates for
the production of export crops, and the resulting massive rural
migration.

When considering their rural development policy options, Third
World governments can no longer neglect the crucial importance
of promoting domestic food production. If they do so, they could
well be held accountable for the dramatic consequences which
result, sooner or later, from misguided and inappropriate policy.

*Small-scale development should take precedence over large-scale
development projects and be integrated in overall economic strategy*
In Chapter 1, we listed the criticisms most often levelled at the
development policies of the past twenty years:

too many large-scale Western-style projects, which were
completely unsuitable to the needs of local populations;

too much money invested for the benefit of too few;

policies which run counter to local and national structures and
are often rejected by the very people who should have
benefited from them.

It is obvious that the emphasis must be shifted from large-scale to small-scale projects, to avoid squandering financial resources and to prevent the negative side-effects of giant development schemes. An added advantage of a 'small is beautiful' approach is that it is easier to monitor project performance and make necessary adjustments before it is too late.

In a time of scarce resources, NGOs in the industrialized world, funding institutions, and international organizations must redefine the criteria they use to identify projects they will support and fund. This means transferring part of the funding earmarked for large-scale endeavours to small projects. Top priority should go to small-scale projects which benefit the largest possible number of people and at the same time require only relatively small investment.

Small projects have the distinct advantage of providing an ideal context for training people in the field and of enabling grassroots groups to take responsibility for projects at village or community level. The project's beneficiaries should retain the initiative, choice, and responsibility for development decisions which are aimed at answering their real needs. This is what NGOs are good at doing.

Larger-scale projects such as roads and dams will continue to be necessary, but if the starting point of development efforts is the village or the community, the entire development process can gradually be extended to a whole region. At this stage large-scale or medium-scale projects become essential if the overall development process is to continue. This is where central government steps in, to co-ordinate and direct the whole development effort, if possible in co-operation with villagers and NGOs.

REDEFINING THE ROLES OF THE AGENTS OF RURAL DEVELOPMENT

It is not easy to gain a global view of rural development, based on new perceptions and priorities, or the options that this implies on the part of governments, international institutions, the media, and NGOs. Nevertheless, such a global view must inspire new strategies if they are to be coherent and successful. All partners in the development process must adapt to this new global awareness, whether it is in the context of policy-making or in terms of patterns of behaviour at national and local levels. The following propositions confirm the vital necessity of such a change of awareness.

Government

Rural development policy presupposes some essential policy options by governments on land reform; population policy; development of networks of small rural clinics for health care; operation of experimental farms and extension services.

To enable small-scale development projects to succeed, governments must strengthen macroeconomic support systems. On many occasions we saw how the results of small-scale projects could be jeopardized by the application of practices and even of policies in direct contradiction to the type of development these projects seek to uphold. At the same time, taxes or similar financial measures levied by national government are particularly resented in rural areas, as this is generally the sector where the lowest income groups are found.

Such government taxation can hamper or even paralyse small-scale efforts, despite any external funding they may receive, because of the economic asphyxia it causes. If governments really are determined to support harmonious rural development, then they must modify their political and financial options by adopting a pricing and taxation policy which favours rural populations and reduces their fiscal burden.

To ensure that rural development remains responsive to local needs, governments must adopt regional development policies which improve infrastructure and promote the creation of intermediate townships between villages and larger cities. In analysing the many projects visited, we have seen to what extent the absence of road infrastructure can exclude villagers from economic activity, forcing them to lead a reclusive, inward-looking existence. Some of the communities we visited had taken upon themselves the task of building roads and bridges to overcome isolation. However, most NGOs are not equipped for this task. This type of regional development must be planned at national level and be integrated in systematic policy-making and implementation.

The same problem arises with regard to secondary education, hospitals, training, and leisure activities (in particular for younger members of the rural population). In the course of our visits, we noted that there was often no intermediate urban development between tiny villages and larger cities, or the capital.

It is up to governments to foster a more harmonious style of development, starting with the village or rural community as the basic unit. This more human approach might help to slow down rural migration by creating badly needed links between rural and urban areas, as well as by providing community services which the rural poor urgently require.

Although it is incumbent on governments to define and implement regional development policies, there is no denying the need for these policies to be felt and expressed by villagers themselves. Moreover, NGOs should not confine development merely to the projects in which they are involved. On the contrary, they should make their programmes as outward-looking as possible. In this way, development will no longer remain isolated in enclaves, but will become part of a general, multi-pronged movement.

International institutions
These bodies have an important role to play in rural development. Although they have always given priority to overall development strategies, they have not always, through the funding they provide and the criteria they have set down, focused efforts at the local level in order to bring development to the most marginalized sectors of the populations of poor countries.

Their actions often appear to be dispersed, their aims not always clearly formulated, and real co-ordination among their leaders is often lacking. In most instances they have hesitated to state clear global development objectives and to promote a better understanding of overall, albeit complex, needs. Many of these inter-governmental institutions, such as the European Community and the World Bank, willingly recognize NGOs and subsidize their activities. It is unquestionably time for them all to adopt a two-fold approach, aimed at supporting a coherent plan to promote rural development in poor countries:

by proposing five-year rural development 'contracts' to governments, who for their part would agree to undertake new policies based on NGO activities and would implement the necessary political and economic measures to support this effort and ensure its efficiency;

by setting up a continuous project evaluation system using joint committees which would include representatives from governments, international organizations, and NGOs.

The media
In a world where communication has become a vital function, the media are rarely perceived as actual development partners.

Nevertheless, they have a duty to observe rural development, to report on it, to identify information and disseminate it. All too often, journalists pay more attention to the spectacular aspects of underdevelopment in rural areas than to the day-to-day reality of development efforts. No doubt they themselves receive insufficient information on these issues, and some of them, in industrialized as well as in poor countries, still lack a clear view and understanding of what rural development really means in poor countries.

NGOs
They must extend their prerogatives in areas where they have proven their capacities:
recognition by governments and international institutions as fully-fledged development partners, while at the same time preserving their specific identity and independence.

This would mean not only that NGOs would be present on the joint project evaluation committees recommended above, but that they would also have to be consulted regularly with regard to the design and implementation of applied development strategies at the country and/or province level.

Lay claim to increased financial resources in order to regroup their activities to increase the number of beneficiaries, estimated at around 100 million at the present time, to the two billion who make up the rural population; this population constitutes the real challenge to the development process, and it should be remembered that its numbers are expected to swell to four billion in the next twenty years.

Develop the vision and adaptability to fulfil their role.
At the risk of repeating ourselves, it must be stated yet again that they must acquire a global view of rural development and be able to update or modify projects in the light of changes in the overall situation. The barefoot peasant movement, the changing political and economic situation — at world, national, and regional level — can very rapidly modify the data we have offered and no doubt the information gathered in the course of this study will change completely in years to come. NGOs must not only acquire this overall view of development; they must also constantly adapt to change.
Acquire necessary qualifications: Special attention here should be drawn to acquisition of technical expertise; improved information on the milieu, its socio-political and cultural environment.

Overcome the inertia and resistance of rural villagers: This study has emphasized the barefoot peasant movement which is starting up more or less everywhere, is spreading, and, thanks to the desire of rural populations to change their living conditions and improve the future for their children, is becoming organized. This movement is taking place in a rural environment where the inertia of the population, its customs, and its resistance to change all constitute obstacles to development. This is an area where NGOs have shown an irreplaceable capacity, through their knowledge of the terrain and of attitudes, to contribute towards changing these attitudes and behaviour patterns. Without exaggeration, they can be said to have accomplished a historic mission in this field.

Be better informed and inform others better: NGOs must improve communication with governments and be better informed of each other's activities. A vast treasure of experience — of successes and failures, of innovative activities — has been accumulated, but this is hoarded away, neither exploited or shared. NGOs must keep themselves informed of the latest developments, and improve the flow of information to other NGOs, their partners and counterparts. The South–South dialogue between NGOs is a vital — albeit modest as yet — element in this exchange of information.

REDEFINING RELATIONSHIPS BETWEEN AGENTS OF DEVELOPMENT

NGOs and governments
Dialogue between NGOs and governments must be promoted and maintained. If, for the reasons which we have stated, co-operation between governments and NGOs is necessary, the absence of such co-operation heads the list of external obstacles encountered by NGOs. The absence of mutual recognition and dialogue between these two types of organization results in negative consequences for rural development, on two different levels;

   insufficient or absence of political desire for development and inappropriate economic options can slow down or even impede the impact of development activities and oppose the extension of such projects;

   on the local or regional level, we have seen that bureaucracy, inertia, indifference on the part of officials are still to be found, more often than on the national level. Frequently local

officials perceive NGOs as alien elements, threatening to
erode their power; and in many cases it can be said that they
feel themselves personally threatened by the vast national
movement implied by rural development in their country.

*Governments and NGOs should co-operate in training officials
to understand and properly support rural development efforts.*
The quality and extent of relations between NGOs and public
authorities can vary considerably from one country to another. Let
us leave on one side the few cases where such relations are good,
and consider instead the majority of cases where they are unstable,
not to say downright bad. Though governments may need NGOs,
the need NGOs have of governments is no less great. In any case,
co-operation is a desirable aim.

It is not easy to establish co-operation between so-called non-
governmental organizations and governments: by their very nature
they would seem more suited to be in opposition to each other.
And any co-operation, if it can be established, will always be
vulnerable. NGOs, which are frequently informal, flexible, and
accustomed to taking decisions rapidly and acting accordingly,
have difficulty in tolerating the dilatoriness and unwieldiness
of authorities. Governments distrust these organizations, whose
motives and method of operation they have difficulty in understanding; nevertheless, governments do recognize the fact that
only NGOs have the capacity to fulfil certain development activities, and they do appreciate the financial resources at the disposal
of NGOs. On the hypothesis that a government has chosen
political options and implemented voluntarily the policy required
to achieve the aims that these options presuppose, then it must
train its civil servants and motivate them, if it wishes them to be
active participants in this policy.

*Governments and NGOs should work together to fight various
forms of corruption.* We have seen that the role played by intermediaries and the effects of corrupt systems together frequently
constitute impediments to the development process. Overcoming
such practices presupposes stability, political courage, and a
considerable amount of time. It is certainly one of the most
difficult steps to take in relation to practices (in many cases
customs which go back over generations), which are constantly
spreading and can wreak havoc in the economic development of a
country.

By identifying the problem and enacting laws, governments should be able to combat this dramatic factor of regression. NGOs can give their support to such a policy and help to make public opinion more aware of the harm done by a few to the general interest, and to that of the rural population in particular.

NGOs and governments should work together to increase financial support and credit for rural development. The number of projects in need of funding is increasing while the amount of money available from the North is decreasing. Extension of development projects will be possible through two complementary means:

transferring to NGO projects and the different rural groups part of the financial resources allocated by large international financial institutions to large-scale development projects;

increased attention by governments in the South to the financing of small-scale projects, either through direct subsidies or through preferential credit policies, with sufficiently low intererest rates to provide additional incentive for this type of rural development.

Although the initiative and example can come only from government, NGOs may play a part by basing their activities on clearly stated policy to act on the local level and by informing public opinion of the significance of the activity undertaken.

NGOs and international institutions
NGOs must satisfy donors and financial institutions through improved project management. NGOs often have the feeling that donors see things from far away and therefore are not able, as they themselves are, to respond to reality and to emergency situations, especially when they are acting outside the terms of the project as financed.

For their part, donors are increasingly demanding with regard to the use made by NGOs of the money received, and are tending to require NGOs to use increasingly complicated accounting systems. It is true that NGOs, in particular small ones which are in the majority, are ill-equipped to organize the financial management of the funds they receive, and this gives rise to conflicts which can be harmful to what ought to be a joint effort. Donors must be aware that the bureaucracy they may be forcing on NGOs could well endanger their specificity and efficiency.

NGOs must provide a regular flow of information and encourage feedback, so that international institutions can draw on the experience of NGOs and adapt their financial policy to the realities as communicated to them by the NGOs.

Partnership between Southern and Northern NGOs

Third World NGOs are showing an increasing tendency to take the initiative in projects and to manage them; Northern NGOs, after having shown them the way, often see their role transformed primarily to that of financing Southern NGOs and becoming their correspondents or spokesmen in the North. The major NGOs in the North, whose budgets are frequently greater than those of the overseas development administrations of the smaller countries of Europe (these are the NGOs which some people like to call the 'multinationals of development aid') support and frequently finance similar types of project. They are tempted to impose the same types of management on them, to apply the same evaluation methods, and thus contribute to standardizing the world of NGOs. In such circumstances, it is not always easy for Third World NGOs to retain their original characteristics, any more than they are able to maintain their independence from governments.

Now, more than ever before, dialogue in a spirit of mutual respect is needed between NGOs from developing and developed countries, in order to maintain a balance difficult to achieve and constantly under threat. It is only through such frank and fruitful dialogue that the specific roles of NGOs in both hemispheres will be seen as complementary and useful.

NGOs and the media

NGOs have often overlooked the important role of advocate and publicist for development which the media potentially constitute. They must learn to communicate who they are, what they do, and the nature of their mission as well as the results they achieve. They must establish a constant dialogue with the media within their reach and make this communication function one of their vital concerns.

Conclusion

The purpose of this book has been to survey a major trend in rural development — the emergence of people-oriented, NGO-sponsored, village-level development initiatives throughout the Third World. In our most ambitious moments we never dreamed we would find such a store of experience and promising perspectives: we had only hoped to point out the way to others, in both the private and public sector, so that further research could be carried out. Yet, in view of the response we encountered in the rural areas of the nineteen Third World nations which took part in the field survey, we soon realized that we were in a position to offer a great deal more interesting data on work under way in a wide variety of projects.

The techniques used to select the projects to be studied and for carrying out the survey in the field served our original purpose beyond expectation. But, like most research tools, they have their limitations. Our one guiding concern throughout has been to pave the way for more systematic research in this field and, above all, to stimulate a wide-ranging international debate on one of the great challenges facing the world today — sustainable and self-reliant development for the two billion people who live in rural areas.

Our conclusions are far from definitive and in many instances largely intuitive. The extremely diverse nature of these projects, their rapid rate of change, and the dearth of reliable statistical information on NGO-sponsored development work (in terms of both levels of funding and numbers of beneficiaries) hindered our research. However, the difficulties encountered were mainly due to the fact that until now the very subject of NGOs' contribution to rural development has been either neglected or considered of little significance. We also came up against a few cases of reticence on the part of NGOs — no doubt fearful of attempts to control their activities — which preferred to remain either tight-lipped or extremely vague when it came to providing precise figures, or which claimed a right to anonymity on the grounds that their operations in politically sensitive areas might be jeopardized.

Rural development certainly deserves to be given priority attention by all those concerned by the economic problems of the Third World. What is needed to make information more available, accessible, and intelligible are universal criteria for evaluation, standard parameters and indicators, and systematic gathering of information. On the basis of our findings, this is the first requirement if progress is to be achieved in development in full knowledge of the facts.

A second conclusion, which has been a leitmotiv of the entire study, is the need for stressing 'people-oriented' development. This is where cost-benefit analysts and economists throw up their hands in despair. Economic growth can be charted, food self-sufficiency calculated, skills, technology, and capital costed, but the most important variable, the human factor, is totally unpredictable. Experts often tend to overlook this fact, forgetting that development must serve real human needs. The ultimate reason for development is the satisfaction of basic human needs which include dignity and human rights. The part of most of the projects visited which is most difficult to quantify, but certainly the most important and encouraging for the future, was that which engaged each participant's imagination, creativity, decision-making, sense of responsibility, and desire to control the circumstances of his or her life in a harmonious environment.

In a sense these grassroots initiatives are workshops of democracy in which groups are rediscovering their capacity to set common goals and achieve them through collective solidarity. Many rural villagers and NGO workers have pointed to the prospects for creating greater social consensus, and the emergence of new and more community-orientated societies in rural areas. While overly optimistic hypotheses or hasty predictions should be avoided, the example of the progress achieved in many rural areas by simple people who have managed miracles could well serve as an inspiration for the marginalized sectors in the industrialized societies.

Solutions to the problems evoked in the early chapters of this book have emerged gradually from the accounts of the participants in developing projects.

NGOs — THE KEY TO SELF-RELIANT DEVELOPMENT

In the great majority of the cases studies, the work of Third World NGOs respected the structures and traditions of the concerned communities, particularly in Asia and Latin America. Examples were even found in which the presence of the NGO helped strengthen traditional village life. In Africa, where the proportion of NGOs from industrialized countries is greater, a better know-ledge of the local environment and populations might improve results.

In general, the results of the surveys show that the activities of NGOs are a great deal more successful than had been originally thought. However, it must be admitted that, in relation to the needs of two billion rural inhabitants of the planet — the challenge facing our world — 100 million rural villagers is still a rather limited number to benefit from NGO-sponsored development work. The crucial question is, therefore, how can NGOs expand their activities to address the needs of this vast rural population effectively?

If the estimated average cost of rural development, $6.50 per capita per year, is correct (see page 213, Chapter 14), an overall programme to push through development benefiting two billion people would entail an annual investment of $13 billion. This figure is given simply to indicate the scope of the problem, but it does not appear excessive if we take into account all the budgets and sums of money devoted by the international community to various development schemes.

It can be asserted that there are no major obstacles to increasing the financial resources which could be allocated to NGOs. It is clear, however, that this measure, though essential, is not suf-ficient. NGOs alone are in a position to determine whether and how they can train a sufficient number of rural educators and project workers to meet the challenge of increasing their present action twenty-fold. NGOs can only take on this gigantic task if the other partners in rural development fully assume their re-sponsibilities and make the necessary policy decisions. This con-cerns, first and foremost, the governments of concerned countries and the funding institutions. The first step in this direction is for NGOs to be recognized as fully-fledged agents of development.

To assume this expanded level of responsibility, NGOs must develop, open up, and improve their dialogue with the govern-ments of the countries in which they are working. They must be willing to sit down with other NGOs and government officials wherever possible to devise co-operative solutions which can enlist the goodwill and resources of both the industrialized and developing worlds in providing concrete technical, educational, and economic solutions.

While NGOs continue their work and projects increase exponentially throughout the Third World, the entire grassroots development movement we have chosen to call the 'barefoot revolution' gains momentum. This movement is truly a revolution, because for the rural poor it signifies a break with the past, a turning away from misery and injustice and overcoming inertia and isolation. It is also a revolution to the extent that within their hearts is being born the tremendous hope that they can break out of individual helplessness, join with others, and through united action build a better future for themselves and their children.

This vast revolution, which is under way on three continents has two striking characteristics: first, it is a peaceful revolution and, second, it is a movement which respects the law. However, the options it implies are political and no one can deny that rural development in poor countries is a political problem. Initially a political problem for Third World governments, it has also become a political burden for the industrialized North which — for better or for worse — will be affected by its evolution.

The barefoot revolution is at present unallied to political or ideological forces, but it could easily change into a political movement or be taken over by extremist political forces. The final outcome of this struggle will depend on the solutions to the problems addressed in this study, and on the speed with which the agents of development can mobilize.

This revolution will either be victorious through peace, or be vanquished by conflict.

Methodology and Procedure of the Qualitative Survey of NGO Rural Development Projects in the Third World

I — PREPARATORY PHASE: OCTOBER 1982–OCTOBER 1983

1 Inventory of NGOs specializing in rural development
First of all, the identification of NGOs operating throughout the world was undertaken through different sets of enquiries: through NGOs, through the OECD, letters to Research Institutes, Universities, the EEC, NGO networks, experts, members of the Club of Rome, etc.

This produced about 3,300 names and addresses of 'Northern' and 'Southern' NGOs, classified as being organizations involving:
    development, not aid;
    operations at grass roots, without access to public opinion in the rich countries;
    rural development, not urban.
The selection was difficult to achieve, because some organizations do not always communicate what they really do; others have a number of activities overlapping the chosen definitions.

2 Inventory of projects
In parallel with the inventory of NGOs research was undertaken about projects in progress in Third World countries, both through NGOs and through opinion leaders aware of what was going on in the rural development of their own country. Projects were identified in the chosen categories and then contacts were established with their leaders, for further information, and eventually for permission to visit the project.

3 Sampling of the countries
This sampling was established according to the following parameters:
    large geographical zones of the Third World;
    climatic and geographical data;
    type of agriculture;
    socio-political organization;
    cultural and religious data, taking into consideration ethnic, etc., diversity.
Nineteen countries were selected:
In Latin America: Bolivia, Brazil, Colombia, Ecuador, Mexico, Peru;

In Africa: Cameroun, Burkina Faso, Togo, Mali, Zaire, Egypt, Kenya, Nigeria;
In Asia: Bangladesh, India, Indonesia, Philippines, Thailand.

4 Sampling the projects
This was established according to the following factors:
nature, origin, location;
size, impact, expected results;
classification according to the context:
characteristics of population, density, age, know-how,
physical conditions (geography, climate, topology),
richness of the soil and the sub-soil,
existing equipment (buildings, machinery),
means of communication, and exchange,
administrative environment, management and support services etc.
classification according to priority objectives:
the improvement of economic, social, and environmental conditions, desertification, pollution, security, etc.,
the transfer of know-how and appropriate technologies,
the replicability of the projects in the villages in the neighbourhood or the region.

5 Preparation of the interviews
a) A letter was first sent to the leaders of the project. It defined the objective of the mission, and the expected results, giving the names of both interviewers and asking for authorization to visit the project.
b) At the same time a technical note was prepared giving the general data concerning the area, its population, the project itself etc. based on the information received from the NGO involved.

On the spot, the survey lasted between three and ten days. Interviews were conducted with the people in charge of the project, the local public administration, opinion leaders, villagers, and those benefiting from the project. When possible, interviews were also sought with farmers belonging to other village communities, to discover if they would like to see the same kind of development projects set up in their own village, or if, on the contrary, they would object to similar initiatives and if so, for what reason (ethnic, religious differences, etc.).

6 Elaboration of guidelines
The guidelines were conceived in order to list all the questions to which it seemed necessary to look for answers. Their purpose was to help the interviewer not to forget any topic which should be tackled during the interview: in no case was it intended to be used as a questionnaire. Such guidelines were drawn up for each category of interviewee.

7 Methodology of interview
The chosen methodology was the in-depth interview, semi-structural. This means that the interviewer explains the objective of the survey, and the

role of the interview, and guarantees the confidentiality of what is said (no mention of name or origin, unless there is specific agreement) according to the professional code of ethics.

These interviews were informal and lasted several hours. Sometimes they went on over several days, depending upon the quality of the relations established and the degree of confidence obtained.

II — COMPLETION OF THE SURVEY: DECEMBER 1983–JANUARY 1985

1 In each country visited, the team of experts made contact with national and international NGOs in charge of the selected projects, but also with the Ministry of Agriculture, central and regional administrations, academic circles, and any person identified as capable of giving useful information.

These steps helped to provide a more global view of the situation and to collect maximum data on the country.

We also left our teams free to visit projects not contained in the initial framework, but discovered on the spot and thought to be interesting for the survey. Such initiatives by the teams led to the study of 93 projects instead of the 60 initially planned.

2 The visit to each project, generally with the leader of the project, tried to collect the maximum information by:

interviews with different categories of people involved in the project, managers, 'animateurs', educators, volunteers, social workers, civil servants of the local administration, farmers, etc.

observation and evaluation (the number and quality of buildings, appearance of the villages, houses, breadth of general culture, behaviour of the people involved, hygiene and health of the population, waterpoints, etc.)

the study of documents such as yearly reports, account books, etc.

3 Each team of experts supplied a detailed report, itself integrated in a global report established country by country, and placed in the socio-economic context, the political climate, and the situation of NGOs vis-à-vis the government.

III — ANALYSIS AND SYNTHESIS OF THE REPORT: OCTOBER 1984–APRIL 1985

The nineteen reports established by the teams in the selected nineteen countries formed the basis of the final report.

IV — BOGOTÀ SEMINAR ON THE RESULTS AND CONCLUSIONS OF THE SURVEY: 10, 11, 12 APRIL 1985

A seminar on the results of the final report was held in Bogotà with the participation of some experts on the Third World, some members of the Club of Rome, and Centro Febbraïo 74.

Comments and suggestions made by the participants led to the definitive version of the report, as it is presented in this book.

APPENDIX II
List of Projects Visited

ASIA

Bangladesh
1. Gonoshathaya Kendra Savar
2. Gono Unnayan Prochesta Rajoir
3. Pullah Kandi Jamalpur
4. Palli Gono Unnayan Kendra Padrishipur
5. Legal Aid Association Madaripur
6. Nigera Kori Narchi

India
7. Seva Sangh Samiti – Amta
8. Seva Sangh Samiti – Jikhira
9. Seva Sangh Samiti – Bankura
10. Seva Sangh Samiti – Barakpore
11. ASSEFA – Utchapatty
12. ASSEFA – Malayapatty
13. ASSEFA – Vadugapatty
14. ASSEFA – Natham Blook
15. ASSEFA – Sethur
16. ASSEFA – Mykudi
17. Brother Muller Hospital Charities Mangalore
18. Darmasthala Mangalore
19. Gujarat Khet Vikas Parishad Ahmedabad

Indonesia
20. Baturaja (Sumatra)
21. Danjarnegara (Java)
22. Poletindo (Java)
23. Hydraulique villageoise (Bali)
24. Trana (Ambon)

Philippines
25. Centre for Rural Technology Development (CRTD – Calanan)
26. International Institute of Rural Reconstruction – Silang
27. Preda Foundation – Olongapo City
28. Negritos of Zambales
29. Kalahan Educational Foundation – Imogan

Thailand
30. PDA Bon Phai
31. PDA Mahasarakham
32. PDA Bandong
33. PDA Petchabun
34. PDA Kanook Njam
35. Girl Guide Association of Thailand
36. Svida Foundation
37. Women's Development through Non-formal Education (Sisters of the Good Shepherd)

AFRICA

Burkina Faso
38. ZECCO – Po Region
39. NIOU Yatenga
40. Project Six/S NAAM Ouahigouya
41. Project GARY – Titao

Cameroun
42. AFVP Gaban
43. M'BEZOA Haute Sanaga

Egypt
44. Deir El Maymoun Beni Suef
45. High Dam Lake Basis Integrated Services Aswan
46. Basaisa Village Integrated Field Project

Kenya
47. Kandito Women's Association – Homa Bay
48. Community Development Ogwedha – Sigawa
49. Centre for Community Development – Saradidi
50. Dol Nyalik Women's Association
51. Kibwezi Women's Association
52. Nakuru New Population Zones

Mali
53. Centre for Training Rural Artisans Ségou
54. AFSC Goundam
55. Mali Aqua Viva à San
56. Integrated project – Dogon Plateau
57. Ile de Paix Tombouctou
58. Co-operative movement – Diré

Togo
61. Maisons Familiales et Rurales Sokode
62. Maisons Familiales et Rurales Bouvoleme
63. Maisons Familiales et Rurales Manga
64. Centre d'animation Rurale Adjengra
65. Projet de cultures de spirulines Farendé
66. Coopérative de crédit Niamtougou

Zaire
67. Madiata – Kimpemba collective
68. Nyamilima – Goma Region
69. Hospital – Jomba
70. JOPAJE (Jomba Pastorale des Jeunes) Jomba
71. Savings and credit co-operative – Rutchuru

LATIN AMERICA

Bolivia
71. CICDA Ambana
73. GORTA Puerto Perez
74. CIPCA à Corta

Brazil
75. MOC Feira de Santana
76. PATAC Campina Grande
77. CDDH/AEP João Pessoa
78. FASE Fortaleza
79. Other FASE

Colombia
80. Nueva Escuela Cali
81. Las Gaviotas
82. Savings co-operative

Ecuador
83. FEPP Cuenca
84. CEAS Riobamba
85. Terra Nova Guayas
86. AICF Latacunga

Mexico
87. Servicio Desarollo y Paz
88. Sociedad Cooperativa la Selva Lacandona
89. Veciños Mondiales

Peru
90. Centro de Estudios Rurales Andinos
91. La Granja de Yucay
92. PISCAA Dept Cuzco
93. CIPCA Piura

The Club of Rome

Founded in Rome (hence its name) in 1968 by Aurelio Peccei and Alexander King, the Club of Rome is made up of a group of prominent world citizens who are convinced that it is vital to promote a better understanding of the challenges confronting our rapidly evolving society so that it may be more wisely guided. An association of 100 members — scientists, economists, sociologists, business and government leaders — from 40 countries on five continents, from East and West, North and South, its membership runs the full professional and ideological gamut, ensuring the group's diversity and at the same time making consensus impractical, if not impossible. Members are nevertheless committed to working together in a spirit of common concern for the future of humanity. Most of the major issues and tensions that confront the world at large find expression within the Club.

From the very outset, the Club of Rome based its thinking and action on

a global approach to the vast and complex problems of a world in which interdependence between nations is rapidly increasing;

seeking a deeper understanding of the interactions within the tangle of contemporary problems — political, economic, social, cultural, psychological, technological, and environmental — for which the Club has coined the phrase, 'the world problématique';

the long-term perspective and issues which will affect future generations.

Since the publication in 1972 of the first report to the Club of Rome, *Limits to Growth*, which sparked world-wide debate, the Club has pursued its study of the world problématique in a variety of areas. Reports have been published on the search for a new world order, the North–South dialogue, human resources, the social impact of new technologies, and so on.

These reports have been debated at large international conferences and at seminars held in the four corners of the globe. Since its creation, the Club has invited world leaders and experts in many fields to attend major conferences held in Rio de Janeiro, Moscow, Toronto, Tokyo, Algiers, Kuwait, Yaoundé, Budapest, Seoul, Bogotá, Philadelphia, Santander, among others.

The Club does not restrict its activities to research studies and the holding of international conferences. It feels that it must ensure that its findings are known to policy-makers at all levels, so that this information can be instrumental in the decision-making process, and also seeks to stimulate world-wide debate on issues that are seldom dealt with in traditional forums. The Club feels it has a duty to help inform public opinion concerning the changes constantly taking place in the world, so that people can better understand the challenges confronting the citizens of all countries in the future.

The Club of Rome shares the conviction of its late founder Aurelio Peccei that men and women need not remain passive and isolated in the face of rapidly evolving phenomena which, for better or for worse, will affect their lives. Once citizens are informed and become involved as true participants in their lives and the events that surround them, they will be able to influence, and at times decisively shape, the future of humanity.

DATE DUE

GAYLORD			PRINTED IN U.S.A.